Military Strategy and Diplomacy

Military Strategy and Diplomacy

Capt. (Retd.) Prem Singh

PRASHANT PUBLISHING HOUSE
DELHI-110094

Published by :
Prashant Publishing House
C-34, 28 Foota Road, Gali-3,
West Karwal Nagar, Delhi-110094
Phone : 011-22963970, Mob. : 9810396373
e-mail.: prashantpublishinghouse@gmail.com

Military Strategy and Diplomacy

First Published 2013

ISBN 978-93-80565-42-2

PRINTED IN INDIA
Published by Mr. R.K. Jha M/s Prashant Publishing House and Published at H.S. Offset House Press, Delhi.

Preface

Military diplomacy, more often than not, does not receive the attention that it merits. Where employed, it suffers from not being fully integrated with the nation's overall foreign policy and diplomatic efforts. Anton du Plessis puts it very succinctly when he states: ...defence diplomacy approximates a military adjunct to diplomacy rather than a distinct type of diplomacy. At one level, its importance in a changing environment and use for foreign and security policy purposes are recognised in principle, whereas, at another level, defence diplomacy has become an overarching term for defence foreign relations. As a result, defence diplomacy does not receive the recognition it deserves. Conceptually, this is due less to the precarious relationship between various foreign policy instruments, and more to an underestimation of the nature, scope and utility of defence diplomacy. Practically, and due in part to conceptual ambiguity, this underestimation is reinforced by a lack of integration with foreign and defence policy and corresponding military policy and strategy, as well as by defence diplomacy being restricted to its military-defence policy context rather than enhanced by its diplomatic-foreign policy context.

As a corollary, there have been numerous instances of peaceful use of military to further a nation's international relations. This peaceful use of the military as a tool of national diplomacy led to the use of the term 'military diplomacy'. Thus 'military diplomacy' could be defined as use of (peaceful) military in diplomacy, as a tool of national foreign policy. It is axiomatic that military diplomacy has to be dovetailed and integrated with the national diplomatic efforts. UK's defence diplomacy is defined by Anton du Plessis, in a narrow sense, as the "use of military personnel, including service attaches, in support of conflict prevention and resolution. Among a great variety of activities, it includes providing assistance in the development of democratically accountable armed forces".

The book deeply highlights the Military Diplomacy.

—Editor

Preface

[illegible]

Contents

1

Military Diplomacy

Militaries, historically, are associated with achieving national aims and objectives in international relations through the use of force. In the 18th and 19th centuries the coercive use of militaries (and navies) by colonial powers led to coining of the term *'gunboat diplomacy'* which refers to the pursuit of foreign policy objectives with the aid of conspicuous displays of military power, implying or constituting a direct threat of warfare. It meant that the military had to have the capability and wherewithal to act; and the decision makers the will to call the enemy's bluff, if required.

As a corollary, there have been numerous instances of peaceful use of military to further a nation's international relations. This peaceful use of the military as a tool of national diplomacy led to the use of the term 'military diplomacy'. Thus 'military diplomacy' could be defined as use of (peaceful) military in diplomacy, as a tool of national foreign policy. It is axiomatic that military diplomacy has to be dovetailed and integrated with the national diplomatic efforts. UK's defence diplomacy is defined by Anton du Plessis, in a narrow sense, as the "use of military personnel, including service attaches, in support of conflict prevention and resolution. Among a great variety of activities, it includes providing assistance in the development of democratically accountable armed forces". Du Plessis goes on to give a broader definition of military diplomacy as "the use of armed forces in operations other than war, building on their trained expertise and discipline to achieve national and foreign objectives abroad". He also gives Cottey and Foster's inclusive definition of defence diplomacy (alternatively international defence diplomacy) as "the peacetime use of armed forces and related infrastructure (primarily defence ministries) as a tool of foreign and security policy" and more specifically the use of military cooperation and assistance".

The words 'military' and 'defence' are used loosely and can be freely interchanged. While the term 'military' could be used to identify activities undertaken by the uniformed components of the nation's defence establishment, the term 'defence' could be used to imply the entire defence establishment to include the nonuniformed components such as ministry, R&D establishments, national training institutions such as National Defence College and national defence universities.

The Indian ministry of defence defines defence diplomacy as exchange of highlevel defence related visits, dialogue on security challenges and port calls; and defence cooperation as those activities covered by training exchanges, combined exercises; sourcing, development, production and marketing of defence equipment and other forms of cooperation. Going by the most obvious meaning of the terms, diplomacy efforts/ initiatives could be unilateral or by mutual consent between two or more countries. Unilateral initiatives could include policing of the high seas by navies. Cooperation, on the other hand, cannot be unilateral as it implies cooperative or consensual actions between two or more nations. While the aims and objectives of nations participating in military diplomacy or cooperation could differ the crux is that they work together to develop an environment of peace and trust.

OBJECTIVES OF MILITARY DIPLOMACY

Defence diplomacy serves specific national foreign and security policy objectives. In the context of global and regional strategic engagement, it creates sustainable cooperative relationships, thereby building trust and facilitating conflict prevention, introducing transparency into defence relations; building and reinforcing perceptions of common interests;

changing the mind-set of partners; and inducing cooperation in other areas. Defence diplomacy can further country specific foreign policy objectives by managing defence foreign relations and supporting the other diplomatic initiatives of government. The author, in his book 'Enabling Military-to-Military Cooperation as a *Foreign Policy Tool'*, details the various activities that can be undertaken as part of defence and military cooperation and which could also contribute towards military diplomacy.

A positive security environment implies that no adversarial or inimical activities are planned, initiated or undertaken or abetted against a country. This assumes greater significance in view of the global network of terror with or without state support. The following actions could be undertaken to achieve this:

Political, security and strategic defence dialogues: Multi-tiered dialogues would serve to enable an understanding of the participants' concerns and establish areas of common and mutual interest. These dialogues could be at the political level of national leadership level – head of state/government/ ministry and the civil and military professional/specialist level within the government and the armed forces.

Defence agreements/MoUs/treaties: These agreements could range from mutual assistance to cooperation. They ensure that respective positions etc, as the case may be, are identified and recorded to enhance trust and to prevent misunderstanding at some later stage.

Transparency in intent with regard to national military policy: Ensuring some degree of transparency in national defence and military policy such as response trigger lines and capabilities through various media - both government/ confidential and open sources as websites, magazines, journals etc, would assist in realistic assessments and appropriate responses.

Of course, while intentions, however, peaceful, could change, capabilities do not change. However, this transparency could facilitate better strategic and defence perceptions resulting in diffusing of tensions and right sized militaries and related budgets and expenditure. A comparison of bilateral relations between India and Bhutan; and India and Bangladesh highlights this point. India and Bhutan - which is host to an Indian Military Training Team (IMTRAT) - enjoy a special military diplomatic relationship and a larger bilateral relationship. In comparison, India and Bangladesh, despite the special role that the former played in securing the independent status of the latter, have a less than happy bilateral military relationship.

Assistance in maintenance of lawful government: Assistance in the maintenance of lawful government through military means; such as India's assistance to the Maldives during an attempted coup in 1988; and through military training, advice and equipment.

Professional personnel contacts: Contact at all levels would serve to create a better understanding of respective positions. It would also reduce animosity and enable a more conducive approach towards problem solving and interoperability.

This is achieved through permitting contacts between military personnel in formal, informal and social settings. Alumni of military training establishments, particularly long courses as at the National Defence College of Command and staff colleges, where spouses are encouraged to participate can be a major means of achieving this.

Exchange of perceptions: In order to establish commonalities, mutual benefit and areas of discord, both formal and informal (Track II) initiatives can be used to exchange views. Participation in exchanges, visits, seminars, conferences, symposia etc, and presentation of papers at these events educate the participants and provide decision makers with necessary inputs for astute decision making.

Participation in United Nations Peace Keeping Operations (UN PKO) or coalitions and humanitarian assistance and relief: A formal commitment to the UN and other regional cooperative organisations or coalitions for provision of forces and equipment for UN PKO, humanitarian assistance and relief and joint operations is a corner stone of military diplomacy as it is indicative, amongst other things, of a country's willingness to stand and be counted in international relations. The setting up of the Indian ministry of external affairs funded Centre for UN Peacekeeping (training) (CUNPK) at the United Services Institution of India, in New Delhi is a small step in this direction. The US has an elaborate training programme and funding for training other nations in peace keeping operations under the former president's Global Peace Operation Initiative (GPOI). GPOI has subsidiary programmes such as Africa Contingency Operations Training and Assistance (ACOTA) and Enhanced International Peacekeeping Capabilities (EPIC). The US funds UN training and simulation facilities in target countries such as Bangladesh and India. This ensures that countries willing to contribute troops for UN missions have the requisite trained forces readily available thereby enabling the US to ensure adequate UN forces without having to commit its own. Similarly, France supports the Zambakro Peacekeeping School in Côte d'Ivoire (Ivory Coast).

Strengthen defence relationships to promote own influence and access: A vibrant and healthy defence and military relationship could provide the desired influence and access to the country and decision makers. This could be achieved through equipment transfers through sale, aid or gifts; defence and military infrastructural development such as operational, training and administrative facilities; and human resource development with the help of in-country advisory / assistance / training teams etc.

Creation of equipment and intellectual dependency through exports and personnel exchanges could also serve to promote its own influence and access. This could result in access to the defence and military establishments and the desired influence in the target country's decision making instruments particularly defence. This could also ensure that its own sensitivities and concerns are considered and kept in mind during the target country's decision making.

Enhance Own Defence Capability in Areas of Defence Equipment

Sourcing and developing of defence equipment: In order to pose a viable deterrent and thereby ensure national security, the nation's military has to be adequately equipped. Military diplomacy could enable cooperative efforts for drawing up of equipment specifications, research and development, technology transfers, acquisitions and production. Some examples of such joint ventures in this field are the Indo-Russian BrahMos cruise missile and four nation (UK, France, Germany and Italy) armaments agency OCCAR (Organisation Conjoint de Cooperation en matiere d'ARmement) to provide improved management of collaborative defence equipment programmes involving European partners, particularly the Eurofighter jet fighter.

Making own defence industry and R&D effective and financially viable: Countries with relatively large militaries with the consequent large volumes of defence equipment may find home production, especially of spares more economically viable. It also gives the added advantage of not being dependent on imports during conflict situations and reduces the vulnerability to sanctions or exorbitantly high prices or economically detrimental contracts. This could be done by promoting own defence exports, technology transfers, joint R&D and joint production.

Leverage big ticket defence purchases: Big ticket sales made from a position of strength could be leveraged both in terms of strategic relations and financial payoffs such as offsets. However, purchases made from positions of urgent or desperate need could be detrimental to the buyer, as in the case of the Indian purchase of the Russian aircraft carrier *Groshkov* and its huge, frequent and arbitrary price hikes/cost overruns and delay in delivery.

Assist friendly foreign countries to develop their defence capability (without impinging on own security): The efforts to develop the defence capability of friendly foreign countries are always fraught with the need to guard against compromising one's own security. Exposure to own systems and assistance in defence development in areas of equipment, concepts, material resource, defence human resource etc could assist other countries in developing their own capability. These efforts could be linked to safeguards for own security through treaties/agreements, compliance with other development/economic assistance/aid etc.

Undertake international military engagement to enhance own military capability: The art of warfare and science of defence management have evolved with technological advances. There are continuous developments in these fields. One has to keep pace with these developments, in order to assess future threats and develop own capabilities. This can be done, overtly, through personnel contacts in the form of professional military exchanges, defence and military human resource development in basic and advanced military skills, war fighting skills at tactical and strategic levels, and in conceptual and doctrinal abilities; and defence management specialisations in resources, techniques and training. Own systems, approaches and procedures could be raised to optimal levels by carrying out comparative assessments and thereafter incorporating best practices, with appropriate refinements.

Promote defence and military interoperability: One of the likely outcomes of defence and military cooperation could be combined operations; either in bilateral and multilateral arrangements such as NATO, the US led coalition in Iraq etc and under the aegis of the UN. NATO has evolved extensive common standards ranging from English language to military terminology to military equipment to operating procedures to ensure complete and effective interoperability. This would have come in useful during the NATO deployment in Kosovo and other areas.

Appointment of defence attaches to foreign countries: Appointing defence attaches to foreign countries has been an old practice. USA and China have amongst the highest number of defence attaches abroad and virtually cover all the nations in the world. India, on the other hand seems to be taking a very conservative approach by not having increased the number of its defence attaches abroad for many decades thereby losing many opportunities to extend and gain from pro-active military diplomacy.

Specific defence diplomacy actions: These vary considerably and range from post-conflict reconstruction actions to participation in international parades and tattoos. Most of these actions can be linked to and may even form part of the previous categories.

THE CHARACTER AND GROWTH OF INDIAN DIPLOMACY

As diverse as the myriad colours of the land the Indian socio-political vision is essentially pluralistic in nature, leaving a strong influence in her secular diplomatic conduct. Diplomacy in India can be traced back to Aryan epic times of the *Ramayana* and the *Mahabharata*, which laid firm literary foundations to Hinduism. Infact the sacred book of the Hindus The *Bhagavat Gita* is perhaps one of the finest examples of diplomacy. It is interesting to note that the text is wholly based on the battlefield dialogue between Arjun, the noble warrior and Krishna, the illustrated Vishnu-incarnate who has taken the role of his chariot driver.

Before delving more into the aspects of the conversation that exemplifies the various forms of social diplomacy it is worth noting what Hinduism is in its real context. Much before being an iconoclastic term that full of religious embellishments and beliefs in divinity, it is rather an accumulation of 'idealistic' thoughts spoken in verses by Krishna to Arjun about the inevitabilities of life (combining the micro and the macro) and the rights and duties of an ideal person. The word Hindu rather than any religious sect originally meant people of Hind or Hindustan another name for *Bharatvarsha* or India.

As universally witnessed that it is characteristic of any ancient civilisation to bask in the misconception before explorations had begun that the world comprises only of its state (being supreme), besides which there are heavenly deities and the fallen underworld of the evil causing good or harm in direct relations to it. Though its a rather sketchy remark but the concept gives an ironic indication of the universal the three-worlds theory in politics through the ages, only to be interpreted in different ways with the changing agenda in international relations!

Thus Hinduism or the ethics of the Aryan Hind formed a logical linguistic outcome of the Bhagavat Gita that essentially spoke of moral truthfulness, happiness in work without attachment and acting dutifully on life's stage as the situation calls. In two terse lines of the heavily extended discourse of righteous action Krishna offers timeless advice on how one speech should be marked by the following qualities, in ordered priority: 'it should not disturb the mind of the listener; it should be precise with correct use of language; it should be truthful, if possible, it should be pleasing to the listener; and again if possible, it should be of utility to the listener.' Truthfulness is not presented as the highest virtue, overriding other qualities. Rather, the premier place goes to the requirement of not causing distress to the listener. Precision and good linguistic craftsmanship are rated as another high quality, which is followed by, the penultimate truth. What more can feature the qualifications of an apt diplomatic dialogue? The ancient book of human rights the *Manusamhita* or Laws of Man transcribed this pithy advice as a good speaker must: "Speak the pleasant but not the untruth; speak the truth but not the unpleasant".

Infact it is interesting to note that like any other ancient civilisation diplomacy is well exemplified in Indian mythology, more specifically in Hindu Polytheism, which is an impressive example of hierarchical representation amongst Gods. The proximity of cosmic forces/deities to kings, influencing and guiding them in the affairs of state, to make important political changes and bring in justice is remarkable.

Diplomacy is thus ingrained in the Indian psyche from time immemorial and has over centuries developed a distinct habit of tolerance inherent in Indian philosophy and tradition. The tradition stresses on tolerance and peaceful conciliation, which forms the fulcrum of Indian diplomacy. Perhaps that explains why it has so strongly sustained dynasty or regime changes through out history.

The group mind psyche that is the idea of commune has governed the spirit of the people from the Aryan age, reflective in its arts, aesthetics, literature, architecture, drama and even in the ethics of its socio-cultural construction. It is embedded in the Indian people to react instinctively to community claims, thus it can be easily understood how people spontaneously adapted to changes brought about by the distinct dynasties like the Lodis, Rajputs, Moguls, Marathas etc. Perhaps this tolerant outlook indulged the people towards equalitarianism and social content of communism. Another important aspect of thought, which has come down through the ages, is a means to achieve ends according to the moral law. The second century Tamil classic, *Kural* frames the notion 'Avoid at all times action that is not in accordance with the moral law. Success achieved without minding the prohibition of the moral law brings grief in the wake of achievement. To seek to further the welfare of the state by enriching it through frauds and falsehood is like storing water in an unburned mud pot and hoping to preserve it.'

This is not to indicate that Indian rulers have always conformed to ethical precepts. The illustrious fourth century B. C. political analyst and economist Kautilya2 for instance in his *Arthashastra* (Science of Material Gain), a textbook that outlined governmental administration and political strategy recommended that the adoption of state craft should be done according to the circumstance and that what produces unfavourable results is a bad policy; a policy is to be judged by the results it produces, for him diplomacy was an art not to be concern with ideals but achieving practical results for the states.

Going back to epic times it would be worth noting that character of Krishna the first and one of best social diplomat India has ever produced, as we see him advising the legitimate truth to kings and being instrumental in building or controlling many events. One can't but appreciate the tact and polish involved when Krishna acts as a special envoy of the Pandavas to the Kauravas before the battle of *Kurukshetra* in an attempt to get the opinion of the other. Though he did not succeed in averting war, his mission showed that like any adept diplomat he had genuine inclination to avoid war and prove that the Pandavas were right.

'Going thither we will remove the doubts of all man who are still undecided as to the wickedness of Duryodhana. Thither in the presence of all kings I will enumerate all those virtues of thine that are not to be met in all man, as also the wises of Duryodhana...I will also recite the wises of Duryodhana before both citizens and the inhabitants of the country, before both the young and old of all the four order that will be collected there. And though askest for peace no one will charge the as sinful while all Chiefs of the earth will censure the Kurus and Dhritarashtra...' The quote is rather important to understand the essence of Indian diplomacy as Krishna's politicness still influences the many procedures as India continues to pay the attention to the world opinion and seeks it support for achieving her ends.

Indian history holds unique examples of international as well as inter-state diplomacy, where the divergent reigning clans at times defended their interests by social, cultural or religious diplomacy. India's first contact with the Europeans started with Alexander's Indus campaign in 326 BC which resulted in a unique cultural diplomatic fusion between several Indo-Greek elements-especially in art, architecture, court administration and numismatics. Since then the Indian courts had heard regularly from the Greek ambassadors and vice-versa.

Following the Greek invasion was in 322 BC, Magadha, under the rule of Chandragupta Maurya, began to assert its hegemony over the neighbouring areas. Chandragupta, who ruled from 324 to 301 BC, was the architect of the first Indian imperial power—the Mauryan Empire (326-184 BC)— whose capital was Pataliputra, near modern-day Patna, in Bihar. Situated on rich alluvial soil and near mineral deposits, especially iron, Magadha was at the center of bustling commerce and trade. The capital was a city of magnificent palaces, temples, a university, a library, gardens, and parks, as reported by Megasthenes, the third-century BC Greek historian and ambassador to the Mauryan court. Chandragupta's success was due in large measure to his chancellor Kautilya who designed the highly centralized and hierarchical government. There was a regulated tax collection system, the government officials almost formed a cabinet ministry structure that saw to trade and commerce, industrial arts, mining, vital statistics, foreign affairs, maintenance of public places including markets and temples, and prostitutes. A large standing army and a well-developed espionage system were maintained. The empire was divided into provinces, districts, and villages governed by a host of centrally appointed local officials, who replicated the functions of the central administration. Indubitably the Mauryan Empire is considered to be the golden age in Indian history with its enormity of territory and time.

Emperor Ashoka (3rd Century BC) the third monarch of the Mauryan dynasty is a remarkable figure to study as he attained 'greatness' by religious diplomacy after having invaded the muchwanted land of Kalinga (present day Orissa). On witnessing the ruthless bloodshed and horrific killings of the Kalinga war he was so guilty that he became a Buddhist and preached non-violence through the rest of his life restoring peace to his state of affairs and the blood drenched kingdom espousing a theory of rule by 'righteousness'. He never fought a single war more in his reign and eventually won the hearts of many ready to acknowledge his supremacy by sending sombre convoys. He also sent his son and daughter to spread the word of Buddha as ambassadors to Ceylon (Srilanka) and Burma (Myanmar).

One of the most exemplary rulers in world history Ashoka's symbol of authority built in his Lion Capital at Sarnath near Varanasi, Uttar Pradesh still stands today as the National emblem of India. Sarnath was chosen by Ashoka to commemorate Buddha's first sermon there of peace and emancipation to the universe. The national emblem is thus symbolic of contemporary India's reaffirmation of its ancient commitment to world peace and goodwill. The four lions (one hidden from view) – symbolising power, courage and confidence-rest on a circular abacus. Four smaller animals- guardians of the four directions gird the abacus: the lion of the north, the elephant of the east, the horse of the south and the bull of the west. The abacus rests on a lotus in full bloom, exemplifying the fountainhead of life and creative inspiration. The motto '*Satyameva Jayate*' inscribed below the emblem in Devanagari script means 'truth alone triumphs'. The British historian H.G. Wells has written: "Amidst the tens of thousands of names of monarchs that crowd the columns of history... the name of Ashoka shines, and shines almost alone, a star." His toleration for different religious beliefs and languages reflected the realities of India's regional pluralism. Ashoka's numerous inscriptions chiselled on rocks and stone pillars located at strategic locations throughout his empire—such as Lampaka (Laghman in modern Afghanistan), Mahastan (in modern Bangladesh), and Brahmagiri (in Karnataka)—constitute the second set of datable historical records. He sent diplomatic-cum-religious missions to the rulers of Syria, Macedonia, and Epirus, who learned about India's religious traditions, especially Buddhism. Ashoka's Greek and Aramaic inscriptions found in Kandahar in Afghanistan also reveal his desire to maintain ties with courts outside India. By the end of the sixth century BC, India's northwest was integrated into the Persian Achaemenid Empire. This integration marked the beginning of administrative contacts between Central Asia and India.

After the disintegration of the Mauryan Empire in the second century BC, South Asia became a collage of regional powers with overlapping boundaries. India's unguarded north-western border again attracted a series of invaders between 200 BC and AD 300. As the Aryans had done, the invaders became "Indianized" in the process of their conquest and settlement. Also, this period witnessed outstanding intellectual and artistic achievements inspired by cultural diffusion and syncretism.

After the Mauryas it is worth noting how India held its first diplomatic conference during the Kushana dynasty The Kushana Kingdom controlled parts of Afghanistan and Iran, and in India the realm stretched from Purushapura (modern Peshawar, Pakistan) in the northwest, to Varanasi (Uttar Pradesh) in the east, and to Sanchi (Madhya Pradesh) in the south. The Kushana Kingdom was the crucible of trade and diplomatic ties with the Persian, Chinese and Roman empires and controlled a critical part of the legendary Silk Road. Kanishka, who reigned for two decades starting around 78 AD, was the most noteworthy Kushana ruler. He converted to Buddhism and convened an International Buddhist council in Kashmir. Besides Sanskrit literature, the Kushanas were patrons of a diplomatic art form called the Gandharan, a cultural synthesis between Greek and Indian styles.

Similarly the amity maintained between the Mughal Emperors and the Rajput Kings of Rajasthan in spite of being Islamic and Hindu clans respectively is noteworthy as the diplomatic interventions besides war were often seen to be resolved with marriages and pompous social festivals like the traditional *Rakhi* ceremonial, tying the knot of fraternity among states. Another way of extending friendliness among states were in the form of exchanging valuable artists or courtiers, it is well acknowledged that Raja Mansingh Tomar of Gwalior gave the legendary classical singer Tansen as 'a gift of appreciation' to the Mughal emperor Akbar along with his ambassadorial convoy to the Delhi durbar. One can't deny that it was the Raja's pride in showing how culturally enriched he was than the Emperor.

With the onset of western explorations India's xenophile nature and tolerance got enhanced as it embraced the initial setting up of trade relations and missionary activities of the Portuguese, Danish, Dutch, French and the British, later conferring them with administrative powers for ruling their own settlements or colonies which ultimately resulted in 200 years of British rule till India got its Independence in 1947.

Ever since India attained her independence to form the parliamentary executive, the vital decisions of foreign policy as in all governments fell on the Cabinet Minister in charge of foreign affairs. Initially Jawaharlal Nehru served as the Minister of foreign policy, besides being the prime minister primarily because of his influential foreign contacts and personality, that was even instrumental for securing the India's independence. In pre-independent India, Nehru guided the Congress Resolutions which catered to set the framework of India's foreign policy and being a leader in the government as well as holding leading positions in the party made him an authoritative speaker in the international forum as he worked closely with his illustrious political advisors Dr. S.Radhakrishnan, V.K.Krishna Mennon and Sir Girja Shankar Bajpai, the founder of Indian Foreign Service (IFS).

INDIA'S EFFORTS AT MILITARY DIPLOMACY

India maintains defence and military relations with many countries including Mauritius, Seychelles, Maldives, Indonesia, Laos, Malaysia, Singapore, Brunei, Cambodia, Japan, Philippines, Republic of (South) Korea, Thailand, Vietnam and ARF, China, Kazakhstan, Kyrgyzstan, Mongolia, Uzbekistan, Tajikistan, Israel, Oman, Iran, UAE, Botswana, Lesotho, Zambia, Namibia, Congo, Ethiopia, Eritrea. Sudan, Djibouti, Tanzania, Kenya, South Africa, USA, Brazil, UK, France, Russia, Czech Republic, Poland, Ukraine, Hungary, Belarus, Germany, Greece, Italy and Australia.

Over the last decade India's military diplomacy contacts and activities have increased exponentially. Rajat Pandit chronicles the list of war games being undertaken by the Indian defence forces in 2010-11. The army has planned 14 to 18 exercises with countries ranging from the US, UK and Russia to Bangladesh, Mongolia, Thailand, Tajikistan, Seychelles and Singapore; both at home and abroad. After the 'Malabar' naval war games on the western coast, the 'Habu Nag' amphibious exercise at Okinawa (Japan) Indian warships will hold combat manoeuvres with French warships, including the nuclear-powered aircraft carrier *Charles de Gaulle*. Indra-Dhanush, air combat war games between IAF and British Royal Air Force are slated to be held at Kalaikunda airbase in West Bengal. While the RAF has deployed its spanking new Eurofighter Typhoon fighters, E-3D AWACS (airborne warning and control systems) and VC-10 mid-air refuellers, IAF is participating with Sukhoi-30MKIs, Mirage-2000s, MiG-27s and the Phalcon AWACS8.

The example of Indo-Singapore military cooperation and the consequent more mutually supportive relations is a case in point. Singapore was looking for training areas and skies closer home and found them both in an India that was willing to explore new ways of defence cooperation. India has endeavoured to combine military diplomacy or cooperation to support its larger strategic interests as in Sudan for its oil, Yemen, Botswana, Lesotho and Zambia in Africa, China's neighbours – Laos and Vietnam, Pakistan's neighbour, Afghanistan and the Central Asian Republic of Tajikistan.

An Analysis of India's Military Diplomacy

The Strengths: India has actively conducted military diplomacy since independence. The initial efforts were a combination of its colonial inheritance (Nepal), the non aligned movement (NAM), support for anti-imperialistic and anticolonial movements (Nigeria, Iran, Iraq, Namibia, South Africa's anti apartheid efforts, etc). India's vast experience in mountain warfare, counter-insurgency/ terrorist operations and its redoubtable military training machinery has been exploited to develop vibrant bilateral relations through the medium of training and joint exercises. Bilateral relations with countries where Indian Military Training Teams are deployed are extra special as evinced in Bhutan, Lesotho, Zambia, Laos, and Tajikistan etc.

The presence of training teams assist in building links with the host country's military thereby supplementing the efforts of the diplomatic corps and at times even off setting not so cordial relations at the diplomatic level. Bhartendu Kumar Singh in his analysis of India's military diplomacy credits Prime Minister Manmohan Singh for the increased military diplomatic activity being undertaken by India in keeping with its rising economic and political profile, that has also been backed by the strategic consensus, for tackling common security threats through cooperative security in the region. Bhartendu Kumar Singh feels that gains are readily visible in the reduced tensions with China (sic) which has allowed the two countries to explore the possibilities of a partnership in the emerging Asian security architecture. It has enabled India to ensure enhanced policing of waters in the Indian Ocean region, through sharing of intelligence with other countries. India's capability to curb piracy and other subversive activities in the region has definitely increased as witnessed in the recent sinking of pirate ships in the Gulf of Aden by the Indian navy. This has allowed India to maintain a peaceful periphery and project its power in a discreet and subtle manner that resonates with the maritime needs and aspirations of small littoral countries in the region.

The Weaknesses: Bhartendu Kumar Singh also highlights the shortcomings in India's military diplomacy. He states that scope of military diplomacy is still limited to a few countries, and is also limited in variety and depth. India is not able to harness military diplomacy due to the demand supply disequilibrium in military modernisation. India still does not have a diplomatic presence in many of the continental countries in Africa as well as in the littoral countries of the Indian Ocean region and its trade linkages with these countries are too shallow to create 'stakes' for these countries. Many of the military diplomatic activities therefore, are a consequence of agreements reached with individual countries, rather than the part of a grand strategy. There are significant players competing with India with more resources and more lucrative terms of engagement. He argues that India's military diplomacy is yet to catch up with its rising power status. With the security situation in South Asia as well as the larger neighbourhood constantly fluctuating, India should focus on re-inventing the basket of military diplomacy. Given the nature of the Indian bureaucratic decision making process India's strengths have not been optimised due to a number of infirmities in the Indian approach to military diplomacy. Some of the infirmities are listed below:

- The over centralised approach of India's bureaucracy aka ministry of external affairs (MEA) and a convoluted and cumbersome decision making process.

- Lack of a definite and structured policy and road map for engaging other countries.
- Lack of a vision to develop a strategic grouping such as the Shanghai Cooperation Organisation (SCO) and the ASEAN Security Community (ASC).
- A general approach within the decision making polity and bureaucracy where a major portion of military diplomacy is considered to consist of leveraging the economic aspects of defence industry rather than relationships built on institutional and personal interactions at all levels.
- Lack of dedicated funding for military diplomacy which prevents the development of a long term approach. It also does not inspire much confidence in bilateral relationships due to the resultant uncertainty.

MILITARY DIPLOMACY – UNDER OPTIMISED

Military diplomacy, more often than not, does not receive the attention that it merits. Where employed, it suffers from not being fully integrated with the nation's overall foreign policy and diplomatic efforts. Anton du Plessis puts it very succinctly when he states: ...defence diplomacy approximates a military adjunct to diplomacy rather than a distinct type of diplomacy. At one level, its importance in a changing environment and use for foreign and security policy purposes are recognised in principle, whereas, at another level, defence diplomacy has become an overarching term for defence foreign relations. As a result, defence diplomacy does not receive the recognition it deserves. Conceptually, this is due less to the precarious relationship between various foreign policy instruments, and more to an underestimation of the nature, scope and utility of defence diplomacy. Practically, and due in part to conceptual ambiguity, this underestimation is reinforced by a lack of integration with foreign and defence policy and corresponding military policy and strategy, as well as by defence diplomacy being restricted to its military-defence policy context rather than enhanced by its diplomatic-foreign policy context.

2

Developing a Pluralist Approach to Security in the Asia-pacific

Coalition operations in the 21st century will be very different from those in which we have participated in the past. Perhaps the most significant consequence of the accelerated process of globalisation that has occurred since the end of the Cold War has been the convergence of states' interests. Contrary to the fevered imaginings of the half-educated, this process is not the product of a conspiracy cooked up by the World Economic Forum, international financiers or even the illuminati.

Rather, the convergence of human, social, economic and political relationships has been inevitable since the introduction of steam power, the telegraph and aircraft dramatically shrank the globe. The unanticipated consequences of the dawning of the information age have produced a paradigm shift in human relationships that is forcing states to redefine the way in which they relate to each other. Arguing that the new strategic environment does not allow us the luxury of a strategic pause, the former Commander in Chief of United States (US) Central Command, General Anthony Zinni, pointed out that states are increasingly interdependent and interconnected. Accordingly, it is no longer possible to claim that the internal affairs of states do not have implications for others. General Zinni has concluded, together with many of his colleagues, that military organisations, and particularly land forces, need to be prepared to respond to a wider range of tasks than ever before. The complexity of information-age politics also means that states are no longer the only players in the global community. Faced with a threat to human security, such as the September 2001 attack on the United States, all legitimate states have little option but to cooperate to preserve their common interests. Unlike formed alliances that are built on longer-lasting perceptions of common interest, 21st-century coalitions are increasingly likely to be formed by default.

The passing of the bipolar world order that dominated the Cold War has created the conditions that have caused coalitions to thrive and flourish over the past ten years. As coalitions are formed to deal with specific circumstances, no military coalition is typical. It is important to distinguish coalition operations—which are common in a multipolar strategic environment—from alliance operations, which are characteristic of an amalgamated security environment. Coalitions may contain alliance partners, but coalitions are put together for purposes other than longterm strategic understandings. A coalition is, by definition, an 'ad hoc arrangement between two or more nations for common action'.

Coalition operations are the product of temporary and relatively informal combinations of states that share common interests and work together for broadly common ends—not the best foundation for the employment of military power in the information age. The first true information-age conflict is beginning to demonstrate the problems of multinational cooperation in the delivery of security. The rather loose characterisation of the international support promised to the United States in the immediate aftermath of the terrorist attack on the World Trade Center as a 'coalition' has significant implications for security cooperation in the Asia-Pacific. Until those that have tendered their support to the United States agree to both the general objectives of the 'war on terrorism' and the measures to be adopted, it is not quite accurate to speak of a coalition. Nonetheless, the approach adopted by President Bush has left no room for doubt—those that are not with the United States are against it. Most countries of the Asia-Pacific have promised to cooperate with the United States. Although the US commitment to bringing about regime change in Iraq served to alienate many governments that supported operations against al-Qa'ida, the comprehensive nature of the war on terrorism is likely to continue to bind regional states to the global effort. Success against the rogue regime of Saddam Hussein will prove its own justification. In the long term, all countries will need to remain focused on combating the threat of transnational fanatic terrorist ideologies.

The emergence of these commitments may well mark a significant shift in the region's security architecture. Since the end of the Cold War, many regional countries have shied away from too close an association with the United States and have placed greater emphasis on multilateral diplomatic initiatives such as the ASEAN Regional Forum (ARF). The demands made by the United States, combined with the palpable air of insecurity generated by the contemporary situation, may well see regional states become more closely associated in developing common security. It has been instructive, in the wake of the Bali bombing, to see a high level of effective international cooperation in the investigation of the outrage. At a governmental level, for instance, the sharing of intelligence and police force-to-police force cooperation has done much to restore the Australian–Indonesian relationship which had declined in the wake of Australia's role in securing East Timor's independence.

The heterogeneous nature of the region makes it difficult to forecast what combinations of national forces will be available to cooperate together in the future. Before the East Timor crisis occurred, no-one anticipated that a multinational coalition consisting of contingents from regional and extra-regional states would be required to sustain extended operations in that country. Before the end of the Cold War, no-one imagined that Australian troops would be employed in multinational operations as far dispersed as Kuwait, Somalia, Rwanda, Bougainville and the Solomon Islands. The challenge that faces force planners as they set about preparing for operations in an utterly novel strategic environment has been spelt out by Admiral Dennis Blair, Commander in Chief of United States Pacific Command: [A]s a combatant commander, I cannot conceive of wars in the 21st century that will not involve coalition partners. And especially in the Pacific, each contingency may require a different set of coalition partners. We cannot expect to rely on alliance protocols such as NATO [North Atlantic Treaty Organization]. We need systems that have been wrung out in the development stage with our coalition partners so that we identify what part of the operational picture needs to be seen in all coalition headquarters, what messages need to be passed back and forth, and how we can solve the daunting information assurance challenge in a coalition environment.

We will return to Admiral Blair's vision for the future of security cooperation in the Asia-Pacific, but first we need to develop an understanding of why coalitions represent the future of military operations.

Regardless of the level of operational intensity and despite the complexity introduced by the demands of information-age conflict in a heterogeneous global community, building and sustaining a coalition of countries with a range of interests and ideologies is the most significant way of bestowing legitimacy on a particular cause. Given the current situation in the Asia-Pacific, however, few states are capable of engaging in coalition activities at anything other than the most basic level. Learning from the international political, military and domestic levels of recent coalition efforts, it becomes obvious that the Asia-Pacific needs to evolve a security architecture that will enable rapid and effective responses to regional crises. The alternative is to accept that the region will suffer conditions of relative insecurity no longer tolerated in the West nor even in much of the Middle East.

In industrial-age conflicts it was possible to circumvent close cooperation between coalition partners. Operations could be carved up and tactical areas of responsibility could be easily apportioned to the armed forces of different states. In the European Theatre of Operations during World War II, for example, the British and American forces conducted their advances independently, coordination of their efforts being managed at the highest level. Even the two air forces divided their strategic bombing campaigns into night and day.

This sort of stovepiping is not so easily accomplished in information-age operations. As opposing forces contend to get inside each other's decision cycle, the coalition that has not established internal situational awareness is starting on the back foot. With the exception of the Russo–Japanese War, the Iran–Iraq War and perhaps the Indo–Pakistan Wars, all major conflicts of the 20th century have been waged by coalitions—at least on one side.

Unlike longterm, formal alliances, their success is founded on the ability of their members to work together and preserve unity in achieving identifiable common objectives. Some members of a coalition might well have a history of cooperation, but most of the combinations of the last decade have seen disparate states forced to improvise the manner in which they work together. In contrast, combined military operations arising from alliance relationships are generally based on firmer political resolve; greater commonality of purpose; and shared training, equipment and doctrine.

Preparing for coalition operations in a complex strategic environment requires much closer attention to detail than was the norm during the Cold War. As the American–British–Canadian–Australian Armies Program (ABCA) *Coalition Operations Handbook* points out: [P]lanners must closely study the political goals of each participant as a precursor to detailed planning. Political considerations weigh more heavily with coalitions than with alliance operations. Coalition operations are not new... Since human nature has not changed, conflicts over territory, religion, politics, and economics, such as those that prompted previous military operations, will continue to be widespread. The precise role of armies in these operations will vary according to each political and military situation.

SECURITY PLURALISM AND PRINCIPLES

If land forces are to be successfully employed on coalition operations, a high degree of cohesion has to be present from the beginning of their mission. This requirement implies that multinational forces will have established a pre-existing level of understanding and functional interoperability before they arrive in-theatre. Looking for ways of improving the conduct of coalition operations, General RisCassi focused on the factors of doctrine and leadership. He argued that doctrine and leadership are the keys to achieving order in the chaos of battle and that this truism rings doubly true for multinational operations. Nonetheless, he noted that, despite long experience of coalition membership, the United States (and by extension all other states) remained remarkably ill-prepared for combined action. Although his comments focused on warfighting, they apply to any coalition force facing armed opposition. The fog and friction of operations, he wrote, were best overcome by:

> accentuating the commonalities that exist: first, between our national interests; second, between how we intend to deal with threats to mutual interests; and then in how we actually apply our combined forces in battle. Where commonalities are required but lacking, we move quickly to create them... The key to achieving this unity is by promulgating a doctrine for warfighting that is commonly understood and applied. Planning systems must be collective and participatory, yet responsive and unerringly timely.

General RisCassi concluded that the friction inherent in coalition operations was best overcome by rapidly analysing and testing combined tactical integration; command-and-control systems; training; and logistic arrangements. Provision could then be made to 'sew' these coalition systems even tighter. The task of developing coalition doctrinal principles that are both capable of being applied by the states of the Asia-Pacific and politically acceptable to them is a daunting one. However, that task is perhaps not as difficult as we might think. Attitudes to multinational operations are often shaped by experiences of UN-run missions. The past record of such operations does not provide an ideal starting point for a consideration of the most efficient way to deploy coalitions—a fact that the UN is honestly, if belatedly, accepting. The *Report of the Panel on United Nations Peace Operations*, which was released in August 2000, frankly exposed the problems that many coalitions faced. Such problems included the overly bureaucratic distribution of responsibility in coalitions; shortfalls in officers qualified to serve in command and staff positions on coalition headquarters; the lack of training and equipment; and the inability of many states to honour the commitments that they had made to the UN.

These findings emphasised the gross disparities that generally exist between forces hurriedly cobbled together for multinational operations. Despite these criticisms of the manner in which the international community currently mounts multinational operations, there is another dimension to the military profession. Whatever their cultural origins, almost every military force recognises a list of principles that guide its actions. Most of these principles are derived from a common body of professional literature and enable officers, despite their own unique backgrounds and disparate force capabilities, to communicate complex concepts to each other. Working from a foundation of commonly accepted principles, professionally trained officers can establish understandings that will form the basis of a coalition and enable command relationships to be formed. Although we often concentrate on the 'bad news' about multinational forces, we should be surprised that they ever work at all. How many other professionals, sent far from home at short notice, could achieve anything in a polyglot team drawn from twenty or more countries?

With coalition operations becoming more common, soldiers can now expect to serve on a number of such missions during their career. The requirement to sustain operations in East Timor has resulted in the rotation of most active-service Australian Army units through that theatre. In addition, many Australian officers have gained valuable operational experience in multinational headquarters or as liaison officers with other forces. Officers from other armies participating in the operation often have even more experience of multinational operations than their Australian counterparts.

From a regional perspective, a middle-level officer in the New Zealand Army is likely to have served on three or four overseas peace operations, and a Fijian soldier may well spend half of his career overseas on operations. If the operational tempo currently maintained by the Australian Army persists, frequent overseas service may well become the norm, not the exception, in a soldier's career.

In these circumstances it makes little sense to reinvent the wheel for each operation. Longstanding, well-trained alliances such as NATO forces, or for that matter the forces of the Warsaw Pact, have demonstrated the value of possessing formed doctrine. The existence of such doctrine does not presuppose a commitment to particular operations, but does demonstrate a capacity to collaborate effectively if required. Different levels of cooperation are achieved within every interstate relationship: military, political and economic connections operate in different dimensions and at distinct levels. For example, the formal treaty-based special relationship with the United States is supported and supplemented by the specific operational synergies with other armies that the Australian Army gains through its participation in the American–British–Canadian–Australian Armies Program. In fact a comparative reading of Australian, US and British doctrinal publications will demonstrate extraordinary conceptual similarities—similarities that often extend to the order of the words themselves. (In the academic world we might call it plagiarism. In the drafting of military doctrine it is considered a full, frank and open exchange of ideas.) The high level of intellectual understanding that English-speaking and other NATO forces can establish only emphasises the problems faced by ad-hoc coalitions, which are often required to coordinate military operations in a matter of days.

Due to their complexity, land forces are particularly reliant on doctrine. Historically, the development of doctrine has reflected the particular national and cultural characteristics of individual forces. Their cultural similarity explains the ease with which English-speaking armies can share operational philosophies. In the Asia-Pacific, where even the simplest level of understanding between disparate forces is difficult to achieve, it is not possible to share common doctrine. In the absence of linguistic and cultural ties, it becomes even more important to seek alternative means of building common understanding. A recent joint US–UK–German–French working group on improving cooperability on coalition operations found that: Coalition partners working with very different doctrines will obviously have problems harmonizing their efforts. Indeed, regardless of the degree of technical interoperability they might achieve, genuine cooperability will be all but impossible to achieve. In simplest terms, forces that operate on different fundamental principles become vulnerable to misunderstandings, poorly coordinated actions, and even working at crosspurposes. Doctrine can, if harmonized, be the glue of coalition operations. Finding ways to harmonize doctrine is, therefore, a priority effort to ensure improved coalition operations.

It is a mistake to believe that the task of improving the level at which land forces can cooperate is fettered to the state of relationships between states in the Asia-Pacific. Nor is it in the long-term interest of regional states that the level of security dialogue should be pinned to formal diplomatic instruments. As Lord Palmerston famously commented: 'There are no permanent friends, only permanent interests.' It is in the interests of states that they be prepared to cooperate at short notice, even if it is impossible to foresee the circumstances that might give rise to joint action.

In a proposal with particular relevance for the Asia-Pacific, Colonel Michael Smith, Director of the Joint Doctrine Directorate in the US Army's Training and Doctrine Command, suggested that: To overcome the problems associated with the lack of common doctrine, regional organizations should develop regional doctrinal publications which identify doctrinal 'considerations' for commanders and planners. The term 'considerations' is used because it is unlikely that anything more detailed or prescriptive would be adopted and endorsed by all potential coalition members from a region.

Unfortunately, the nature of the strategic environment in the Asia- Pacific militates against the creation of a 'strong' security community. The region is simply not ready for developed multilateral cooperation in the way that Europe is. Not only does the region not share a monolithic security architecture, but historically it has not shared many of the presumptions on which international law and the notion of collective security are based. The security implications of the heterogeneous nature of the region are particularly clear in the case of the member states of the Association of South-East Asian Nations (ASEAN). In a paper published in 1996, Nicola Baker and Leonard Sebastian highlighted the extreme reluctance of ASEAN states to commit themselves to formal alliances:

> Formal multilateral security agreements and structures were not considered feasible or desirable by the founding member states of ASEAN for three... reasons: they lacked the defence capacity for any form of collective security, their relations were complicated by unresolved territorial disputes, and they had quite different threat perceptions. Regional defence capabilities have since improved significantly but few have reached the point where adequate forces could be committed to, and sustained in, any form of collective action beyond the occasional military exercise.

To a certain extent, operations in East Timor have disproved this last assertion. Regional forces have established a precedent for cooperation on active service. Importantly, both INTERFET and its successor, the peacekeeping force element of UNTAET, have enjoyed regional leadership— in turn generals drawn one each from Australia and the Philippines, and two from Thailand.

Despite initial worldwide and regional support for the US-led 'coalition' against terrorism, we are unlikely to see overtly formal cooperative security structures established in the region in the near future. At the intergovernmental level, such an initiative—particularly if it originated in a Western state—is likely to be unwelcome. Although initially most East Asian governments pledged support for the planned US retaliation against the al'Qa'ida organisation, these governments have often had to face hostile domestic constituencies. The promises made to the United States have placed many regional countries in a difficult position—particularly those countries where the United States does not enjoy domestic popularity. As Bruce Gilley of the *Far Eastern Economic Review* wrote: Domestic pressures in every country will force most governments to keep their cooperation with the U.S. low profile. Anti-American sentiment, and more commonly a lack of support for a U.S. response, runs deep within the region. Some countries—particularly Singapore and Malaysia—are wary of making themselves targets of terrorists. Yet a failure to support U.S. efforts would put a country in danger of being labelled an undependable ally, or a rogue regime. So far, that is providing a formidable incentive to stand up and be counted.

While current circumstances provide indications that regional resistance to security cooperation may not be permanent, we must not be naive about the political constraints on the task of creating the preconditions for military coalitions. Over and above questions of language, culture and technical interoperability, many regional military forces play political and economic roles in their own countries. In some instances they have been implicated in human-rights abuses. The usual Western response to this concern was summarised by the Canadian scholar Brian Job, who made the quite valid point that: expansion of the extent and scope of military to military activities is viewed positively by Asia-Pacific security analysts who see substantial longer term benefits from opening dialogues among national militaries, as preliminary steps toward creating understanding, advancing transparency, and promoting important functional [links].

Nonetheless, liberal democracies cannot afford to be seen to be providing implicit support to the armed forces that might not fully represent the legitimately expressed aspirations of the populations that they are meant to protect. It would be naive to believe that we would never act in concert with such forces; instead, we can expect to belong to coalitions with a diverse composition when our national interests are involved and the particular operation or cause is demonstrably legitimate. Issue-based coalitions— rather than formal, standing defence relationships—will continue to be the norm so long as regional military forces remain active participants in their countries' political and economic affairs. The question that confronts us in the immature strategic environment that is the Asia-Pacific is how to create cooperative synergies with essentially dissimilar militaries.

Although multilateral diplomatic engagement has its place, post-Cold War regional diplomatic initiatives have singly failed to improve conditions of security. As Frederick the Great is credited with saying, 'diplomacy without arms is like an orchestra without instruments'. Security needs to be backed up by potent military force, and in the information age the talisman of military power needs to be transnational. At the level of military-to-military cooperation, US strategic engagement in the Asia-Pacific provides a model that regional forces need to embrace wholeheartedly. The challenge to US Pacific Command and its regional partners that Admiral Blair enunciated requires an information-age response that can only be achieved when armed forces have developed a high level of familiarity with each other. In the Asia-Pacific the US policy has been to support the growing pattern of security pluralism in the region. Admiral Blair has been particularly active in promoting the notion of 'security communities' that will enable specific-issue cooperation between military forces, even if more comprehensive political links do not exist between countries.

The notion of security communities—which was the brainchild of Karl Deutsch, the noted Harvard-based political scientist—is used to describe a group of nations that share dependable expectations of peaceful progress. Recognising that many regions were not yet ready for amalgamated security arrangements, much less shared political and economic systems,

Deutsch identified three factors that could substantially enhance the prospects of a pluralistic security community. The first of these was the widespread unattractiveness of war as a means of resolving conflict among the potential members of the community. The second factor was the spread of intellectual movements favouring security interdependence. Thirdly, Deutsch promoted: the development and practice of skills of mutual attention, communication, and responsiveness, so as to make possible the preservation of the autonomy and substantial sovereignty of the participating units, and the preservation of stable expectations of peace and peaceful change among them.

The first factor is almost a foregone conclusion in a region that seeks stability for economic growth and where most countries would regard war as a calamity. The second process is certainly in train, through measures such as the second-track diplomacy of the ARF and the Council for Security Cooperation in the Asia-Pacific (CSCAP). The third process is one that could be substantially enhanced by the practical security collaboration that will arise from preparation for coalition efforts.

The concept of the security community is particularly useful for those states that are likely to come together to form coalitions and that need to prepare their forces to do so. As already demonstrated, land forces require the most preparation for multinational operations, and they have the most to benefit from the sort of cooperation envisaged by regional security cooperation.

Admiral Blair has pointed out that: An attractive feature of security communities for Asian states is the absence of any requirement for security institutions or regimes specified by treaty. Communities may be based on a non-military organization such as the ASEAN Regional Forum; or their membership may be based upon geography or common concerns rather than any multilateral security forum. The key is that the members are committed to policy coordination, including combined military cooperation on a particular regional security issue, or a series of related security issues, to advance peaceful development of their region over time without major conflict.

As far as land forces in the Asia-Pacific are concerned, cooperation can be engendered by practical measures to prepare regional land forces for the most common operations that they will have to carry out. In the current strategic environment, this requirement entails preparing for peace operations and countering transnational threats such as terrorism, smuggling, piracy and other crimes that threaten regional order. In the absence of more formal cooperative instruments, a useful expedient would be the formation of a multilateral army-to-army program, modelled on the highly successful ABCA system and building on the excellent relationships formed in recent regional peace operations.

The ABCA program provides the region with a useful model for inter-army cooperation since it is not an alliance, nor has an ABCA force ever been employed under the program. The program began after World War II to take advantage of the unprecedented levels of standardisation achieved by the American, British and Canadian armies. Australia joined the program in 1963 and New Zealand joined as an associate member two years later. The member armies conduct formation-level exercises on a biennial basis in order to identify technical interoperability issues and to test the abilities of the armies to operate in coalitions should the need arise. These exercises do not, however, imply a commitment to alliance operations; rather, they are a recognition of the common interests of the member states and signify an awareness of the fact that the member armies are likely to continue to serve together in the pursuit of common objectives. The program produces standardisation agreements, advisory handbooks and planning guides that help the armies to operate together when they are called on to do so. Although achieving total technical and doctrinal interoperability between armies from such varied operational environments is not likely, or even desirable, the experience of the synergies that they have been able to achieve demonstrates the value of this arrangement. The adoption of an ABCA-style model in the Asia- Pacific would not commit regional land forces to common doctrine, but it would enable them to harmonise their operational styles. Nascent infrastructure for army-to-army cooperation already exists. The Pacific Armies Management Seminar (PAMS), which is annually cohosted by the US Army and the army of one other Pacific Rim country, has been in existence since 1978. Representatives from 33 countries attended the seminar in 2001. Similarly the biennial Pacific Armies Chiefs Conference (PACC) involved fifteen army chiefs at its second meeting in Kuala Lumpur in September 2001. Although significant adjustments to the circumstances of the Asia-Pacific would be necessary, the adoption of a standardisation program would build on the goodwill and shared experience established by the Australian Army's participation in recent operations in Cambodia and East Timor.

THE DISTINCTIVE ROLE OF LAND FORCES IN A COALITION ENVIRONMENT

The Australian Government's recent Defence White Paper identified the need to develop a 'professional, well-trained, well-equipped' land force that: is available for operations at short notice, and one that can be sustained over extended periods. This type of force will have the flexibility to deal with operations other than conventional war, and contribute to coalitions.

The requirement that Australia's Army be capable of contributing to coalitions recognised the particular challenges faced by armies when they are required to integrate their efforts with those of dissimilar coalition partners. Unlike the other services—which are traditionally 'platformbased'— land forces are human-based organisations. When we think of deploying air and naval assets, aircraft and ships immediately spring to mind. By contrast, the range of capabilities that land forces bring to a coalition are diverse and complex. Consequently, the way in which land forces are structured, commanded and employed on coalition operations must be distinguished from the way in which air and naval forces might be used. While we are accustomed to thinking of coalition operations as joint efforts involving the synergy of air, land and maritime forces, we must recognise the particular characteristics of land forces that affect ground-based operations. These characteristics are cultural, organisational, tactical and political. It is important to appreciate how the complex interplay of relationships between different forces will affect land operations. The way in which armies operate reflects the culture from which they are drawn, as well as their particular history, their longstanding alliances and the doctrinal influences that have shaped their thinking. Although soldiers from many countries have the opportunity to train and conduct operations overseas, armies are inherently parochial and self-centred organisations— and this is not meant as a criticism. The history of land forces deployed as part of a larger effort bears out this observation, regardless of whether they are engaged in warfighting or military operations other than war. Any contingent assigned to an operation is a cultural microcosm, a unit or formation sealed in time and defined by its constituent elements. In contemporary operations, national forces can find themselves deployed at short notice into an unfamiliar environment and as part of an ad-hoc multinational force. In those circumstances the national characteristics of the forces deployed become particularly evident.

The considerable differences that exist between national forces are nowhere more obvious than in the Asia-Pacific. The lack of cultural and organisational compatibility between forces is obvious to most observers, but in recognising these 'soft' factors we must not forget the significant differences that exist in the capabilities of many forces. As the revolutionary potential of information-age warfare opens up to us, the gap between cutting-edge military forces and industrial-age organisations is likely to widen. Nowhere is that gap more obvious than when assigning tasks to the disparate land forces that countries contribute to coalitions.

As the former Commander in Chief of the United Nations and US–Korean Combined Forces Command, General Robert RisCassi, observed in 1993: Air and naval forces, because they must operate in international mediums, are equipped with communications gear and common protocols and procedures to provide for organized space management. All of the 'vessels' that operate in the air or the sea can be readily classified for their strengths and weaknesses to perform the various missions of air and naval warfare. Ground forces come in all shapes and sizes, and their equipment may be entirely dissimilar and incompatible. Technological differentials, particularly in this era of revolutionary change, can be vast. Therefore, fundamental commonalities become even more important. As we have already seen, for most crises requiring a military response, there is no dispensing with land forces. The temptation in recent coalition operations has been to employ platform-based weapons rather than the much messier option of troops on the ground. In asymmetric conflicts the Western democracies see distinct domestic advantages since ships and aircraft are less likely to incur casualties and are easier to deploy, being mobile by their nature. By comparison, soldiers are more vulnerable to both conventional and unconventional weapons. Nonetheless, land forces are required in both peace operations and warfighting—since only they can enforce compliance on the ground.

The employment of land power does present operational planners with a particularly complex set of problems. As Colonel Anthony Rice pointed out in an article published in *Parameters*, the journal of the US Army War College, the 'ground component has invariably been the most difficult to integrate, because doctrinal and equipment differences affect the lowest echelons of command in all armies'.

The tempo of operations can, however, make a significant difference in the level at which forces need to be integrated. Where a major conflict such as the Gulf War raises problems of sustaining resource-hungry, high-intensity operations that require a common logistic system capable of rapidly supplying the needs of the whole force, low-intensity operations such as peacekeeping may allow forces to be resupplied at a much lower level. On low-intensity operations, countries can take direct responsibility for maintaining their own forces and thus relieve the strain on the coalition's logistical arrangements. Air and naval units can more easily establish a symbiotic relationship with dissimilar forces. Navies can do this by matching capabilities to needs, and air forces achieve it by matching the characteristics of their aircraft to specific missions. As these functions are highly automated, or at least essentially platform-based, they do not involve the political dimension of human interaction in the same way that integrating ground forces does. Ostensibly, platform-based units appear to be better suited to coalition operations, but it is a mistake to think that all coalition operations will lend themselves to stand-off weaponry. Low-level operations will always require a human presence, and any operation that requires troops to take and hold ground to achieve the mission's political objectives involves the need for ground forces.

Ground forces devoted to coalitions raise particular problems for commanders. The prominent US scholar of coalition operations, Thomas Durrell-Young, has demonstrated that land commanders require a greater level of command authority when conducting coalition operations than that required by their naval and air counterparts. In addition, land forces are extremely vulnerable and their presence on an operation raises specific issues of force protection, interoperability and operational autonomy.

To develop the same level of symbiosis between ground forces as is possible with platform-based services, armies need to train together. Also, as part of their preparation for command, commanders need to develop specific skills and aptitudes in order to meet the demands of ad-hoc combined operations at every level of conflict. As US Navy Captain Terry Pudas pointed out, senior officers need to appreciate the effect that different coalition combinations will have on key planning factors, and accordingly officers at all levels need to conduct exercises in order to familiarise themselves with the variables that are inherent in multinational operations.

WAR FIGHTING AND PEACEKEEPING: KEEPING OUR OPTIONS OPEN

The Asia-Pacific region has not the same tradition of coalition operations as has Europe, or for that matter, the West as a whole. In the past, the disparate nature of the region has militated against the formation of broadbased coalitions. However, global pressures now mean that there is a greater co-identity of interests between states than was the case during the Cold War and before. While the likelihood of major global war between the great powers appears to have receded, the possibility of aggression by marginalised states and failing states remains. In addition, we now face the threat of asymmetric attacks by non-state actors such as terrorist and criminal groups. The proliferation of novel threats to human security in the Asia-Pacific has resulted in more willingness on the part of regional countries to employ their forces in coalitions for purposes other than war.

During the past ten years, within our immediate region alone, Australia has been involved in multinational peace operations in Cambodia, Bougainville, East Timor and the Solomon Islands. While these operations have not involved warfighting, the ability of the Australian Army to prosecute military operations offshore, and to bring with it the promise of potent warfighting skills, has made it a valuable asset to these multinational forces. The same can be said of Australian contributions to extra-regional coalitions such as those in Somalia and Rwanda. Australia's willingness and ability to take command of INTERFET demonstrated its commitment to regional stability and enhanced its credit within the region. Like those of our neighbours in the Asia-Pacific, the direction of Australian national policy and our current pattern of deployments indicate the likelihood of involvement in future cooperative partnerships. As the current Defence White Paper points out: Over the next ten years the ADF will continue to undertake a range of operations other than conventional war. Preparing the ADF for such operations will therefore take a more prominent place in our defence planning than it has in the past.

We must therefore consider those factors that might influence the use of land forces once they are committed to a multinational force. It is also important that we identify the roles that Army units will have to undertake in regional coalitions. In many military forces there is considerable resistance to the notion that they will be called upon to execute operations short of 'warfighting'. The conservative argument is that armies are designed to fight wars and that other functions, such as peacekeeping and humanitarian relief efforts, more properly belong to other bodies, for example, police forces or non-government organisations. As well as being short-sighted, this argument does not follow history. Land forces have traditionally fulfilled a range of roles. During the 19th century, European forces performed constabulary tasks around the world. During the postwar period of decolonisation, troops across the globe took on the thankless task of preventing the independence process from descending into total chaos. Not for nothing do we speak of the Pax Britannia—and in retrospect that period of vile imperial repression is beginning to take on a roseate hue. Commencing with the Roman legions, soldiers have generally spent more of their active careers serving as engineers, administrators, lawgivers and police than in combat roles. Their authority is, however, only as good as their capacity to enforce their will.

In the aftermath of the Cold War we are experiencing a variety of challenges to international security. Some of the most immediate threats requiring the potential employment of military force include the disintegration of states; ethnic and religious conflict; small wars and large displaced populations. Consequently, there is a greater demand than ever before for legitimate and militarily capable armed forces that can enforce order and lay the foundation for reconstruction. As the former Chairman of the US Joint Chiefs of Staff, General John Shalikashvili, used to joke, the US Armed Forces did not have the option of hanging a large sign outside the Pentagon saying 'I'm sorry, we only do the big ones'. Soldiers have to be able to fight wars, but that is not a sufficient condition. In the fluid strategic environment that is the Asia-Pacific today, we require forces that can win on the battlefield and provide the conditions that will guarantee the peace—in either a pre-conflict stage or the aftermath of violence.

Given the need for such forces, as well as the fact that they will almost inevitably be employed in a coalition context, we need to question why in the information age we should adopt the comparatively messy option of deploying land forces, rather than avoiding personnel-intensive operations. The answer is simple: whether conducting peace operations or fighting a war, the task of pursuing political objectives through the use of force in a land-based environment requires the physical presence of troops. Conrad Crane of the US Army's Strategic Studies Institute recently made the point that: Army units are the preferred forces to form the core of the joint force required for the type of enhanced conventional deterrence that can compel an aggressor to back down and defuse a crisis. Not only do Army forces possess significant capability, the deployment of heavy units also is the strongest possible signal of American intent. The effort that goes into their movement and relative permanence of their placement shows the maximum national commitment to defend US interests. Lighter Army units also clearly signal commitment intent and usually serve as the spearhead for American ground involvement in any crisis.

What applies to the actions of a superpower also applies to the efforts of a multinational effort seeking to demonstrate its legitimacy in a situation where order has either broken down or is in the process of breaking down. However, the very potency of wielding land power in a multinational context brings its own challenges. It is important that we identify what these potential pitfalls are.

3

The Changing Nature of Military Forces

The growth in the number and importance of peace operations and other non-traditional security roles is said to be part of a broader shift in the general nature of military organisations generally whereby the existing modern military organisation is evolving into a new, postmodern form. According to Charles Moskos and his colleagues, modern and postmodern militaries differ in quite significant ways.The modern military organisation is a product of the Westphalian and Weberian eras. It consists of volunteer and conscripted lower ranks operating under the command of an increasingly professionalised officer corps. It is 'waroriented in mission, masculine in makeup and ethos, and sharply differentiated in structure and culture from civilian society'. The postmodern military, by contrast, is 'more multipurpose in mission, increasingly androgynous in makeup and ethos, and [has] greater permeability with civilian society'. A related trend has been the recent expansion of the types of military forces beyond state-based ones.

Military forces are becoming, on the one hand, increasingly transnationalised with national forces being deployed under the control of such regional and international organisations as the United Nations, NATO and the Commonwealth of Independent States. We are also seeing a growing array of private military services and mercenary organisations that are often 'organised around a charismatic leader' or 'attached to political movements or organized criminal networks or both'. While they may not have cruise missiles and the other hightechnology weapons that are owned by national and transnational forces, these 'post-Fordist' militaries can easily access the range of small arms that have flooded the world in the wake of the end of the Cold War. They are likely, too, to benefit from what Kaldor and her colleagues describe as the increasing 'informalization' of the international arms trade, a process whereby surplus weapons from the arsenals of the rich countries are sold 'downstream' to Third World governments or newly independent states in the Balkans or the former Soviet Union. Redundant soldiers sell their weapons or services for hard currency. Weapons scientists sell their knowledge to outlawed governments. Obsolete bases or stores are raided by black marketeers. Often, illegal small-scale craftsmen copy light weapons to arm informal groups.

These trends are part of a much wider process in which the sovereignty of the state and its longstanding relationships with the military and society are being challenged from both above and below. In a rapidly globalising world, the economic, physical, cultural and psychological underpinnings of state sovereignty are being eroded or circumscribed by the unimpeded flow of goods and capital, ideas and information, lifestyle cultures, criminal activities, drugs and pollution. Governments are having to contend with increasingly powerful transnational economic actors as well as global social movements of various kinds. They are also being confronted by a growing array of what Anthony Giddens calls 'manufactured risks'—nuclear oblivion, global environmental pressures of various kinds, AIDS and other pandemics, and so on—which are a product of human activity and against which individual states are relatively powerless.

As a result, the image of the state as posited by classical realist and neorealist thinking is becoming increasingly problematic. In some places, the 'sovereign' or 'territorial' state is being reduced to what some describe as the 'residual state' and others the 'enabling state', one that is more and more the agent of global capitalism and less and less the representative of civil society. In other areas we are witnessing the emergence of so-called 'phantom states', or 'failed or failing states'—states that exist on paper, that may have a government and be represented at the UN, but have ceased to provide the services that are paid for and expected by people within their borders.

These pressures are producing in turn, a 'crisis of governance' in which people everywhere are beginning to question traditional sources of authority and to look to other institutions and ideals for meaning and leadership. Citizens in the postmodern era are assuming multiple identities or have multiple loyalties which are often locally and globally as well as nationally based. Military organisations are not immune from these processes. As James Rosenau describes, today's service men and women are likely to identify themselves, not only with a particular service or country, but with specific religious, ethnic or secular groupings that exist within the state—and which also often have global connections—as well as broader social movements concerned with such global issues as gender, human rights and environmentalism. This 'disaggregation of interests' within the military itself is likely to have important operational and other policy consequences ranging from the need to adhere to a range of global norms and expectations through balancing the interests of the state with those of self or family, to dealing with soldiers who refuse to fire on fellow or like-minded citizens.

THE CHANGING NATURE OF WAR

The stated primary purpose of modern militaries is to be able to fight and win wars against other states. Yet there is a growing view that major interstate wars may be becoming a thing of the past. This view, which admittedly is not shared by everyone, is seen to be heightened by the end of the Cold War, the continuing spread of democracy and the phenomenon of globalisation itself which is facilitating growing levels of interaction within and between states, and the gradual spread of globalised cultures and associated norms. The decline in the prospect of war between industrialised nations does not mean, however, that armed conflict will disappear completely—for the foreseeable future at least. As evidenced in the upsurge of violence in Africa and the Balkans, the post-Cold War political landscape is witnessing a range of armed disputes and conflicts that are variously called 'new wars', 'uncivil wars' or 'wars of the third kind'.

These conflicts differ from their predecessors in a number of important ways. They are taking place largely within society rather than between bordered states, and in relatively remote regions on the periphery of the developed world. Unless taken up by the international media, they usually have little relevance much beyond the immediate vicinity of the site of the conflict. They often arise in the wake of the disintegration of existing states or the destruction or marginalisation of local economies. They are more often directed at civilians than opposing military forces. They are marked by a decline in earlier patron–client state relations and the emergence of a range of new external connections and actors including various diaspora communities, transnational commercial networks (both legally and illegally based), foreign mercenaries, and non-government organisations. And they are more about the politics of identity than traditional concerns with *Realpolitik*.

These and the other changes described earlier are raising questions about existing military mindsets, doctrines and structures. Donald Snow questions, for example, whether the high-technology weapons and forces flowing from the 'revolution in military affairs' are entirely relevant or appropriate for most of the conflicts likely to be faced by the United States and its allies in the future. Carl Builder of the RAND Corporation suggests that the size of active forces required for warfighting roles will almost certainly decrease, whereas missions and associated forces 'involving the rapid projection of infrastructure (transport, communications, surveillance, rescue, medical, humanitarian assistance, civil emergency and security) are likely to increase disproportionately'. Mary Kaldor argues that security planners are failing to recognise the importance and character of the 'new wars' taking place around the globe, seeing them as secondary to traditional interstate conflicts, and when they are engaged, responding to them in largely Clausewitzian terms.

Others, including those from the environmental, feminist and critical security movements, suggest that it is time to broaden our traditional and largely militarised understanding of security to include the various non-military sources of insecurity described above, or to have individuals or the globe as a whole replace the state as the key referent in future security calculations.

As evidenced by the proliferation of workshops, journal articles and conferences on such topics as the 'revolution in military affairs', the 'future of warfare', the 'military after next', 'new era security', 'information warfare' and 'asymmetric warfare', defence and security establishments around the world are aware of many of these changes and, as noted earlier, are beginning to adjust their thinking and policies accordingly. Yet Western military planners still tend to ignore the social and political roots of continuing ethnic conflict. They often overstate the incidence and potential impact of intrastate conflict in order to argue that the world is becoming a much more dangerous and unstable place.

They continue to posit non-military sources of insecurity as dangers to be defended against rather than problems to be solved. And, in many countries, they continue resolutely to resist suggestions that the concept of security be extended beyond traditional politico-military concerns usually on the grounds that this would divert attention from more serious threats to national security and overly complicate defence planning. Yet as we have seen, the world is becoming more complex, not less, requiring policy makers to develop more sophisticated and nuanced ways of examining and responding to the global security *problematique*.

THE ROLE OF MILITARIES IN COSMOPOLITAN WORLD ORDERS

Just as the roles of national military forces stem from a statist approach to international politics, so the roles of cosmopolitan militaries are shaped by the key principles that underlie the notions of cosmopolitanism. As described above, these include, at its most basic level, the idea of the world as a single moral community in which people everywhere share certain basic rights. These rights are enshrined in a growing body of international cosmopolitan or humanitarian law which is upheld and, where necessary, enforced by the key actors in this Kantian world. In the case of the military, this involves a capacity to be ready and able to protect the citizens of the planet, wherever they may be located, against gross violations of human rights whether by states or by other actors. The conduct (or not) of such humanitarian interventions will be determined, in part, by the circumstances surrounding the violation. The recent experiences of UN or UN-sanctioned humanitarian interventions provide us with an indication of the kinds of operations and basic roles that may be required to be mounted by cosmopolitan forces in the future. As described above, these include such things as the protection of ethnic or other communities, the delivery of humanitarian aid, and the establishment and policing of 'safe havens', 'humanitarian corridors' or 'no-fly zones'.

Those who see cosmopolitanism as a political as well as a normative project would see the role of militaries extending beyond protecting individuals against gross violations of their human rights to helping facilitate the transition to a humane system of global governance and its subsequent protection. Just as, within a realist world, military force is used to advance the political interests of the state, so in this case they would be used to advance and defend key cosmopolitan values and objectives. Therefore cosmopolitan militaries might be expected, first, to be used to help defend and, where necessary, restore civil society especially in areas where it is under threat from criminal activities or various destructive forms of particularist politics.

This is certainly the view of Mary Kaldor. In her analysis of the 'new' or 'uncivil' wars that have become a feature of the post-Cold War political landscape, she argues that the international community and their militaries should be less concerned with the negotiation and oversight of agreements with the warring parties as with enforcing cosmopolitan norms largely through the 'provision of secure areas in which alternative forms of inclusive politics can emerge'. In her view, such a role lies: somewhere between soldiering and policing. Some of the tasks that international troops may be asked to perform fall within traditional ambits, for example separating belligerents and maintaining ceasefires, controlling airspace. Others are essentially new tasks, e.g. the protection of safety zones or relief corridors. And yet others are close to traditional policing tasks—ensuring freedom of movement, guaranteeing the safety of individuals, especially returned refugees or displaced persons, and the capture of war criminals.

The position taken by Kaldor is not entirely removed from that advocated by certain mainstream military thinkers. In his 1995 essay on 'The Guardian Soldier', for example, Gustav Daniker, a former Major General in the Swiss Army, suggests that the military's primary missions are now to promote peace and to facilitate the current transition from an era of confrontation to one of cooperation. Military forces are 'no longer solely an instrument of countering enemy power, but increasingly an instrument for building and cementing a new era of inter-state relations'. This is said to require a 'paradigmatic shift' in strategic and defence thinking involving, first, the view that military victory will become a tactical goal, sublimated to the broader strategic purpose of creating 'favourable conditions for new, more comprehensible and durable peace settlements' between the combatants. As such, the ultimate goal of military doctrine is reconciliation, and combat plans must endeavour to minimise not only friendly force casualties but those of the adversary as well. This requires that existing military roles and structures must also be expanded and provide for much greater flexibility and multifunctionality than previously. This cannot, in Daniker's opinion, be improvised but must be included in the military's force structure calculations and its training and equipment schedules.

In a contingency, combat troops can carry out aid missions, but technical or logistics units would be better qualified. It would be even better to train in advance for such missions. Armed forces which will be equally well prepared for combat, protection, aid and rescue missions—apart from a certain degree of specialization which is indispensable—will be best suited to measure up to the variety of challenges which may arise. Even in the past, armed forces had to comply, for different non-military reasons, with various and costly regulations which were sometimes contrary to their combat missions. Therefore it should be possible in the future, in the light of clear requirements, to develop organisational patterns, operational principles and equipment for a multiple employment of modern armed forces.

While there is considerable overlap in the positions of Kaldor and Daniker, there are nonetheless some important differences or potential differences. Cosmopolitan militaries would be seen to be acting in the interests of the victims of the conflict—usually the local population— rather than its interested parties (externally as well as internally located). They would be guided by the precepts of cosmopolitan rather than international law which they would seek to carry out both impartially—no distinction made on the basis of nationality, race, religious beliefs, class or political opinions—and effectively (ordinary people would be persuaded of the advantages of abiding by the rules whereas those who seek to break them are both isolated and marginalised). While the peace enforcers must be prepared to use force against those who threaten the local population or seek to undermine the operation's mandate, the use of such force would be demonstrably reasonable, proportionate and appropriate. Thus 'unlike warfighting, in which the aim is to maximize casualties on the other side and to minimize casualties on your own side, and peacekeeping, which does not use force, cosmopolitan law-enforcement has to minimize casualties on all sides'.

A second purpose of militaries in a cosmopolitan world order might be to help protect and defend the global environment or global commons. As described earlier, traditional, militarised approaches to environmental security tend to see environmental degradation and resource depletion as further sources of insecurity and potential conflict between states. They therefore focus on identifying and dealing with the consequences of environmental decline rather than its causes. Scarcities in water resources, arable land and other environmental services are posited as potential threats to be prepared for or overcome rather than environmental problems to be solved. Thus military planners focus on maintaining access to certain 'strategic resources' only. Their involvement in the mapping and monitoring of the environment is driven by operational rather than normative considerations (information that provides an operational edge or advantage is not shared). And, in the event of conflict, environmental obligations under both national and international law are ignored. Cosmopolitan militaries, by contrast, would give priority to securing the environment over securing states. Their roles could include the physical clearance of landmines and other 'leftovers from war'; the decontamination and clean-up of land and other toxic sites used for military purposes; the clean-up of pollution and restoration of environmental damage in areas that are outside the jurisdiction of states or that are beyond the capacity of individual states to deal with; the monitoring and policing of global environmental agreements and laws; and the protection of specific world heritage areas, resource zones or even endangered species.

Constituting Cosmopolitan Militaries

There is some debate over how such forces should be constituted. In his 1995 book, *Democracy and the Global Order*, David Held thought it reasonable that 'a proportion of a nation-state's military (perhaps a growing proportion over time) ... be "seconded" to the new international authorities and, once moulded into coherent units, placed at their disposal on a routine basis'. He preferred, however, that the global authorities 'increase enforcement capabilities by creating a permanent independent force, recruited directly from among individuals who volunteer from all countries'. In an article published in Peace Review two years later, Held argued that the main problem with existing means of enforcing international law is that they depend too much on powerful states, such as the United States, which are likely to operate on the basis of their own interests rather than those of the community as a whole. A true system of cosmopolitan democracy, he continued, required new enforcement mechanisms that are genuinely transnational, and thus transcend the boundaries of nation-states and existing geopolitical interests. International law enforcement should not depend on particular nation-states lending part of their military apparatus to regional or global democratic institutions. To the contrary, a global military force should be internationally recruited, based on individuals not countries.

Mel Gurtov similarly argues that a key agent in a 'truly new world order' in which the world community does not 'walk away from mass violence on the basis of narrow calculations of national interest', may be a permanent international peace force (IPF) that acts under UN command and is deployed in the 'event that non-violent measures fail to produce compliance with UN resolutions'. This force, which would comprise national military contingents that are brought together for training in advance of actual need, would Act on behalf of the international community, not an individual government or regional organization. Its primary purpose would be rapid deployment to prevent or minimize large-scale threats to human life, such as by creating safe havens for civilians. A specific threshold of violence would automatically trigger the deployment. Secondly, and not automatically, the IPF might be used in select instances of 'peace enforcement', meaning the use of deadly force to assert the world community's will.60 Like many others who have proposed or examined the establishment of some kind of permanent UN-based force, Gurtov acknowledges the concept of an international peace force is a contentious and problematic one which 'must answer to a large number of political and ethical questions'.

MILITARY FORCE(S) AND COSMOPOLITAN WORLD ORDERS

The cosmopolitan project responds to the imperatives of limiting transnational harm, controlling and overcoming violence, and reconstructing democratic legitimacy in a globalising world characterised by both intensified spatial and temporal interconnectedness and increasing exclusion and marginalisation. A cosmopolitan approach to security takes into account the security of individuals and communities and is concerned as much with the conditions for peace as the causes of war. It anticipates an emerging post-Westphalian order in which 'sovereign statehood and territoriality are loosening their grip on modern political life'. A cosmopolitan approach identifies statist approaches which are associated with particularist and exclusivist values as inadequate or even counter-productive in the search for just and equitable responses to many contemporary challenges. The cosmopolitan project is not simply an intellectual or theoretical account of the good political community, rather, as McGrew points out, it 'identifies the political possibilities inherent in the present', and seeks to put in place the means to translate these into future actualities.

In developing alternative and transformative models for the practice of world politics, contemporary cosmopolitan thought rests on a number of key propositions. The first is that humankind is bound together as a single moral community with shared rights and obligations which 'transcend the morally parochial world of the sovereign state'. The consequences of such a world, cosmopolitan scholars argue, is that a right violated anywhere is felt everywhere and so we have a moral commitment to those who are not our co-nationals. Thus, as Andrew Linklater argues, many exponents of cosmopolitan citizenship 'support the project of enlarging the moral rather than the political boundaries of community'. In line with Kant's original conception, they believe that if citizens (and leaders) of bounded states imagine themselves as 'co-legislators in a universal communication community', this would be enough to 'place powerful moral and psychological constraints on the wrongful exercise of state power'.

But others believe that cosmopolitan citizenship needs to go beyond a moral commitment not to exploit others. In their view, political action is also required to form a global democratic political community in which centres of power are diverse and overlapping and in which structures and practices of governance are representative, accountable and equitable. A second feature of contemporary cosmopolitan thought therefore is that compassion to outsiders must extend beyond Kant's cosmopolitan right of hospitality to include a powerful normative commitment to the creation of democratic or humane forms of global governance. This notion of cosmopolitan democracy recognises that our world is becoming increasingly complex and interconnected. It is a world where states are not the only and, in some cases, not the most important actors in the management of international affairs, where citizens have multiple and often conflicting identities and responsibilities, and where problems affecting the wellbeing and security of citizens everywhere have to be dealt with locally and globally as well as nationally. This expanding notion of citizenship, responsibility and accountability requires the creation of new institutional arrangements and universal frameworks of communication that are based on the principles of dialogue and consent rather than power and force.

Exactly what these new arrangements should be and how they might be implemented is the subject of some difference and contention. Daniele Archibugi argues, for example, that cosmopolitan democracy should be concerned with utilising the positive features of both the confederal and federal models of state systems while avoiding their pitfalls. In his view the actions of states can be constrained by strengthening existing world judicial powers, including the International Court of Justice, changing the membership of the security council, and establishing a UN Peoples' Assembly. While not ruling out such measures, others, like Andrew Linklater, call for the development of new forms of political community in which 'citizens and aliens come together as co-legislators within a wider public sphere'.

Citing the European experience as a possible model, Linklater sees these new structures complementing and extending existing state-based arrangements by providing representation to people with both sub-state and transnational allegiances. Such structures are said to be necessary in part because the vast number of existing international organisations are neither democratic nor publicly accountable and, in part, because without them the considerable achievements of national citizenship will be increasingly at risk.

The third feature of cosmopolitan thought suggests that these expanding political arrangements need to be embedded in a growing body of cosmopolitan law which embodies both democratic and humanitarian principles including international humanitarian law and the laws of just warfare.

Among other things, cosmopolitan law permits and facilitates military intervention in the internal affairs of states in order to protect the rights of individuals or groups of individuals against the actions of others or their own state. As a consequence, military forces of some kind are likely to be needed to underpin and, if necessary, enforce the emerging *pax cosmopolitica* and its body of cosmopolitan law. This is the fourth (and possibly most contentious) proposition of cosmopolitanism and the one that informs the remainder of this essay.

Cosmopolitan Militaries

While much has been written in recent years on cosmopolitan citizenship and cosmopolitan democracy, no significant work has been done on the place and role of military force(s) in a cosmopolitan world order.

What are the theoretical arguments for, and the operational expectations of, military force and military forces in a cosmopolitan world order? Should they be defined primarily by the purposes for which they are deployed or by their normative structures and value systems?

Can state-based militaries, traditionally hierarchical, closed and non-democratic, be deployed as agents of what is an essentially and inherently democratic, open and non-hierarchical normative purpose? Can they serve both cosmopolitan and statist objectives at the same time? What follows are some preliminary thoughts about some of these questions grouped under three key headings: the perceived roles of militaries in cosmopolitan world orders; how cosmopolitan militaries might be constituted; and their preferred organisational and ideational structures.

IMPLICATIONS FOR THE ROLE OF MILITARY FORCE(S)

States and their military forces are the products of the Westphalian age. Yet in the view of many commentators, the Westphalian age has ended and we are entering a new era in international politics. Just what the post Westphalian world will end up looking like remains a matter of considerable contention. Some see the world returning to the kind of situation that existed before the Treaty of Westphalia—a world of chaos and anarchy as portrayed on the screen by the Mad Max movies, and we find in reality in countries like Rwanda, and other places in West Africa. Some see a continuation of existing state-centric structures based around realist, rationalist or liberal internationalist systems of world order in which states remain the key actors. Some suggest that future fault lines will occur between civilisations or so-called 'zones of peace' and 'zones of turmoil'.

Others argue that existing state-based systems are being complemented or replaced by a complex, increasingly interconnected and globalised international political economy and associated global society, a world that has porous or no borders, and is increasingly dominated by a range of non-state entities, transactions, structures and norms. These contending world visions have different implications for the meaning of security—in particular who or what is being secured and against what—as well as the future roles of military force and armed forces. It is difficult to tell at this stage which one or combination of these visions of the future is the most appropriate or will prevail. Depending on when and where we look, some models seem to be more valid than others. Certain parts of Africa, for example, seem closely to fit the 'new medievalism' thesis, while western Europe is a clear exemplar of the economic security community postulated in both the liberal internationalist and zones of peace–turmoil models. Given that the process of globalisation cannot be reversed, it would seem reasonable to suggest that we are slowly moving towards some form of system of global order or geogovernance. How quickly and how uniformly we complete this transition and what kind of system of geogovernance we end up with, however, remains uncertain and will depend, in large measure, on the actions and decisions we take now.

Depending on these decisions, we could move towards a system of world order that is inequitable, unjust, unrepresentative, and, for many, profoundly insecure; a system of predatory globalisation' marked by structural inequalities, global economic apartheid, and continuing conflict 'between the forces of globalisation and the territorially-based forces of local survival seeking to preserve and to redefine community'. Or we could oversee the transition to a world that is both enlightened and humane, in Richard Falk's words: an imagined community for the whole of humanity which overcomes the most problematic aspects of the present world scene ... [and where] difference and uniformities across space and through time are subsumed beneath an overall commitment to world order values in the provisional shape of peace, economic well-being, social and political justice, and environmental sustainability.

How such a system of humane geogovernance might be organised, and the role of military force and forces in such a system are the subjects of the second half of this chapter which examines the cosmopolitan project and cosmopolitan militaries.

4

Preventive Diplomacy and Peacekeeping

Since the termination of the Cold War and the resulting alterations in the global and regional power balances, the world has witnessed a proliferation of low intensity conflicts. The international response, mainly via the United Nations, has been to promote preventive diplomacy and, in a number of cases, to implement peacekeeping operations. This new world order trend is obviously a most welcome and positive development. Through peacekeeping, military assets that have been originally designed and deployed to destroy human life, are now being used, albeit on a limited scale, to prevent conflict and to save lives. The peacekeeping revolution is a significant step towards increased human co-operation and the development of a functional international society. Although peacekeeping operations may require significant commitments on the part of participating states, specifically the willingness to accept financial costs and casualties, all governments should seriously consider taking part in these operations in the interest of promoting international and regional stability.

Post-Cold War conflicts may be largely divided into two categories. The first category includes civil wars caused by long standing historical differences, or new nationalism. The second category, which dominates on the African continent, are conflicts based on ethnic, national or religious divisions. Africa is additionally affected by a complex array of problems which have not been remedied over the last three decades. Many problems can be traced to colonialism, while other difficulties are part of the socio-political systems which have evolved in the post-colonial era. The specific nature of each dispute consequently requires appropriate responses in order to limit or to prevent conflict.

A great deal has been written on both preventive diplomacy and peacekeeping, and an increasing number of conferences have been held to address these issues in recent years. This intellectual process, while in some cases far removed from the reality of international diplomacy and military operational activity, is to be welcomed as a way of further promoting the use of diplomacy and war machinery to serve peaceful and positive ends. Research in the field of peacekeeping has focused on a wide range of issues and, as is the fashion in the nineties, has attracted a large and impressive academic following. Regrettably, much of this research has concentrated on what is theoretically desirable, while the political and practically possible has been neglected. This approach has promoted enormous expectations of the UN, which clearly cannot be met.

In the African context, South Africa has been identified by many observers as the one state able to execute effective peacekeeping operations on the continent. On paper, South Africa's military capabilities appear impressive, but in reality there are many impediments to a major role for the South African National Defence Force (SANDF) in peacekeeping. However, these impediments are not unique to South Africa and apply to all democratic countries. There are a number of central issues which the promoters and supporters of preventive diplomacy and peacekeeping have not paid sufficient attention to in their analyses.

KEYS FOR SUCCESS

The four important issues which have not received adequate attention by peace operations studies and which are of critical importance to any government contemplating involvement in preventive diplomacy or peacekeeping are:

- early warning and the early response to a crisis-the key to preventive diplomacy;
- adequate financial support for peacekeeping;
- an accurate assessment of casualty tolerance in peacekeeping operations; and
- sufficient information for successful peacekeeping.

The above issues are fundamental to any political leader's decision-making process. Without dealing adequately with these issues, no decision-maker can realistically be expected to make a major contribution to crisis diplomacy, or to undertake an even more risky peacekeeping operation.

EARLY WARNING AND PREVENTIVE DIPLOMACY

The idea of 'early warning' as "information that can provide a timely alert to potential conflicts" has been emphasised by a number of scholars as an important component in conflict resolution. In the African context, the Organisation of African Unity (OAU) has sought to develop an effective early warning system in an effort to deal with continental conflict. The OAU Secretary-General appears to favour a system which would provide sufficient information of an impending inter-state conflict, or internal political crisis. Once the problem has been tabled at the OAU, a high-level mediation mission can be mandated to initiate discussions with the objective of resolving the crisis.

Any successful early warning system should involve the synthesis of a range of information inputs from different sources, including governments, non-government organisations (NGOs), academic and research institutions.

By implication, any early warning system or activity may be perceived to be infringing on a state's sovereignty and could be rejected as an unwelcome form of foreign intervention. Nevertheless, crisis management and resolution have the best chance of success if action is taken early. A continental early warning system, as proposed by the OAU is extremely ambitious and is unlikely to be successful in the short term. The OAU's

Conflict Management Centre (CMC) in Addis Ababa is a major step towards the prevention of conflict in Africa, but lacks the funding and resources to provide an effective continental service. Rather, individual African countries, armed with sufficient early warning information, should be able to initiate regional crisis diplomacy, while the OAU mobilises broader support. The OAU's 1993 resolution on Conflict Prevention, Management and Resolution serves as the foundation and guiding light for preventive diplomacy on the African continent, but the difficulties in mobilising sufficient support for speedy action necessitates a more streamlined procedure.

In the former UN Secretary-General's An Agenda for Peace, member states were asked to mobilise regional organisations and actors in co-operation with the UN to lighten the burden of peacekeeping. The OAU Early Warning Seminar, held in January 1996, acknowledged the importance of the 'sub-regional level' in early warning and preventive diplomacy processes. A multinational organisation located far from the crisis area can never compete with the speed and co-ordination of a national government. Former UN Secretary-General Boutros-Ghali had plans to abdicate some or all of the UN's peacekeeping functions to regional organisations. In November 1996, the UN's Joint Inspection Unit (JIU) indicated that there was a need for the UN to find partners "who would share responsibilities in collective security." In addition, the JIU study suggested that regional organisations "should be the first port of call for the prevention and pacific settlement of local disputes." There is a growing international consensus that conflicts could more easily be prevented or resolved through regional initiatives.

A recent British proposal to the UN on conflict prevention and peacekeeping in Africa has stressed that early warning is vital for successful preventive action. In most cases, especially conflicts in Africa over the last few years, there is no shortage of information indicating an impending crisis. However, the complex causes of conflict and the difficulty of processing and analysing different pieces of information require a co-ordinated and concentrated intelligence effort. Moreover, the sharing of processed information among all potential peace operation participants is a necessity for a timely and appropriate response. The UN, as well as its specialised agencies, should improve their information collection, analysis and distribution capabilities. Specifically, real time information should be readily available to the OAU headquarters, supplied by the UN and available to all OAU members involved in any regional peace operation.

In support of international efforts to provide information for preventive diplomacy, individual states should allocate intelligence assets for early warning. Indications and warning (I&W) or 'warning intelligence' are based on an interdisciplinary approach incorporating current, estimative intelligence with broader political, historical and geographical analyses. The warning intelligence process results in the production of an accurate warning statement for decision-makers. The peace operation warning process, however, requires some modification to the traditional approach of attempting to identify and predict possible surprise attacks by regional or ideological opponents. Traditionally, the raison d'être of an early warning system was to ensure that the nation's decision-makers were not surprised by an enemy attack.

The peace operations early warning system requires a different approach with less emphasis on direct threat analysis. In order to respond adequately to a regional crisis, decision-makers require strategic warning and tactical warning. Strategic warning ensures that the decision-makers have a clear overall picture and sufficient quality time to make the necessary decision. Strategic warning should provide decision-makers with regular updates on regional developments with specific emphasis on the potential for internal or inter-state conflict, thereby ensuring an opportunity to prepare effectively for a decisive peace support intervention. Tactical warning requires more detailed and specific information for the decision-maker willing to commit a direct response. In this context, the leaders of the conflicting parties, as well as the central issues in dispute should be identified and analysed in detail. Psychological and biographical profiles of the leaders concerned should be provided along with possible diplomatic solutions. Tactical warning should also provide the decision-maker with a number of options which could be pursued if preventive diplomacy is to be initiated.

States should allocate key defence and intelligence assets to the prediction of conflict and thereby provide the means for an early settlement. The warning analyst should be trained to think in terms of probabilities, predictions and possible short term courses of action. The goal is to discern the intentions of major players in any potential regional conflict. Military and other reconnaissance satellites should be more directly used in providing early warning and support for diplomacy. For example, Russia's earth observation satellite, the Resurs-F3 is capable of delivering film negatives of 2,2 metre in diameter.

Images, costing between $3 000 and $5 000, would be adequate to identify the movement of troops, or refugees. The United States Air Force white paper entitled Global Presence 1995, outlined the US' ability to maintain 'virtual' presence via space-based and air-breathing reconnaissance systems along with other information gathering technologies. The use of these technologies to support preventive diplomacy, rather than simply to promote the national interests of the US, would be a major contribution to conflict resolution. The mobilisation of satellite observation platforms for peace operations could be decisive in empowering early warning organisations. Last year, then US Defence Secretary William Perry undertook to provide Israel with near real time satellite early warning information from Colorado Springs via secure US military downlink stations in Europe. A similar service, with the emphasis on information for preventive diplomacy, would be extremely useful for the UN and OAU. Details on the positioning, or movement of military forces combined with other open sources of information may be the key in preventing the initial outbreak of conflict and accompanying loss of life. At the same time, any early warning system should respect the sovereign equality and territorial integrity of all states.

The key factor in the success of any early warning system is an early response, not simply the ability to identify an impending problem: in other words, the earliest possible application of preventive diplomacy. The former UN Secretary-General defined preventive diplomacy as "the action required to prevent existing disputes from escalating into conflict and to limit the spread of the latter when they occur." The method of choice for preventive diplomacy is based on intensive 'shuttle diplomacy' to organise one-to-one meetings with all stakeholders. In addition, the involvement and support of regional leaders is clearly important for the success of such an exercise. The institution of preventive diplomacy early in 1994 in response to the growing political instability in Lesotho, serves as a useful model for this form of activity.

The co-ordination of a regional initiative combined with a rapid response to an impending crisis were the keys to success. Moreover, the willingness of the protagonists to accept external intervention cannot be overemphasised. In the ideal case, regional crisis negotiators should be invited, rather than impose themselves, to lead negotiations for a peaceful diplomatic settlement. Events preceding the Rwandan crisis of April-June 1994 provided extensive evidence of an impending outbreak of violence. For more than a year prior to the eruption of the crisis on 6 April 1994, the increasing tension and violence in the country pointed towards a disaster. There is strong evidence to suggest that the UN was in possession of information indicating an impending outbreak of major conflict. The failure to respond appropriately and speedily to early warning information allowed the genocide to occur. The spark of the recent Zairian crisis occurred on 7 October 1996 when the deputy governor of Zaire's South Kivu province demanded that the 300 000 strong Banyamulenge community (ethnic Tutsis) leave Zaire within a week, or "be hunted down as rebels."

Within fourteen days, serious conflict erupted between the Banyamulenge and Zairian troops leading to the flight of over 250 000 refugees into Zaire. It took almost one month before an emergency summit was held to discuss the crisis. By this time, the refugees were faced with severe problems and the conflict had escalated significantly. An effective early warning system should have been able to warn of the impending conflict and should have facilitated the launch of a diplomatic initiative before the crisis began on 7 October 1996, or immediately thereafter.

Thus, the appropriate standby arrangement for crisis management and resolution are experienced and respected 'shuttle diplomats', supported by the necessary secretariat and rapid transport.

Additional requirements include satellite telephones, IT support, data communication systems, along with the necessary technical skills to manage a complex negotiation process. In this context, South Africa could play a leading role on the African continent. South African diplomats, complemented by President Mandela's immense prestige, along with the necessary secretarial personnel and executive aircraft could provide the means for African solutions to continental conflict without the intrusion of external powers.

IMPLICATIONS FOR MULTI-TRACK DIPLOMACY

These trends present a sober picture indeed of the world of the 21st century. The realm of multi-track diplomacy, as one small player in the global drama, exists within this context, yet brings a perspective, a commitment and a set of methodologies that are at humanity's leading edge for dealing with these most difficult issues. In fact, I would go so far as to suggest that the work of peace-building is at the forefront of our planet's evolutionary journey in these times.

The very dangerous conditions described in the section above arise from, and thrive in, a worldview and set of assumptions about the world as a place of separation. Separative consciousness sees duality and difference as opportunity for superiority, dominance and control, and breeds materialism, greed and violence. For many centuries the dominant western world organized its political, social and economic systems on this basis. The general breakdown in the global (and environmental) environment we are seeing now can be understood as the natural ripening of the inherent seed of destruction in the separative worldview, for when only the parts are seen, without reference to the whole, duality will play itself out in struggle, contest and conflict indefinitely.

We live at a time when large numbers of people on the planet are discovering that there is another worldview, a holistic or unitive view, that acknowledges the parts as inherently interrelated and part of a larger innate wholeness. Beyond the duality we share a common human experience, a common spiritual source, and a common capacity for connecting through that source to ways of being that will honour both the diversity and the unity in the family of life. The world is living through a major period of transformation, as the bankruptcy of one worldview becomes apparent, while the new worldview is still in its infant stages. This produces both the potential for chaos and the potential for great creativity. The peacebuilders of the world, and the multi-track approach to peace in particular, because of its systems orientation, carries that creative potential and is, therefore, a vehicle for humanity's evolution into a new state of consciousness.

In addition to these obvious activities, multi-track diplomacy can face the unique challenges of this transformational period in seven quite specific ways:

Maintaining Flexibility in the Face of the Unknown

The state of world affairs is, as we have seen, in a period of great flux. Many events that we can reasonably anticipate may or may not occur. Others that we have not considered may happen tomorrow. A single event of biological terrorism, for instance, could easily change the face of life on this planet as we know it. A single expansive move by China, or new confrontation in the Balkans or the Middle East, could re-configure political relations for many years to come. The truth is, peacebuilders need to be prepared to move in several directions at once, both responding to whatever opportunities present themselves for positive and effective work for peace, and also being pro-active in turning challenges into opportunities. To maintain this flexibility as a whole field of endeavour requires greater reflexivity, discourse and coordination among theory builders and practitioners from all parts of the world.

Recognizing Healing as the Key to Transformation

Because of the profound human trauma discussed earlier, and the brokenness of many systems, healing and reconciliation are critical aspects of any multi-track diplomacy process. New and sustainable peace systems must take into account the mending process that comes with acknowledgement of the harm done, apology and forgiveness when possible, completion of mourning, and healing at the individual and group levels. One of the greatest challenges facing peacebuilders today is not just how to engage individuals in this type of healing, but how to engage whole systems, and especially the leadership, for unless humanity learns how to heal itself, the trauma will condemn us to repeat the same cycles of violence from generation to generation.

Building the Infrastructure for Peace

The forces of war have an existing infrastructure that enables them to mobilize and actualize their aims -they have armies and arms suppliers; transportation, commerce and communication systems; banking, taxing and other funding methods; media, education and propaganda systems; and government ministries, clans, villages, political parties and other entities capable of taking action.

The forces of peace have little of this. We have come a long way in recent years toward developing organizations and networks that can serve as vehicles for carrying and coordinating peace-building activities, with an accompanying research, education and media capability as well. Much more needs to be done to create both a human and an institutional infrastructure for peace-building, in order to concretize these methods and approaches in social, political and economic systems that can both stand on their own and work together toward a shared goal. In addition to such institutions, we need the capacity to move money, materials, people and technologies rapidly and efficiently to wherever needed on the planet. In this way the transformation of consciousness is assisted by building alternative structures so that as the old collapses, there is something in place to sustain that which is being birthed.

Taking the Holistic and Positive View

One of the hallmarks of a multi-track approach is the capacity to see the whole, and the inter-relationship of the various parts. We know that development and peace are mutually interdependent, for instance, and that democratization requires the capacity for conflict resolution and problem solving at a group level, so we see the natural interface of several disciplines. This kind of relational awareness is critical to building peace systems, for it encourages the kind of connections, bridges, alliances and networking that are essential to the ongoing support of the change process. Stepping back and seeing the whole picture, especially that of the evolutionary moment in which we stand, allows us to hold the gate open for a new range of possibilities. It also allows us to affirm the positive view that, despite all the problems in the way, peace is indeed possible. In this way we energize the potential rather than the despair, and keep hope, that precious and fragile flame, vibrant and alive.

Making Peace From the Inside Out

People whose life is given to peace-building, whether as outside third parties or actors within conflict systems, are generally motivated to service, and as servers, may be prone to work themselves beyond the point of balance. Certainly working in war zones, with wounded people and in tense and violent circumstances can produce symp oms of secondary trauma, compassion fatigue and burn-out.

Because multi-track diplomacy is a systems approach, in which even the intervenor is part of the system, and because it is a multi-level approach, in which the personal level is just as important as the inter-group level, those involved in this field have the opportunity to use our own technology with ourselves, becoming agents of peace in our being as well as in our doing. When we are taking the time to integrate what we teach about peace in the outer domain with our deep experience of peace within, we can be much more effective, at the individual and at the institutional levels, in two ways: we are clearer and stronger channels for the outer work when we take time to reconnect with our own inner source of peace, and we are better models for others, showing by our presence as much as by our actions that peace is a viable and dynamic state.

Creating New Pathways for Shifting Consciousness

A colleague, Robert Fuller, once spoke about finding 'a better game than war.' Peacebuilders taking a multi-track approach are engaged in this endeavour. We know that the 'war option' is a lose-lose game; we come offering a better way, a way that goes even beyond win-win toward the transformation of the consciousness that would allow us to build truly just and peaceable societies. Because the methods and pathways for this shift are inherent in the principles and practices of peace-building with a holistic view, we occupy a position in the world analogous to the early road or railway builders. We are opening the paths, setting the tracks in place, laying down the rails, making clear the direction that will shape the future of our planet.

Our tools-methods for cooperation, creative joint problem solving, reconciliation, prevention, dialogue, mediation, negotiation, and communication, among others-are the tracks that we are setting down, so people will be able to transport themselves across old territory in new and better ways. As with all road building, once we open a path, more and more travellers will use it, especially if it carries them to where they want to go. The ways of thinking and acting we are inviting people into is a different, and a better game than war, and our work makes it possible for people in large numbers to make that shift. Knowing this, we can be more intentional about it.

Empowering Peacebuilders for Local Action

Multi-track diplomacy invites everyone into the game of peace-building. It says that there is a place and way that people from any sector of society can make a contribution to peace. Those of us engaged in travelling to places of conflict to make interventions there realize that building peace is primarily a local task. What we can offer is to give people a view and a direct experience of what is possible, help them do what they want to do faster and better, and perhaps strengthen their capacity to use appropriate tools and skills. We can motivate, catalyze, inspire, instruct, facilitate, encourage, support, assist, demonstrate, and convene. We can present possibilities, open minds to new ways of thinking, and cheer people on as they take charge of changing the systems they live in. We can articulate theories and best practices, provide a safe space where people can meet 'the other', or elicit inner individual and cultural wisdom about peace and conflict resolution. What we can never do impose our solutions on others, or build their new systems for them.

Our power to empower is perhaps the most important role we can play in the 21st century. The more individuals who feel empowered to work in their own systems for peace and conflict transformation, the closer the world comes to that critical mass that will allow for a massive leap in consciousness, allowing new processes for peace that were previously unimaginable to become normative, and easy.

Exercising our power to empower means generating more stories like those shared elsewhere in this book, building a base of success from which we can all learn and draw. It means enabling people to have that critical understanding of what true power is, the very opposite of the power of domination and control that characterizes war systems. Ultimately, exercising our power to empower means that the next article written on the role of multi-track diplomacy will have infinitely more peacebuilders-like those mentioned in the very beginning of this article-to showcase as examples of those engaged in the courageous act of creating viable, sustainable peace systems on this precious planet we all call home.

INFORMATION SUPPORT FOR PEACEKEEPING

Adequate preparation for a peacekeeping operation should include detailed and quality intelligence. This issue was emphasised in former UN Secretary-General Boutros-Ghali's An Agenda for Peace. Peacekeeping forces need what NATO calls the 'Commander's Critical Intelligence Requirements (CCIR)'-the minimum information required for operational success. Information systems which provide instant battlefield awareness are essential for combat supremacy in any military operation. This information should be provided by the UN, or by participating states. Without CCIR, peacekeeping operations are unlikely to succeed. The UN has acknowledged this point and have debated the launching of 'spy' satellites to support peacekeeping, but high costs have led to the idea being shelved.

The use of the word 'intelligence' immediately promotes a negative image. During the Cold War, opposing intelligence organisations became increasingly powerful and secretive. Intelligence became a key component in the ideological struggle between East and West. The elements of Cold War intelligence included collection; analysis (forecasting); counter-intelligence (protection); and covert action.

The fourth element of the Cold War intelligence menu raised the most concern and controversy. The use of covert action to eliminate opponents or overthrow foreign governments clearly brought into question the process and function of intelligence organisations. At the same time, the nature of the ideological struggle between East and West enhanced the role of intelligence organisations and promoted secretive covert action activities which in turn undermined the legitimacy of the organisations themselves.

Post-Cold War intelligence activities no longer resemble the programmes of the past. Collection is based more and more on the almost overwhelming supply of open sources. Traditionally, the majority of intelligence information was obtained from open sources in any event. Counter-intelligence relates increasingly to a very small area of activity.

The era of obsessive information protection has been replaced by a new culture of transparency, the Internet and a world-wide flow of information which clearly benefits mankind as a whole. Covert action is irrelevant in the more open, interdependent and democratic international system.

Modern intelligence activities thus focus on analysis, or strategic forecasting. Making use of mostly open sources, supplemented by advanced processing technology, the average intelligence officer joins together the relevant pieces of the intelligence puzzle and provides the intelligence product to the decision-maker. In one sense therefore, "intelligence [remains] fundamentally a service required by those who have to make decisions."

The quality of the intelligence product is of vital concern to the decision-maker. The ideal intelligence officer should thus be a highly qualified and skilled individual, capable of assembling, analysing and communicating information. In the post-Cold War world, intelligence is nothing more than processed information for use by decision-makers. The trained assassin, or disguised undercover agent, are no longer part of the modern intelligence agency and no longer relevant to the modern intelligence agenda.

The new intelligence process is guided by the broad definition of security. In 1968, former US Secretary of Defence Robert McNamara published a book entitled The Essence of Security in which he proposed a definition of security which included a wide range of non-military elements. McNamara stressed that "security is development and without development there can be no security."

Since then, other scholars have come to realise that security is a broad concept which cannot be limited only to military force and the identification of enemies, or potential enemies. In 1980, the UN's Independent Commission on Disarmament and Security Issues concluded that military strength alone could not ensure security in an ever-changing international system. More recently, the security 'definition debate' was highlighted by Buzan and Thomas, both of whom agreed that security had been too narrowly defined in the past. The intensity of the Cold War and the danger of surprise nuclear attack, possibly resulting in planetary devastation, preoccupied security experts and led to a neglect of the broader and, in many ways, obvious security issues. With the end of the threat of nuclear war, or the threat of a limited regional war escalating to a nuclear exchange, broader security issues have come into focus.

The new agenda contains a vast array of different elements each requiring specialist attention and analysis. Ekins, for example, suggests that there are "four highly credible, but also totally avoidable threats to our existence on earth-war, hunger, repression and eco-disaster." Mankind no longer faces the prospect of a quick and devastating nuclear exchange, but rather needs to contend with what may be called broad-based, steadily increasing, threats to human survival. In response to new threats, intelligence organisations need to master international information networks as providers of relevant security information and recruit the services of specific field specialists able to add value to the intelligence product. The modern day intelligence officer is concerned with a completely open research and analysis agenda which represents the interests of society as a whole and not the particular interests of any ruling élite, party or ideology. Thus, in the post-Cold War context, national intelligence organisations are well suited to support peacekeeping and conflict resolution.

The UN has neglected to set up a comprehensive information gathering and processing system to support peacekeeping operations. Clearly, the implementation of an advanced information processing system by the UN would significantly benefit peacekeeping operations at both the planning and execution stages.

With regard to planning, intelligence could be used to accurately calculate troop requirements, the availability and utility of facilities (especially airfields), local infrastructure (roads) and logistic requirements. Quality planning would positively influence calculations with regard to the supply of troops and support personnel for peacekeeping, thereby minimising costs and maximising chances of success.

In addition, the potential for hostile action and the capabilities of potentially hostile forces need to be carefully evaluated to avoid tactical surprises, especially in the early stages of operational deployment. The use of air transport to deploy peacekeepers implies that information on possible belligerent anti-aircraft capabilities are crucial. Moreover, where a peace enforcement operation is envisaged, the identification of the hostile forces' centre of gravity becomes critical.

The UN process of ad hoc ground reconnaissance has resulted on a number of occasions in serious time delays in the deployment of troops, as well as the insufficient provision of supplies. The use of both aerial and ground-based surveillance, using sensors and imaging technology, would significantly improve any peacekeeping force's ability to monitor the theatre of operations. Lockheed Martin Corporation is presently developing a reconnaissance vehicle, known as 'DarkStar', which will provide near real time, continuous, all-weather, wide area surveillance to tactical commanders.

Moreover, it is specifically designed and constructed to operate in high threat environments. Technology of this kind would be ideal to provide intelligence support to peacekeeping operations. Intelligence specialists have identified unmanned aerial vehicles (UAVs) as potentially one of the greatest force multipliers. The Pioneer UAV was used extensively during the Gulf War (483 missions, totalling 1559 hours) with good results. The Predator UAV's multiple sensors provide an effective close-up picture of ground operations capable of revealing objects as small as 20 centimetres in diameter from an altitude of 4 000 metres.

The development of an aerial border patrol system similar to the US counter-narcotics Command and Management System (CMS) to monitor cease-fire agreements in support of peacekeeping operations would also be useful. Other options for the provision of quality intelligence includes the Hughes synthetic aperture radar system capable of providing 1,8 metre resolution images from an orbital distance of 110 kilometres.

The Sinai Support Mission, established by the US in 1974 at the request of both Israel and Egypt, used sensor technologies to successfully monitor military activity in the Sinai. In April 1982, the Multinational Force and Observers began to make effective use of ground sensors, aerial photography and on-site verification to ensure the implementation of the Camp David Agreement. Advances in the field of satellite imagery have provided tactical information support for peacekeeping forces. During Operation Restore Hope, the US' operation in Somalia, the US Army Space and Strategic Defence Command provided the 10th Mountain Division with a multi-spectral satellite imagery terminal capable of accessing civilian LANDSAT satellites. This ensured a quick response mapping capability for tactical use by unit commanders.

The US operation in Somalia confirmed Sun Tzu's two thousand five hundred year old thesis-good intelligence is vital for any military operation. In his book entitled Somalia Operations: Lessons Learned, Kenneth Allard points out that "while 'information' is the term of choice, operations in Somalia proved that, whatever it is called, intelligence has a crucial role to play at the lower end of the conflict spectrum." US forces in Somalia made use of a wide range of information gathering equipment, including night-vision devices, ground-surveillance radars, tactical air reconnaissance and unmanned aerial vehicles. An important source of intelligence proved to be soldiers in the field using eyes and ears to provide commanders with quality "situation awareness."

The UN operation in Somalia suggests that peacekeeping operations have created a new form of 'information warfare' within which the peacekeepers compete with those who oppose the peace process. Success in this new information environment however, requires a mindshift away from the traditional intelligence approach of identifying and assessing the 'enemy'. In peacekeeping operations there are no enemies, but there may be factions or groups which use force to undermine the peace process. Nevertheless, the approach towards peacekeeping, as with any form of military deployment or conflict, should be based on the logic and science of war. In the case of Somalia, the forces of Mohammed Aideed became the central opponents of peace and were therefore identified as hostile. At the same time, it is clear that in every peacekeeping operation there is a possibility that the peacekeepers themselves will become the target of hostility. Good intelligence will be able to predict and prepare for this eventuality. In Somalia, despite the technological aids outlined above, the US did not have sufficient quality intelligence and thus paid the price. The issue of intelligence is therefore one of approach, more than technological barriers.

PEACEMAKING BY CONSENSUS

'Let me repeat again today the pride that I feel to be at the head of a nation which has made tolerance and dialogue its cardinal virtues. As a modern state, Mali needs to add to its ancestral heritage of dialogue, a modern institutional infrastructure which demonstrates there is a real democratic process taking place.' (...) 'With this in mind, I shall ask my government to organize a series of regional Concertations in which every current of opinion will be able to express its views. Each participant will be invited to contribute to the debate, seeking to define solutions for tomorrow's problems. Our purpose will exclude systematic opposition to the ideas of others; nor will there be room for narrow sectoral demands. The government will bring to the discussion both its point of view and its proposals for change and together we shall seek the necessary consensus to achieve the transformations which we have started.' (President Alpha Oumar Konaré on 8th June 1994, the second anniversary of his inauguration as Mali's first democratic elected President)

The West African Republic of Mali ranks among the world's least developed and poorest countries, and in this vast and impoverished land, its northern regions are by far the least developed. With the exception of the 'interior delta' area of the Niger River and a few oases and mountainous areas, the entire zone is an infertile desert covering an area greater than France. Education, health care, water, communications, and transportation infrastructure are almost totally non-existent. In this area lives a ethnically diverse population numbering something less than one million inhabitants, of which the Songhoys and the Touaregs are the most numerous.

Like many of the nations of Africa, Mali has been governed for extended periods of its post-colonial history by non-democratic regimes. From 1968 until 1991, President Moussa Traoré presided over a repressive, corrupt, and incompetent one-party regime. Throughout the Traoré period, very little economic development took place, and that which did was largely restricted to the Bamako region and other regions of the south. The poverty of northern Mali was further aggravated by repeated periods of drought.

Traditionally, the Touaregs and Arabs have looked more to the north for trade relations than to the southern areas around Bamako, the capital of modern Mali. In the late fifties, northern peoples had pushed for the establishment of an independent central Saharan state, and in 1963, a revolt by Touareg supporters of this state was brutally suppressed. During the drought years, many young Touareg refugees ended up in Libya, where Libyan leader Muammar Gaddafy was both able and willing to exploit their alienation from Bamako. The Mouvement Populaire de Libération de l'Azawad (MPLA) was founded in Libya in 1988, by exiled Malian Touaregs who were serving as mercenaries in Libya's Arab Legion. When its leaders returned to Mali in 1990, they launched the rebellion of Mali's northern peoples against 28 years of repressive central government.

General-President Moussa Traoré reinforced his army in the north and launched a brutal and violent campaign to crush this rebellion. Many of the victims of the military's efforts to put down the rebellion were innocent civilians. The inevitable result of the military heavy-handedness was to turn previously uninvolved Touareg youths into rebels, and to antagonise other ethnic groups.

As the violence continued, the Touareg fighters issued a 21-point declaration which included various demands for improved economic development, better social conditions, reduced military presence, multi-party democracy, a greater political role, and amnesty for their rebel activities. The northern rebellion coincided with increasing civil unrest in Bamako and the south, as demands for multi-party democracy and an end to the Traoré regime grew louder. Traoré needed to bring troops back to the capital to prop up his tottering regime, and so, in January 1991, the government of Mali signed a peace agreement with the rebels.

It made little difference. In March, 1991, Traoré was arrested, and Mali began a transition process to multi-party democracy under the leadership of General Amadou Toumani Touré (known as A.T.T.) And in the north, despite the agreement, which was, in any case, viewed by many in the south as a 'capitulation', the violence continued. The MPLA, which had already split into separate Touareg and Arab factions, splintered further, and fighting among the factions was often as intense as battles between rebels and government forces. Military units carried out summary justice, in one case killing a group of rebel leaders who had been imprisoned in Timbuktu. Government officials could no longer safely travel outside of the northern towns. Traditional leaders, who were viewed by the rebel leaders as too closely allied with Bamako, were also perceived as enemies. Anarchy and banditry prevailed throughout the north.

There were continued efforts to put an end to the violence. Algeria, in particular, played a crucial role in promoting efforts to reach a negotiated settlement. The new regime also attempted to bring more northerners into the government. A Peace Agreement was signed in April 1992, a 'National Pact' which accorded a 'special status' to the north. The Pact also provided for the demobilisation of armed rebels and their integration into the Malian military or police forces or into civilian life, an exchange of prisoners, the return of refugees, economic development for the north (and commitments to seek international funding for that development), local responsibility for law enforcement, and, significantly, the establishment of a commissioner for northern Mali, reporting directly to the

President. This pact provided a framework for an end to the violence, but real peace would still prove elusive.

Conditions improved for short periods, but would then deteriorate. More than two hundred thousand people fled the fighting and banditry, taking refuge in neighbouring countries, or moving southwards.

Acts of ethnically motivated violence were also reported in some of the larger cities and towns. As the elected civilian administration headed by President Alpha Oumar Konaré took office, the economy came under severe pressure from the combined effects of years of mismanagement and war. In May 1994, a new element was added to the already highly explosive mix-an armed movement known as Ganda Koy (Masters of the Land) was launched by sedentary peoples who were fed up with the violence and banditry.

Mali was on the Verge of Civil War

That this did not occur is to the credit of President Konaré and his new Prime Minister, Ibrahim Boubacar Keita, who both understood that they could never impose a military solution on the rebels, as well as a large supporting cast of local and international actors who persisted in working with the warring parties to find a way to re-establish the rule of law.

The construction of a stable peace in Northern Mali did not come about as the result of any one single action, but as the result of a complex of efforts to rebuild trust, to address legitimate grievances, and to reward combatants who chose to give up the fight. Building incentives into the peace process that would assure the continued commitment of people on both sides of the conflict to peace.

Six essential aspects of the Malian peace process:

(1) Building civilian-military relations

(2) Discreet mediation by national and international figures

(3) Decentralisation of governance

(4) Promotion of reconciliation through civil society

(5) A process of disarmament and demobilisation

(6) Investment in the re-integration of former rebel combatants

Even while the violence continued, the government convened a series of meetings at the local level beginning in 1994. In convening these meetings, the government was embracing the African tradition (and following the pattern it had already used to effect the transition to democracy following the 1991 popular revolution) which goes beyond the traditional western democratic process where elections are the determining factor in shaping government. In the African tradition, decisions are taken at the village council, where elders preside over a discussion involving the entire community. Participants at the hundreds of meetings that took place from 1994 through 1996 included political parties, the administration, trade unions, religious groups, and NGOs, but subsequently, and more importantly, the local leaders, women's organisations, social organisations, economic co-operatives and associations, and other institutional representatives of civil society. All these meetings stressed the inseparable relationship between security and peace.

The administration also undertook to reform the military, improving conditions and training for soldiers, and improving communications both within the military and between the military and civil society. While both security and development were considered to be crucial to achieve stability in the north, the approach adopted by those involved in peacemaking efforts has been described as 'security first'. This followed from the logic that the armed civilian population would only give up its weapons if they believed that the security forces were capable of defending their families.

Also the kind of development required to build trust and improve living standards in the north could only be achieved if donors felt confident that hostilities would not break out again and that development professionals could safely work in the former areas of conflict. Interestingly, one element of the overall peace plan was an attempt (with only limited success) to persuade development agencies to make modest contributions to the implementation of security projects.

Beyond Symbols: Weapons for Development

In 'The Weapon Heritage of Mali', authors Van der Graaf and Poulton argue for a programme tying weapons collection to community development assistance. Instead of providing cash payments to individuals who hand in their weapons, development assistance is provided to communities for programmes like improved water systems, health care, and education.

While a 'Flame of Peace' is in and of itself both practically and symbolically valuable, a development for weapons programme helps not only to reduce the number of weapons in circulation, but it also to bring communities together to provide for both security and development, and quite possibly to prevent those who hand in a weapon from simply going out and acquiring a new one.

As discussed above, Mali's northern peoples felt little connection to Bamako. Part of the wisdom of the reconciliation process pursued by the Konaré administration was to accept this reality and to work with it, by offering to extend more power to local authorities. Decentralisation has been a central plank of Konaré's vision of society. During the many meetings of civil society, one goal was to convince people to support locally elected authorities, consistent with one of the points agreed to in the National Pact, and this is now moving ahead with the establishment of a nearly 700 locally elected 'communes' throughout Mali.

Robin-Edward Poulton, Senior Research Fellow at the United Nations Institute for Disarmament Research, who has worked on conflict resolution for many years in West Africa, describes the Konaré approach as 'ambitious' and 'visionary'. He observes that 'most of Africa's states will flourish in the 21st century only if they are able to reconcile the need for broader economic or monetary unions with the pressure from local groups to assume their cultural identities.' Poulton concludes that 'decentralisation is the new framework which will make people responsible for their own lives, for mobilising national resources and using them locally for productive investment.'

These activities certainly contributed to reduced tensions between the government, the northern non-combatants, and the rebel fighters. But peace could only be truly secured by a process of demobilisation and re-integration of the rebels into the fabric of Malian society.

This was largely accomplished by setting up a programme which provided for the cantonment of former combatants, the turning in of weapons, the closing down of rebel bases, and the integration of some of the former fighters into either the armed forces or the civilian sector.

Participants in the programme were paid $200 pocket money, free food and training, uniform and a small monthly payment during the duration of cantonment. Those who came in without a weapon received $100 and were accepted into a UNDP credit programme to help them establish themselves in civilian life. While fewer than 2000 of the ex-combatants were actually integrated into the police, the military, or civilian administration, between November 1995 and January 1996, another 9000 individuals benefitted from the civilian integration programme and nearly 3000 weapons were collected. The cycle of violence had been definitively broken.

On March 27, 1996, President Konaré, Ghanaian President Jerry Rawlings (chairman of the Ecowas at that time), leaders of the Mouvements et Fronts Unifiés de l'Azaouad (the MFUA, uniting the various rebel factions), Ganda Koy, and a large delegation of international observers gathered in Timbuktu for the highly symbolic destruction of all collected weapons in what was called a 'Flame of Peace'. The weapons were stacked into a giant pyramid, doused with fuel, and then ignited by the presidents of Mali and Ghana. The rival movements issued a joint declaration in which they affirmed the indivisibility of Mali, pledged their support to the Malian constitution, renounced the use of violence, exhorted their fellow African fighters across the continent to 'celebrate their own Flame of Peace', and finally, proclaimed the irrevocable dissolution of their respective organisations.

Citizen Carter: The Statesman

What happens to Presidents after their term in office ends? Once voluntarily departed, or shoved out the door, do they spend long leisurely days by the leafy pond? Play endless rounds of golf? Covet high-profile memberships of corporate boards? Not so for former American president Jimmy Carter.

In June 1994 Carter could be found in Pyongyang holding intensive talks with Kim Il Sung, the North Korean dictator over a way out of a nuclear crisis with the United States. A few months later, Carter's name was back in the news. This time he was part of a three-member delegation trying to mediate the departure from office of Haiti's military rulers. By the end of the year, the former US president was trying to negotiate peace in Bosnia. As one American columnist described Carter, 'He goes everywhere, doing good.'

The visit to North Korea was made under a cloud of scepticism, and even some opposition, back in Carter's homeland. But there was more than grudging applause when the ex-President announced in a television interview a credible agreement with North Korea to 'freeze' the illegal nuclear programme, which President Bill Clinton had said publicly North Korea could not be allowed to pursue.

That deal effectively aborted a US campaign to press for international sanctions against North Korea. It also eased military tension between South and North Korea. In the same way-by talking, and attempting to find common threads for agreement-'Citizen Carter, the statesman', as he has been described by the newspaper USA TODAY, pulled another rabbit out of the hat by brokering a deal that led to the United States calling off a planned invasion of Haiti. The dramatic events in which Carter became involved in 1994 marked the culmination of an activist post-White House role the former President has carved out for himself since leaving office in 1981. Working through The Carter Center, a non-profit, privately run body based in Atlanta, which he set up with his wife, Rosalynn, in 1982, Carter has used the considerable weight of his office as former president to become one of the world's most effective peacemakers. In sometimes last-minute visits to disparate parts of the globe, the trademark charm and a reputation for caring, have opened doors closed to others.

Carter was president of the United States from 1976 to 1980. He was succeeded by Ronald Reagan. During his time in office, he was a central figure in the historic 1978 Camp David peace accords between Egypt and Israel. But the popular perception in the United States is that his presidency was marked by the Iran hostage crisis, an oil embargo, high inflation, and the like.

Run in partnership with Emory University, The Carter Center has set lofty goals which underpin some of the very ideals that were hallmarks of a Presidency which pursued a foreign policy based on human rights considerations. Already, the Center's work has erased some of the bitter memories of its founder's presidential years. Its Mission Statement include promoting peace and human rights, resolving conflict, fostering democracy and development, fighting poverty, hunger, and disease throughout the world.

Carter Center programmes are wide-ranging: eradication of Guinea worm disease in Africa, India, Pakistan and Yemen; working to promote democracy and human rights; increase farm yields in the developing world; child immunisation; the prevention of river blindness. In the United States, the Center runs projects to erase the stigma of mental illness and improve access to and quality of services and treatment for Americans who experience mental disorders. It runs various youth projects as well as in preventive health care programmes.

In addition, Carter Center monitoring teams have overseen multiparty elections in Haiti, Ghana, Panama, Paraguay, Guyana, Suriname, Zambia, Nicaragua and the Dominican Republic. The Atlanta-based centre has assisted the strengthening of the economic and institutional foundations of emerging democracies. Carter personally, and members of the Center's International Negotiation Network (INN)-a 25-member conflict resolution body comprising Nobel Peace laureates, former heads of state, conflict resolution practitioners, representatives of international organisations, governments, and non-governmental organisations-have mediated many of the 30 major armed conflicts taking place somewhere in the world at any one time.

Described as an informal network of eminent persons, the INN is chaired by Carter, whose high personal profile tends to make less pronounced the contributions made by other INN members to activities undertaken by the Center's Conflict Resolution Program (CRP) in Sudan, Bosnia, the Great Lakes region, Liberia, Ethiopia, the Korean Peninsula and elsewhere. INN also ran a successful project in the Baltics which brought together Estonians, Russians living in Estonia and Russians from Moscow, to discuss integration of the Russian-speaking community into Estonian society.

In the words of The Carter Center, 'The CRP regularly monitors many of the world's armed conflicts in an attempt to better understand their histories, the primary actors involved, disputed issues, and efforts being made to resolve them. When a situation arises where President Carter has a unique role to play and specific conditions have been met, the CRP directly supports his intervention.'

INN member Kumar Rupesinghe says non-governmental organisations (NGOs) such as The Carter Center, being 'unofficial organisations', have the advantage of building trust and confidence between two sides and using their resources to work toward negotiation. 'With no strategic or political motivations, NGOs have greater flexibility... in responding to the needs of people,' says Rupesinghe.

But such is the profile given to The Carter Center by the man who founded it and who remains its driving force, that it is not likely to be perceived as just another NGO. In fact, at times the Atlanta-based body could be criticised for conducting a milder version of the Clinton administration foreign policy in North Korea and Haiti-supporting Washington's policy doves over the more hawkish elements. Before visiting North Korea, Carter obtained President Clinton's nod, although some officials in the State Department opposed to the trip. And while his initiatives in Haiti were undertaken in an unofficial capacity, the former President was thoroughly briefed beforehand and in turn reported on the outcome of his missions to Washington.

Others say by holding negotiations with Somalia's Mohamed Farah Aideed, North Korea's Kim Il Sung, Haitian military ruler Raoul Cedras, and Bosnian Serb leader Radovan Karadzic, the former President merely enhanced the reputations of despots. The more cynical view of Carter is that the ex-President is driven by a determination to erase the memory of a failed presidency, and restore his place in history, possibly by receiving the Nobel Prize for Peace.

Not that such considerations matter to beneficiaries of the Center's varied programmes, who will no doubt argue that the ends are justified by Carter's high-profile and high-octane energy means. For it is the case that Carter's status and reputation-the sheer weight of the name-have opened doors and forced parties at loggerheads to explore the possibilities of reconciliation. Gritty diplomacy and refusal to take 'no' for an answer, have been Carter's hallmarks. And his approach have become so much an embodiment of the Center, there will doubtless be a big gap when he leaves.

'He's quite unusual,' notes Erwin Hargrove, a political scientist at Vanderbilt University. 'Most ex-presidents write their memoirs and retire. But Carter has a tremendous amount of energy and a desire to do good.'

Away from the fanfare, Carter and his team, including wife Rosalynn, used various other devices to bring warring parties around the negotiating table, or at least to consider that as a course. One year after that sequence of headline-generating ventures in North Korea, Bosnia and Haiti, Carter sponsored a major drive among Central African nations to secure the return of two million refugees displaced by the ethnic bloodletting in Rwanda. Meeting in Cairo, leaders of Zaire, Rwanda, Burundi, Tanzania and Uganda, agreed on various confidence-building and security measures in this regard. In the following year, the five leaders met again in Tunis, Tunisia to follow up their African initiative to promote peace, justice, reconciliation, stability and development in the Great Lakes region. In the Tunis Declaration on the Great Lakes Region, issued on March 18, 1996, the parties agreed on additional measures to meet commitments approved the previous year in Cairo.

Implementation of that initiative was subsequently overtaken by the pace of political events, including the overthrow of Zairian leader, Mobutu Sese Sekou, but focused world attention on the region, and galvanised involvement in efforts to deal with one of the major causes of instability. And the meetings secured, at the very least, a blueprint of commitments-pledges even-by Heads of State regarding improvement in the refugee situation, and reducing military conflict.

INSPIRING STORIES OF PEACE-BUILDING

'This conference could augur well for the coming century. It would unite into one mighty whole the efforts of all States sincerely striving to make the great idea of universal peace triumph over strife and discord.' Count Mikhail Nikolayevich Muravyov, Russia's Foreign Minister, expressed the hopes of many when he spoke of the prospects for peace at the First Hague International Peace Conference in 1899.

One hundred years later we know these hopes to have been in vain. The first international gathering to promote world peace-the event brought together representatives of 26 countries-proved incapable of stopping Europe and the world from marching toward the general war that was the opening event of what British historian Eric Hobsbawm has called 'the age of extremes.' The 20th century was to become the most violent of all ages in history, unprecedented in the scale and intensity of killing and destruction.

One of the considerations that played a part in the birth of this book was the fact that, exactly one hundred years after the First Hague International Peace Conference, a large scale global conference will be organised by The Hague Appeal for Peace in The Hague (the Netherlands, May 1116). A few days earlier, an international gathering will take place in Belfast, Northern Ireland, organised by the Coexistence Initiative of the State of the World Forum. The conference (Diversity and Community in a Global Context: Learning from Europe) will deal with creating a greater understanding of the issues of coexistence and community building.

With 'People Building Peace', due to be presented at the conferences in Belfast and in The Hague, we aim to promote these issues which are crucial global challenges for the 21st century. The initiative for this publication was taken by the European Centre for Conflict Prevention, together with IFOR (International Fellowship of Reconciliation) and the Coexistence Initiative of the State of the World Forum.

One could argue, however, that the need to organise these events makes clear that not much has changed. At the end of the century, the world seems to be more insecure than ever before. Deadly conflict has become a prominent feature of the transition period from the Cold War to the 21st century. With over 30 active internal conflicts and scores more potential trouble spots within and between states, the international community is anxiously asking itself whether and how such deadly conflicts can be prevented.

Searching for an answer to these questions, the group of prominent people who produced the Carnegie Commission's 'Preventing Deadly Conflict' report2 came to this conclusion: 'First, deadly conflict is not inevitable. Second, the need to prevent deadly conflict is increasingly urgent. Third, preventing deadly conflict is possible.'

The prevention of deadly conflict, the report argues, 'is over the long term, too hard intellectually, technically, and politically to be the responsibility of any single institution or government, no matter how powerful. Strengths must be pooled, burdens shared, and labour divided among actors.'

The time was not ripe for this kind of approach at the first Hague conference. But it is now! Modern foreign policy is no longer the monopoly of very small groups of statesmen and diplomats. Gone are the days when diplomats could conduct policies of which the citizens were unaware.

In the past decade the number of peacebuilders working at all levels of society in places of ethnic and civil conflicts around the world, has mushroomed. The contribution of civilians, whether working from the bottom up or the top down, to resolving the conflicts of our time can no longer be ignored. Churches, women's organisations, the media, and business have all demonstrated their potential for building peace. So too the role of education, the arts and sports is gaining increasing recognition. 'Multitrack diplomacy', as it is called, is flourishing, and provides a major reason for hope of a more peaceful world.

This hope is rooted, as one of the great thinkers on peace-building and reconciliation, John Paul Lederach, writes in this book, 'in the resiliency of people (...) who, in spite of decades of obstacles and violence, keep taking steps toward peaceful coexistence with their enemies.' Hope is also rooted in the fact that the second half of the 20th Century, though rife with violent conflict, 'engendered the most prolific advancement of non-violent conflict transformation activities systematically known in human history, setting the stage for a potential singularity of peace-building in the 21st Century.'

In this book the reader will find many excellent examples of the valuable and frequently successful, initiatives taken by citizens of many countries, to resolve conflict, to prevent violence, and to reconcile parties that have been at war. Apart from introductory chapters written by experts in their particular fields, the book also presents a global overview of the most important organisations.

Aiming at a broad audience, we have chosen to employ a journalistic approach. Almost all of these casestudies have been written by journalists, on the basis of their independent research and documents from the organisations involved. We hope to have given credit to all actors involved, especially in projects initiated by Northern organisations in Southern countries where information was sometimes hard to find. People from all around the world have contributed to this publication. That cultural diversity is reflected in both the content and the style of the articles you will find collected in this book.

It has not been our aim to promote certain projects or programmes at the expense of others. What we were looking for were 'real-life stories', which give a true account of the possibilities of peace-building by small groups or even individuals, without down-playing the many difficulties involved.

We hope the readers will gain more insight into the potential as well as the possibilities of the several tracks involved. We aim to inspire people and local communities working for peace and to support the work of educators, policy makers and international networks. Our intention is to raise the profile of the subject, provide links to organisations dealing with conflict resolution, citizenship, democracy and the longterm promotion of coexistence, peace-building and reconciliation.

Of course, one could argue that despite all efforts for peace in countries like Israel/Palestine, Bosnia or Angola peace is still a very distant dream. We should however realise that peace is a process, to which many of the initiatives described here have given an impetus, relatively small sometimes, but still meaningful.

The building of peace is a multiparty effort, including setbacks as well as inspiring steps in the right direction. We should try to learn from both of these! One of the lessons which can be learned from the inspiring developments in countries like South Africa and Northern Ireland to mention two peace processes which are extensively covered in this publication, is the importance of a coherent and integrated effort involving as many tracks as possible. The multiplier effect which is created this way greatly enhances the chances for sustainable peace.

The People to People Programme in Israel is another example of the importance of building peace at the governmental level as well as within the community at the same time.

The potential contribution to conflict resolution, peace-building and reconciliation of some of the sectors described here, is still relatively unknown.

Arts and cultural activities as well as sports are tracks that offer many possibilities, amongst other reasons, because of the wide public they are able to reach. Also relatively unknown is the peace-building potential of a powerful segment of society, the corporate sector. Peace is profitable. A fact that has come to be realised by the business communities in South Africa and Northern Ireland. We can only hope that the management of many more companies, Chambers of Commerce, etc. will come to the conclusion that they too can play an important role in the transition from violence to peace and democracy.

Another thing we can learn from the stories presented here is that 'ordinary people' as well as minority groups can make a difference.

By means of their creative approaches, their perseverance and compassion, many individuals around the world have succeeded in transforming apparently hopeless situations. We are able to achieve much more than we are sometimes inclined to think!

We feel that, apart from anything else, these case-studies clearly illustrate the potential of multitrack diplomacy. A substantial additional investment in these kinds of initiatives-which in many cases are relatively inexpensive would greatly enhance the chances for peace in many places around the world. To stimulate this, more publicity is a prerequisite. We aim to contribute to the making of video documentaries of several of these cases for television broadcast as we believe this is the way to really reach and inspire large audiences. We should also mention here the decision to produce a Swedish-language edition of this publication. We hope more translations will follow and contribute to the aim of reaching as many people as possible.

The response to our initiative in publishing this collection of inspiring stories, has been overwhelming. At the same time, we have noticed how hard it was in many cases to collect the necessary information. Some of the cases presented here have never previously been described! That is why we have already decided to further pursue this initiative by publishing another collection of peace-building stories in the near future. All suggestions of cases which could be included in this second edition are welcome (preferably before the end of this year). We are especially interested in examples of peace-building in sectors which are not included in this edition, like youth organisations, exchange programmes, trade unions, the academic world, the military, etc.

5

Defence Modernization and Strategy

MILITARY MODERNIZATION

The military modernization begun in the late 1970s had three major focuses. First, under the political leadership of Deng Xiaoping, the military became disengaged from civilian politics and, for the most part, resumed the political quiescence that characterized its pre-Cultural Revolution role. Deng reestablished civilian control over the military by appointing his supporters to key military leadership positions, by reducing the scope of the PLA's domestic nonmilitary role, and by revitalizing the party political structure and ideological control system within the PLA.

Second, modernization required the reform of military organization, doctrine, education and training, and personnel policies to improve combat effectiveness in combined-arms warfare. Among the organizational reforms that were undertaken were the creation of the state Central Military Commission, the streamlining and reduction of superfluous PLA forces, civilianization of many PLA units, reorganization of military regions, formation of group armies, and enactment of the new Military Service Law in 1984. Doctrine, strategy, and tactics were revised under the rubric of "people's war under modern conditions," which envisaged a forward defence at selected locations near China's borders, to prevent attack on

Chinese cities and industrial sites, and emphasized operations using combined-arms tactics. Reforms in education and training emphasized improving the military skills and raising the education levels of officers and troops and conducting combinedarms operations. New personnel policies required upgrading the quality of PLA recruits and officer candidates, improving conditions of service, changing promotion practices to stress professional competence, and providing new uniforms and insignia.

The third focus of military modernization was the transformation of the defence establishment into a system capable of independently maintaining a modern military force. As military expenditures remained relatively constant, reforms concentrated on reorganizing the defence research-and-development and industrial base to integrate civilian and military science and industry more closely. Foreign technology was used selectively to upgrade weapons. Defence industry reforms also resulted in China's entry into the international arms market and the increased production of civilian goods by defence industries. The scope of PLA economic activities was reduced, but the military continued to participate in infrastructure development projects and initiated a program to provide demobilized soldiers with skills useful in the civilian economy.

Civil-Military Relations

Lines between civilian and military leadership and institutions in China are indistinct. All high-ranking military leaders have high-level party positions, and many high-ranking party officials have some military experience. When military leaders participate in national policy making, therefore, it is not clear whether their positions reflect PLA corporate interests or the interests of groups that cut across institutional lines. In general, in times where there was national leadership consensus on national policy, such as in the 1950s, the PLA was politically quiescent. Once the PLA was drawn into civilian politics during the Cultural Revolution, the military became divided along the lines of civilian factions. As long as the national leadership remained divided on a number of policy issues, the PLA, fearing factional struggles and political instability, was reluctant to leave the political scene. When Deng Xiaoping was rehabilitated in 1977, however, the stage was set for the withdrawal of the military from politics and a partial return to the PLA's previous political passivity.

Political Role of the People's Liberation Army

Deng Xiaoping's efforts in the 1980s to reduce the political role of the military stemmed from his desire to reassert civilian control over the military and to promote military modernization. To accomplish his objectives, Deng revitalized the civilian party apparatus and leadership and built a consensus on the direction of national policy. He also established personal control over the military through personnel changes, and he reduced the scope of the PLA's domestic political, economic, and social roles. Finally, he strengthened party control over the military through institutional reforms and political and ideological education. The revitalization of the party and the establishment of a consensus on national policy assured top military leaders of political stability and a vigorous party capable of handling national and regional affairs without extensive military participation.

Deng's personal political control was established over the military through his assumption of the position of chairman of the party Central Military Commission in June 1981 and through his appointment of his supporters to key positions in the party Central Military Commission, Ministry of National Defence, and the PLA's General Staff Department, General Political Department, and General Logistics Department. Occasional replacement of military region and military district commanders also strengthened Deng's hand. Military leaders who objected to Deng's policies were replaced with more amenable personnel.

The creation of the state Central Military Commission in 1982 aimed to further strengthen civilian control over the military by stressing the PLA's role as defender of the state and by establishing another layer of supervision parallel to party supervision. The civilianization of several PLA corps and internal security units reduced the size of the PLA and the scope of its involvement in civilian affairs. The placement of defence industries under civilian control and the transfer or opening up of military facilities, such as airports and ports, to civilian authorities also limited the PLA's influence in economic and political matters. Propaganda using the PLA as a model for society also diminished, and emphasis was placed on the PLA's military rather than political role.

Party Control

In addition to making personnel changes, Deng revitalized party control over the PLA and diffused the military's political power by designating provincial-level, municipal, district, and county party committee secretaries to serve concurrently as the first political commissars of their equivalent-level units in the regional PLA. The percentage of PLA personnel permitted to join the party was limited by restricting party membership to military academy graduates. Political and ideological training stressed the military rather than the social, ideological, or economic role of the PLA. Special effort was made to discredit the PLA's role in the Cultural Revolution; the PLA's support for the left was described as incorrect because it caused factionalism within the military. While emphasizing the necessity and appropriateness of reforms to modernize the military, political education also sought to guarantee military support for Deng's reform agenda. Beginning in 1983 a rectification campaign (part of the party-wide rectification campaign aimed primarily at leftists) reinforced this kind of political and ideological training.

Beginning in the late 1970s, Deng Xiaoping succeeded in decreasing military participation in national-level political bodies. Military representation on the Political Bureau fell from 52 percent in 1978 to 30 percent in 1982, and military membership in the party Central Committee declined from 30 percent in 1978 to 22 percent in 1982. Most professional military officers shared common views with the Deng leadership over military modernization and the fundamental direction of national policy, and they willingly limited their concerns to military matters. Nonetheless, some elements in the PLA continued to voice their opinions on nondefense matters and criticized the Deng reform program. Dissent centered on prestigious military leaders, notably Ye Jianying, who feared that ideological de-Modification, cultural liberalization, and certain agricultural and industrial reforms deviated from Marxist values and ideals. The Deng leadership contained these criticisms with the help of the personnel changes, political education, and the rectification campaign just mentioned. In this way it was able to keep military dissent within bounds that did not adversely affect civil-military relations.

Popular Attitudes Toward the People's Liberation Army

Starting in the late 1970s, popular attitudes toward the PLA also underwent considerable changes. In the 1950s and 1960s, the military's prestige was very high because of its wartime exploits, because it was held up as a role model for society, and because of its participation in civilian construction projects. But the power gained by the PLA during the Cultural Revolution reawakened civilian resentment of military privileges and abuses of power. By the early 1980s, with the circumscription of the PLA's domestic role and the implementation of agricultural reforms offering greater opportunities for rural youth, the PLA's reputation as a prestigious, elite, Marxist-model organization and a promising channel for social mobility was severely tarnished. Society's perception of the military appeared to be returning to the traditional viewpoint that "one doesn't make nails out of good iron; one doesn't make soldiers out of good men." To restore this damaged image in the late 1980s, the media extolled the PLA's martial virtues and the great strides made in military modernization in recent years.

Military Organization

By 1987 changes in military organization indicated the importance Chinese leaders attached to structural reform in building military forces capable of waging modern, combined-arms warfare. These reforms included the creation of the state Central Military Commission parallel to the party Central Military Commission, reduction in force, reorganization of military regions, formation of group armies, enactment of the new Military Service Law, and reorganization of defence industries.

State and Party Central Military Commissions

At the apex of Chinese military organization stood two bodies— the state and party Central Military Commissions. The 1982 state Constitution created the state Central Military Commission as the state organ subordinate to the National People's Congress responsible for "directing the country's armed forces". The state Central Military Commission was the state's decision-making body in military affairs and directed and commanded the armed forces. The state Central Military Commission consisted of the chairman, who was commander in chief of the armed forces, an executive vice chairman, two vice chairmen, and four other members.

The party Central Military Commission, elected by the party Central Committee, exercised de facto, authoritative policy-making and operational control over the military. In addition to the chairman, the party Central Military Commission in 1987 included a permanent vice chairman who was concurrently secretary general, two vice chairmen, and four deputy secretaries general. The leadership of the state and party Central Military Commissions was identical, but the membership of the party Central Military Commission below the top leadership was thought to include regional commanders and service chiefs. Because the PLA has been under party control since its inception, the leadership of the party over the military did not change with the establishment of the state Central Military Commission. Although parallel leadership blurred the distinction between the two groups, the party Central Military Commission retained its traditional, preeminent position in charge of military affairs.

Ministry of National Defence and National Defence Science, Technology, and Industry Commission

Beneath the two Central Military Commissions were the Ministry of National Defence and the National Defence Science, Technology, and Industry Commission (NDSTIC), which separately took orders from the two Central Military Commissions but had no operational control over the PLA. The Ministry of National Defence was responsible for military modernization and provided administrative support for the PLA. It was responsible for planning, manpower, budget, foreign liaison, and training materials, but it possessed no policy-making or implementation authority. The NDSTIC—formed in August 1982 by merging the National Defence Science and Technology Commission, National Defence Industries Office, and Office of the Science, Technology, and Armaments Commission of the party Central Military Commission—was responsible for military research and development, weapons procurement, and coordination of the defence and civilian economic sectors.

Operational Control

In 1987 operational control of the PLA ran from the two Central Military Commissions to the PLA's three general departments: General Staff Department, General Political Department, and General Logistics Department. Below the department level ran parallel chains of command for operational, political, and logistical matters, each with its own separate communications facilities. Military policy originated in the party Political Bureau or the party Central Military Commission, became an operational order at the General Staff Department level, flowed through the military regions, and arrived at a main-force unit. Orders to regional forces also passed through the military district (provincial) level.

General Staff Department

The General Staff Department carried out staff and operational functions for the PLA and had major responsibility for implementing military modernization plans. Headed by the chief of general staff, the department served as the headquarters for the ground forces and contained directorates for the three other armed services: Air Force, Navy, and Strategic Missile Force. The General Staff Department included functionally organized subdepartments for artillery, armored units, engineering, operations, training, intelligence, mobilization, surveying, communications, quartermaster services, and politics. Navy Headquarters controlled the North Sea Fleet, East Sea Fleet, and South Sea Fleet. Air Force Headquarters generally exercised control through the commanders of the seven military regions. Nuclear forces were directly subordinate to the General Staff Department. Conventional main, regional, and militia units were controlled administratively by the military region commanders, but the General Staff Department in Beijing could assume direct operational control of any main-force unit at will. Thus, broadly speaking, the General Staff Department exercised operational control of the main forces, and the military region commanders controlled the regional forces and, indirectly, the militia.

General Political Department

The General Political Department was responsible for ideological indoctrination, political loyalty, morale, personnel records, cultural activities, discipline, and military justice, and it provided the party structure for the PLA. It also published *Jiefangjun Bao* (Liberation Army Daily), the PLA's influential newspaper. The General Political Department director was at the head of a system of political commissars assigned to each echelon in the PLA. One of the primary tasks of the political commissar was the supervision of the party organization through party committees at the battalion level and above or through party branches in companies. Virtually all high-ranking officers in the military were party members. Until the early 1980s, when party membership in the PLA was restricted, an effort was made to have a party or Communist Youth League member in every unit down to the smallest maneuver element. Political commissars were equal in rank and authority to the commander of their echelon in peacetime but theoretically deferred to the commander during war. Commissars assumed many time-consuming chores, such as personnel problems, relations with civilians, and troop entertainment.

General Logistics Department

The General Logistics Department, headed by a director,

was responsible for production, supply, transportation, housing, pay, and medical services. Historically, much of this support came from the civilian populace, and before the establishment of the General Logistics Department it was organized most often by commissars. PLA logistical resources in 1980 were far fewer than those of Western or Soviet forces; in the event of war the Chinese military would be heavily dependent upon the militia and civilians. In 1985 the General Logistics Department was reorganized, its staff cut by 50 percent, and some of its facilities turned over to the civilian sector.

DEFENCE MODERNISATION CHALLENGES AND STRATEGIES

When we talk of defence modernisation, we normally focus on weapons systems and their procurement — in other words, the nuts and bolts issues. But the core issue for modernisation is the strategy that should guide it. For a country like ours, this assumes even greater importance since large sums of capital are involved and technology acquisition itself is a major challenge which, if tackled correctly, should support economic-industrial growth and also reduce the need to plough our export earnings substantively into import of weapons systems.

Military technological differential is the key to competitive advantage in wars of today and tomorrow. And whoever controls superior military technology in the 21st century would dominate in war and peace, on the battlefield and in the market. Force multiplication is no substitute for force where technological differential become low.

Defence modernisation is one area where trends in weapons manufacture and markets abroad have a major influence on not only costs and technology, but also access to them.

We had relied heavily on Soviet weapons and equipment since the mid-1960s, and the European industry provided an alternative, supplying one-fifth of our total needs. We have had negligible access to American weapons systems and military technology over the decades. But things are changing and it is necessary to look at them carefully to work out our defence modernisation strategies.

The end of the Cold War resulted in contraction of defence industry worldwide. Smaller production runs increased the unit costs of weapon systems; and rapid advances in technology have pushed costs further. Defence establishments worldwide have resorted to upgrades to enhance the operational capabilities as a via media to replacements. But this remains a partial solution in modernisation strategies. Meanwhile, collaborations and mergers became the norm in defence manufacturing, with an obvious strengthening of American hold over military industry worldwide. While some access to American weapons systems has opened with the sale of the artillery Firefinder radars to India, this process still could only amount to a marginal opening of a small window. The European option for weapons acquisitions remains. But the European defence industry is in a difficult situation for a variety of reasons that we need not go into detail here. Its consolidation has resulted in deeper linkages to US industry. We faced its implications after the 1998 sanctions, when naval aircraft and helicopters which we had purchased from the UK were held back while being overhauled at the manufacturers. It took a couple of years before the problem could be resolved, and the costs obviously went up. The disintegration and collapse of the Soviet Union, which has been our primary source of defence equipment since the mid-1960, resulted in serious disruption and decline in the output of the former Soviet defence industry. What Russia retained in reasonably good shape were the Soviet Union's outstanding design bureaus.

We must also note that the comprehensive self-reliance model put into place during Prime Minister Jawaharlal Nehru's time underwent change since the 1960s. This was based on three parallel tracks: Buy weapons, licence manufacture as much as possible, and undertake design and development (with foreign collaboration to build our own expertise). Unfortunately, as licence manufacture increased, providing significant indigenous capabilities and a degree of independence from imports, this also led to a sort of strategic complacency in that the key area of our needs for future modernisation, design and development of weapon systems, started to suffer. Notable examples are combat aircraft where the LCA design was started 30 years after we had undertaken the design and development of an excellent multi-role combat aircraft, the HF-24 Marut, while technology galloped! Similarly, the design and development of the Mainbattle Tank, Arjun, started just after the 1971 War, has yet to enter operational service. Meanwhile techno-operational environment has changed substantively forcing us to buy the T-90 tanks.

The Indian Navy has fared better, although resource crunch delayed its shipbuilding programmes, forcing us to now buy the Gorshkov aircraft carrier when the indigenous Air Defence Ship should have been in service by now. Other examples abound. But the point that we need to note is that a comprehensive strategy for modernisation has been practically absent since the 1970s.

Our weakness since then actually lies in design and development of weapons systems. The DRDO has made valiant attempts, but seems to have shied away from collaborative projects. Scientific professional pride decried collaboration on grounds that it would hamper indigenous development; politically, foreign collaboration aroused negative passions; and the defence establishment was looking to immediate needs rather than long-term capacity building in defence industrial capability. Acquisition of military technology, therefore, has been localised to import of production technology rather than building design capabilities.

It is in this context that a unique historical opportunity opened up just at the time the most severe crisis for defence modernisation occurred with the collapse of the Soviet Union. The former Soviet Union looked for collaboration in design and development of military systems. The West plugged in where it suited them. But it was China, not India, which took advantage of the situation. By mid-1990s over 3,000 Russian engineers and engineers were reported to be working in Chinese defence industry, upgrading and working on design and development of numerous systems which China had not been able to achieve for decades. China is investing in military R&D programmes in Russian institutions and in collaborative programmes where our recent attempts at joint development of the Brahmos missile pale in comparison.

It is still not too late to plug into Russian design base and capabilities, although as it picks up economic strength it may seek to apply tougher terms. Similarly, we have been the largest customer of British Aerospace's weapons and equipment for five decades. But there is little in the country in the shape of joint production, leave alone joint design and development programmes. Regardless of the level of budget being allocated in any particular year, the backlog of modernisation and the needs of future high-technology weapons systems would require investment of the order of $20 billion over the next decade. And that is why most of the global arms manufacturers are setting up shop in India in the hope of selling arms. But this also provides us with a powerful bargaining chip to build indigenous design, development, manufacturing and export capabilities through joint collaborative programmes. What we need is to be clear on our strategy for modernisation that goes beyond mere procurement and licence production. This is also where the private sector can play a crucial role.

In a developing country like ours, there are additional complicating factors in the modernisation processes. First, a large proportion of our defence equipment is still purchased from abroad. Our traditional supplier, the former Soviet Union, disintegrated and landed up in serious socio-economic crisis. Bilateral trade also suffered heavily. The negative impact on supplies of weapons equipment and spares created additional complications for us. Also, many inefficiencies and complexities had crept into our procurement system and decision making for modernisation. Some of these have been sorted out by implementing the decisions of the Group of Ministers taken three years ago to improve the management of national security. But the result has been that with a system that allocates funds on an annual basis, with a review half-way down, large amounts of funds budgeted for defence and modernisation have been lapsing at the end of the financial year for the past few years.

For example, for the three-year period ending March 2003, a total of Rs 25,699 crore remained unspent out of the total budgeted figure of Rs 1,85,587 crore. The effect has been that while defence modernisation had suffered earlier due to lack of resources, now the inability to spend available resources within the stipulated financial year has adversely affected defence preparedness.

Establishing a DMF of Rs 25,000 crore would go a long way in assuring that modernisation processes do not suffer due to procedural delays and other unavoidable reasons. Both the National Security Advisory Board and the bipartisan Standing Committee on Defence of Parliament have been pressing the issue for years. The actual functioning of the DMF, of course, must be evaluated carefully over the coming years, since this is a deviation from the traditional budgetary approach. Its utility may remain less than optimal if the five year plans are not finalised well before the Plan period commences. Also, we need to redefine the budget heads to clearly indicate the resource allocation and utilisation under three functionally different heads of modernisation, maintenance and operating costs of the defence forces separately rather than the current system that does not indicate functional segments of a large amount of the tax-payers' money in an area so crucial to our security and defence.

BLACKLISTING FOREIGN VENDORS

India has a penchant for blacklisting foreign arms producers without considering negative effects it has on India's military preparedness. This is the reasons why recent reports of irregularities in the procurement of seven Barak anti-missile defence systems and 200 missiles from Israel Aircraft Industries Ltd (IAI) have caused serious concern to the Indian armed forces. They fear that the Government may get forced to blacklist IAI as per the provisions of defence procurement procedure. Should that happen, India's defence modernisation plan would suffer irretrievable damage. Having seen the adverse effects of banning Bofors, HDW and Denel, they dread a similar fate for a large number of ambitious plans under implementation.

IAI is deeply involved in most of the major modernisation plans of the three services. In addition to the upgradation of fighter aircraft (Jaguar, MIG-21, MIG-29 and Mirage-2000), transport aircraft (AN-32) and all helicopters of MI series, it is supplying three Airborne Early Warning and Control System (AWACS) systems to India. It is also the prime supplier of unmanned aerial vehicles to the three services. Most importantly, IAI is involved in a number of developmental projects. India simply cannot afford to cut off all dealings with it. The saga of banning Bofors, HDW and Denel cannot be repeated.

Bofors

After carrying out trials of various guns on offer, India opted for Bofors 155 mm FH-77B towed artillery system. A contract for 410 systems was signed with the Swedish firm in 1986 for Rs1437.72 crore. The contract included transfer of technology for subsequent manufacture of guns in India. India had planned to produce 1,840 pieces within the country to equip 92 artillery regiments. However, with the exposure of kickbacks, the Government banned Bofors for all future dealings. It had the following effect:-

- Although India had paid for transfer of technology, it failed to utilise it. India lost an opportunity to create a base for further development of artillery weapon systems. As a result, indigenous competence to manufacture and maintain guns remained stunted.
- As spares could not be procured from Bofors, middlemen thrived making huge profits. In the absence of adequate spares, the Army had to cannibalise parts from some guns to keep other guns functional. Essential maintenance also suffered.
- Without help from Bofors, India is struggling to carry out overhauling of guns in the stipulated time frame. It

is feared that delay in overhaul will adversely affect extension of useful life of the gun systems. Indigenous capacity installed with a Base Repair Workshop is far too less and it will take unacceptably long to overhaul the complete inventory.

- The Navy was already using Bofors guns on some ships and they faced difficulties in ensuring regular supply of spares.
- Indian inventory of 84 mm Carl Gustav Rocket Launchers suffered as Carl Gustav subsequently became a subsidiary of Bofors and thus, came under the ban.

Denel

Discussions were in final stages with Denel of South Africa for 155 mm howitzers (both towed and self-propelled) when it emerged that Denel had employed unacceptable means to grab contract for the supply of NTW-20 Anti-Material Rifle. It was alleged that Denel had engaged middlemen to offer bribes to obtain sensitive information about the internal proceedings of the Commercial Negotiation Committee. The Government decided to blacklist Denel in 2005 and cancel all orders placed on it. The development was highly unfortunate. Bhim project was almost concluded with Denel's T-6 155mm turret from the G-6 being mounted on Arjun hull. An initial order had also been placed on a public sector undertaking. With the blacklisting of Denel, Indian Army's Field Artillery Rationalisation Plan suffered a crippling blow. The total requirement envisaged by 2025 is 3600 artillery guns of 155mm/52 calibre. The current inventory is of 410 Bofors guns only. Therefore, India desperately wants to procure 400 additional gun systems (220 wheeled and 180 tracked) on priority to meet inescapable minimum requirement.

Field trials in respect of wheeled systems were carried out in 2003 to ascertain compliance of Services Qualitative Requirements. Three competitors participated - Denel, Soltam Atmos 2000 and FH77 of SWS Defence. All the three systems failed to meet specified standards. Retrials of duly improved versions were held in 2004. With the blacklisting of Denel, the choice got limited to Soltam and FH77. As per the press reports, FH77 emerged far superior to Soltam and was the choice of the Army. However, due to politically sensitive reasons, the Government incorrectly termed the case as a single vendor situation and decided to float fresh tender enquiries with reformulated Qualitative Requirements. Tender for wheeled guns was floated in March 2007 and the second tender for tracked guns followed soon thereafter. It is learnt that 12 producers of guns have been invited.

Nearly 20 years have passed since the induction of Bofor guns; no new gun system has been procured. Due to ban on Bofors and Denel, India has shut doors on two major producers of guns and thereby limited its choice. Continued shortage of suitable 155mm/52 calibre gun systems implies major gaps in India's defence preparedness. Additionally, India's quest for indigenous production of 155 mm ammunition also suffered a major blow. Work on a new ordnance factory in Nalanda to manufacture 155mm ammunition for Bofors guns has got stalled, as Denel was to provide technical know-how. Hundreds of crores of rupees have also gone down the drain.

HDW

The case of HDW makes instructive reading. A contract was signed with the German firm in December 1981. India was to get two HDW 209 class fully built submarines and sub-assemblies and components for assembling two other submarines in India. HDW was also to provide required training to Indian personnel.

HDW delivered two submarines in 1987 and two more were assembled in India in due course. As allegations of bribery and kickbacks became public, the Government decided to blacklist the company. It was also decided not to build any more submarines of the same class. Marlog, a company jointly owned by HDW and Ferrostal, took over the responsibility to fulfil all contractual obligations. There are just a handful of competent submarine manufacturers in the world. By blacklisting HDW,

India antagonized one of the leading producers and thereby deprived itself of the benefits of latest technological advancements. HDW is the world leader with the most advanced air-independent propulsion system. Continued collaboration would have given a boost to indigenous submarine building competence. Additionally, India would have acquired wherewithal as regards maintenance, overhaul and repair support.

As India had not received the complete drawings and NATO identification numbers for all spare parts of the submarines, it faced immense problems in procuring them from other sources. Middlemen made huge profits. The Navy wanted to increase the offensive punch of the submarines by mounting Exocet missiles on it. As HDW could not be engaged, others laid unacceptably harsh conditions. Indian plans for the upgradation of the submarine entailed an increase in their length and that could be done only by HDW. To sum up, by blacklisting HDW India deprived itself of maintenance support, upgradation opportunities and development of indigenous skills.

MILITARY TECHNOLOGY

Following the withdrawal of Soviet aid and advisers in 1960, which crippled the defence industry and weapons production for several years, China stressed self-reliance in developing its own weaponry. The acquisition of foreign military technology became a contentious issue at times, particularly in the 1970s, when Maoists stressed complete self-reliance and more moderate leaders wished to import some foreign technology.

The signing of an agreement to coproduce Rolls Royce Spey engines in 1975 signaled the resolution of that debate in favour of selective importation. Beginning in 1977, Chinese military delegations traveled abroad, particularly to Western Europe and, in the 1980s, to the United States, to visit Western defence manufacturers and to inspect the state of the art in military equipment. Chinese representatives showed great interest in a wide variety of weapons systems, but they made few purchases of complete weapons systems, concentrating instead on acquisition of selective components, equipment, or technologies and on concluding coproduction agreements.

China's selective approach to acquiring foreign military technology stemmed from the limited funds available for military modernization and the desire of Chinese leaders to avoid dependence on any one supplier. The selective approach also reflected the knowledge that assimilation of foreign technology could present problems because of the low level of Chinese military technology and lack of qualified personnel. Finally, the leadership realized that China's past emphasis on modifying foreign weapons and on reverse engineering had greatly limited China's weapons development capacity. To overcome weapons deficiency in the short run and achieve indigenous military research, development, and production in the long run, China's leaders combined the selective import of weapons and technology with improved technical training of defence personnel and development of the civilian economy.

China primarily was interested in obtaining defensive weapons from abroad to correct the PLA's most critical weaknesses. These weapons and equipment included antitank and antiaircraft missiles, armor-piercing ammunition, helicopters, trucks, jeeps, automobiles, and tank fire-control systems, engines, and turrets for the ground forces; antiship missiles, air defence systems, antisubmarine warfare systems, and electronic countermeasures systems for the Navy; and avionics, including fire control and navigation systems, for the Air Force. Observers opined that the entire military needed improved command, control, communications, and intelligence equipment and computers for command and logistics.

Arms Sales

China's entrance into the international arms market in the 1980s was closely related to reforms in the defence industry and the leadership's desire to acquire the foreign technology needed to modernize PLA weaponry. Before 1980 China provided arms to friendly Third World countries at concessionary prices. Because China transferred arms based on ideological and foreign policy considerations, terms were generous. Around 1980 China decided to sell weapons for profit to absorb excess capacity in the defence industry, make defence enterprises more economically viable, and earn the foreign currency required to purchase foreign military technology. China continued to sell military hardware at generous terms to some of its traditional friends and weapons customers, such as Pakistan, North Korea, Egypt, Sudan, and Somalia.

Hard-currency sales to Middle Eastern countries, however, particularly Iran and Iraq, accounted for the rapid increase in Chinese weapons sales in the 1980s. United States Arms Control and Disarmament Agency studies indicated that from 1979 to 1983 Chinese arms sales ranked eighth in the world, for a total of about US$3.5 billion, of which an estimated US$2.1 billion went to Middle Eastern countries. In 1979 arms sales accounted for 0.9 percent of total exports; in 1983 arms sales rose to 6.3 percent of total exports. By 1987 China had jumped to fifth place, ranking behind the United States, the Soviet Union, United Kingdom, and France.

In the 1980s the defence industry and the PLA established a number of trading corporations to sell Chinese military hardware and to acquire foreign technology. The most prominent of these corporations were the China Xinshidai Corporation, affiliated with the NDSTIC; China Northern Industrial Corporation (commonly known as NORINCO), affiliated with the State Machine-Building Industry Commission; China National Aero-Technology Import and Export Corporation (CATIC), affiliated with the Ministry of Aeronautics; Great Wall Industrial Corporation and China Precision Machinery Import and Export Corporation, both affiliated with the Ministry of Astronautics; China Electronics Import and Export Corporation, affiliated with the Ministry of Electronics Industry; China Shipbuilding Trading Corporation, affiliated with the China State Shipbuilding Corporation; and China Xinxing Corporation, affiliated with the PLA General Logistics Department. In 1984 these corporations began promoting Chinese weapons, actively seeking technology transfer and coproduction agreements with foreign defence companies at international defence exhibitions in 1984.

Civilian Production

In late 1978 China initiated a policy of integrating civilian and military industry more closely in order to promote overall civilian economic development. This policy entailed civilianizing the machine-building ministries to make the defence industry more responsive to civilian control and needs; increasing defence industry production of civilian goods, particularly consumer goods; and transferring technology from the more advanced defence sector to the civilian sector of the economy. Production of civilian goods totaled 6.9 percent of total defence industry output in 1975. In 1980 it rose to 18 percent, and by 1985 it had jumped to 41.8 percent of total output. Chinese officials predicted that by 1990 about 80 percent of defence industry output would be civilian goods. The large excess capacity of the defence industry, resulting from declining orders from the PLA, made possible the rapid growth in civilian output. The defence industry manufactured a wide variety of goods for civilian use, including motor vehicles, optical equipment, television sets, electrical appliances, pharmaceuticals, and medical instruments and prostheses. Many of these products were consumer goods in high demand. For example, in 1985 the Ministry of Ordnance Industry manufactured 500,000 motorcycles, representing two-thirds of total motorcycle output, as well as 250,000 cameras, 450,000 bicycles, and 100,000 refrigerators.

Following the formulation of regulations and mechanisms for such transfers, defence industries began transferring technology to civilian industries on a large scale in the mid-1980s. Technology transfers provided defence enterprises with additional, lucrative sources of income and furnished civilian enterprises with a wide range of useful, advanced technology to modernize production. For example, the Ministry of Astronautics disseminated aerospace technology to light industry and to the petroleum, chemical engineering, machine-building, textile, communications, medical, and electronics industries.

Economic Roles of the PLA

The PLA played a role in economic development practically from its inception. Beginning in the late 1930s and early 1940s, when the party was headquartered in Yan'an, the Red Army raised its own food. After 1949 the PLA became involved in economic reconstruction tasks—building railroads and factories, reclaiming wasteland, digging irrigation canals, establishing state farms, and participating in disaster relief operations. The PLA accepted its role as a force in economic construction and devoted segments of its structure, such as the Engineering Corps, Railway Engineering Corps, Capital Construction Engineering Corps, Signal Corps, and Production and Construction Corps, to building up the national infrastructure. However, PLA regional- and main-force units played a much smaller role in aiding the civilian economy.

This pattern continued into the 1980s. The PLA remained self-sufficient in food, participated in selective infrastructure development projects, and aided in disaster relief. From 1981 to 1985, the PLA contributed 110 million workdays to 44,500 construction projects, including the diversion of river water from the Luan He to Tianjin, construction of the Shengli oilfield in Shandong and the Huolinhe open-cut coal mine in Shaanxi, expansion of Zhanjiang port in Guangdong, and afforestation work involving the planting of 290 million trees.

DOMESTIC IMPLICATIONS OF MILITARY MODERNIZATION

Military modernization will likely produce two distinct consequences. Politically and socially, the role and influence of the military in Turkey is bound to change once the effects of the modernization program begin to be felt. Economically, the design of Turkey's modernization will have a profound impact on Turkey's industrial development, because it will propel the country's defence industry into a whole new league.

Regarding the military, the modernization program was started to counter specific military challenges that Turkey faces in the post-Cold War era. These include primarily the changing geopolitical role of Turkey as an emerging regional power, the need for greater Turkish military compatibility with the United States and the rest of NATO, and the increasing reliance on the military to provide for internal security as well (the military's objectives in the context of foreign policy will be discussed later). Regardless of the legitimate motivations on the part of the Turkish military, the modernization program also has the potential to partially restore the military's stature in Turkish society and perhaps in politics as well. The Turkish military views itself as the guardian of Kemalism, the state-based ideology of secularism, Westernization and modernization. In this context, the program will reinforce Turks' historical image of the military as leading the country's overall modernization.

Already considered a source of national pride and ranked as the most prestigious and respectable institution in Turkey today, military modernization will further enhance the army's prestige. Also, the military's perceived success in country's Southeast against Kurdish rebels both strengthened the military's respect within Turkish society, and may have also increased the country's ability to deter future insurgents. Military modernization is certain to further augment this deterrence.

Moreover, training with the most up-to-date equipment and earning international respect from other NATO countries will ensure strengthen the military's domestic image of professionalism, which had been declining in recent years following the soft coup of February 28, 1997. This image will once again guarantee large numbers of quality applicants for the officer corps and may re-establish the military as a powerful social and political force.

Furthermore, as Dietrich Jung has pointed out in his examination of Turkish society, the original elite officer class has frequently found itself at odds with the emerging new elite of businessmen. Yet, these two groups' interests may increasingly converge due to military modernization, because the Turkish military will also be an important industrial actor as the military-industrial complex grows. Domestic military industries typically draw their contracts from the national armed forces and their staff are primarily former military servicemen. Consequently, a network of formal and informal contacts evolves linking the defence industry closely to the military. Through this osmotic process, there is greater awareness among the military class of political-economic considerations that arise from industry ownership.

A major goal of military modernization is precisely to build a substantial Turkish military industry. Currently, Turkey's military industry averages about one billion dollars in sales annually, of which exports made up only $70 million in 1999—equivalent to 0.3 percent of all Turkish exports. Moreover, the lack of a domestic military industry is evident in the fact that only 21 percent of Turkish military needs are met domestically, hence the large procurement of foreign-made equipment.

Therefore, "virtually all purchase plans require corresponding offsets by foreign investment in Turkey or a co-production arrangement with local arms manufacturers."

Also, most purchases cover high-technology equipment that could hypothetically be reproduced in Turkey. Initially, these high-technology products will be co-produced with one of the traditional suppliers, leading to a transfer in technology that is hoped will lay the groundwork for future independent Turkish production. The goal is to modernize the military while simultaneously boosting Turkey's fledgling defence industry, allowing it to eventually become independent of increasingly less reliable foreign suppliers.

In fact, when analyzing Turkey's capabilities, it is evident that Turkey fundamentally has the potential to develop a major defence industry. According to Luis Bitencourt, in order to succeed in defence industrialization, a developing country needs to have a perception of threat, access to financial resources, a diversified industrial base, a domestic procurement budget, sufficient domestic education, and superpower support. Indeed, even if the country's recent economic crisis casts doubt on

Turkey's financial and industrial development, Turkey does fulfil all of Bitencourt's prerequisites. If Turkey succeeds, the relationship between the military and private business may improve, contributing to further democratization and economic liberalization.

Ironically, military modernization—i.e., strengthening the military institutions—may produce a more democratic society because it links the military with business interests, which are mainly concerned with creating stable macroeconomic conditions through liberalization and good governance.

MILITARY MODERNIZATION AND TURKEY'S FOREIGN POLICY

Turkish military modernization is a central pillar in Turkey's new foreign policy. First, military modernization is in itself a policy goal, one which is supposed to underpin Turkey's new claim to regional leadership. Second, modernization should advance Turkey's traditional orientation towards the West by increased inclusion of Turkey in NATO operations, which is hoped will strengthen otherwise strained ties to the West. Lastly, Turkey has discovered in the process of military modernization that large defence contracts can become a tool for conducting foreign policy.

The end of the Cold War transformed Turkey's strategic position. Instead of being a poor, small country at one of the frontiers of the Cold War, Turkey found itself as a "pivotal state" in several strategic regions: the Balkans, the Middle East, the Caucasus, and Central Asia. Turkey's successful economic policies of the 1980s contrasted with the decline of neighboring states. Notably, the Soviet Union disintegrated into Russia and several weaker small states, some with an affiliate Turkic character. Iran at the end of the decade was still suffering from its eight-year war with Iraq and the international isolation which followed the 1979 revolution. The 1990-1 Gulf War massively crippled Iraq, and Syria was weakened with the disappearance of its Soviet patron. This elevated Turkey's regional status and encouraged Turkey, as former President Turgut Ozal said, to "leave its former passive and hesitant policies and engage in an active foreign policy."

Specifically, Turkey was interested in engaging in international peacemaking and peacekeeping efforts, improving relations with regional partners, furthering integration with the West, and grasping opportunities in neighboring regions. A necessary element for this foreign policy is a military equipped to project power, manage interventions, make credible threats, and act as a reliable ally. As the modernization program has only just begun, the country's more active foreign policy still encounters difficulties because the military is not entirely prepared to handle this expanded role. For example, peacekeeping in the Caucasus (Nagorno-Karabagh in 1994) was ruled out partially due to lack of military capability; in general, Turkish peacekeeping missions are still limited, although growing in number. Nevertheless, Turkey already proved its resolve to take advantage of the shift in the military balance with its neighboring foes. In the fall of 1998, Turkey amassed troops along the border with Syria and issued several demands regarding Syria's support for Kurdish terrorism. Without challenging Turkish intent, Syria caved in to Turkish demands and even expelled PKK rebel leader Abdullah Ocalan. As the Syrian example demonstrates, a modernized military will surely give policymakers in Ankara even greater flexibility in their conduct of foreign policy.

Looking westward, military modernization is necessary for Turkey to maintain and advance integration with the West. Turkey has always been a reliable NATO ally, with the second largest army in the alliance. However, its comparably less sophisticated military has not always been entirely useful in NATO missions, and NATO itself is now undergoing full-scale modernization. Moreover, the EU member states in NATO are seeking to concentrate increasingly on the West European Union (WEU), of which Turkey is just an associate member without permanent membership prospects. This encroaching exclusion based on the emergence of a European security identity may be reversible by upgrading the Turkish military, raising Western recognition of Turkey's military contribution to NATO, and demonstrating that Europe remains partially dependent on Turkey for its security, as emphasized in the October 2004 European Commission report. In that respect, Turkish military modernization is also indirectly improving Turkey's overall prospects for EU candidacy.

Finally, Turkish military modernization has become a Turkish foreign policy tool. Although the dynamic is discussed at length in the next section, the structure of defence industries in the West empowers Turkey to utilize its large defence contracts also in order to achieve other political goals. For example, in 1999, Germany was designated to deliver a series of its *Leopard* tanks to Turkey. However, Germany's coalition government quickly realized the political divisiveness of this arms sale. The Social Democrats were running on a platform of fighting unemployment, while their Green Party counterparts have a political identity that prescribes adherence to certain values, foremost among them upholding human rights. Hence, the government underwent an internal quarrel on the issue, eventually approving a smaller sale while tabling the larger contract. Ever since, when Germany criticizes Turkey on human rights, Turkey reintroduces its demand for the tanks. This strategy has made German criticism boomerang: instead of the Turkish government being confronted with its human rights problems, the German government finds itself repeatedly in turmoil over its arms sales to an ally with a poor human rights record. Conversely, given Turkey's attempt at achieving EU accession, potential military contracts serve to induce Germany and other EU states to support Turkey's candidacy.

One of the bilateral relationships most obviously affected by the modernization program is Turkey's strategic partnership with Israel, whose cornerstone has been industrial defence cooperation. It is no coincidence that the military modernization program was announced at the same time that the cooperation agreements with Israel were signed in 1996. (These agreements were initially exclusively of a military nature and were aimed at fulfilling Turkey's modernization requirements.) Israeli supply of arms is a Turkish strategy that allows Turkey to circumvent anti-Turkish and pro-human rights lobbies in Western capitals when ordering arms. Turkey has other strategic interests the Turkish-Israeli alliance is supposed to help ensure. In order to cement these interests, Turkey has found industrial defence contracts to be a great incentive for increased Israeli military cooperation. In 1996, the first two agreements signed covered aircraft upgrades and missile production valued at $800 million. For the comparatively small Israeli defence industry (which at the time had about $500-$600 million in annual exports), international sales of that magnitude are difficult to find—especially due to Washington's veto power over Israeli arms sales. The economic significance to Israel's defence industry gives Turkey unusual leeway in its conduct of relations with Israel. For example, exceptionally harsh public criticism of Israel issued by Turkey's Prime Minister Erdogan in May 2004 received a discreet Israeli response, as the latter was eager not to sabotage current procurement decisions. The Turkish-Israeli relationship hence exemplifies the utility of military modernization programs in bilateral relationships as well as the remaining influence of the Turkish military in shaping foreign policy.

MILITARY MODERNIZATION IN STRATEGIC ASIA

On September 29, 2005, the Asia Program joined with the Seattle-based National Bureau of Asian Research (NBR) to host a conference exploring the ramifications of military modernization in Asia and the implications of defence transformation for the grand strategies of the region's principal powers, including the United States. Conference attendees sought to examine the drivers and gauge the progress of military modernization in Asia, and to assess the influence of these developments on the regional balance of power. This event was timed to mark the publication of the NBR report Strategic Asia 2005-06: Military Modernization in an Era of Uncertainty, edited by Ashley J. Tellis and Michael Wills.

China's rapid military modernization – in the context of a rising China more broadly – dominates the strategic thinking of the United States and the other major powers in Asia. George Washington University's David Shambaugh predicted that China's military power and regional reach will steadily increase in the years ahead, and will alter the balance of power in Asia. Nonetheless, Shambaugh cautioned against overestimating Chinese capabilities, or concluding that double-digit increases in China's military spending in each of the past 15 years mean that the Chinese military will be able to transform itself into a first-class fighting force with global reach in the near term.

China's military possesses numerous deficiencies in both quantitative and qualitative terms, especially when compared to American capabilities. But when viewed in the context of a Taiwan Strait conflict, Shambaugh added, China has made steady and even surprising progress in increasing its strength. China's aspiration and plans regarding defence modernization, he judged, are much what one would expect for a nation of China's size, wealth, location, national interests, and global role.

The remainder of the first panel focused on the military modernization programs of Asia's other major powers, Japan, Russia, and India. Christopher Hughes argued that Japan is gradually forsaking its post-1945 pacifist tradition, and moving along a long-term trajectory toward assuming the military capabilities and security roles customarily expected of nations of Japan's size and wealth. Japan is acquiring enhanced power projection capabilities and will inevitably play a more active role in both regional and global security. While Japan has no realistic option other than to maintain its close security links with the United States, Washington can expect Tokyo to become a more assertive ally, one that demands greater reciprocity and more equal treatment from the United States.

Stephen Blank contended that despite rising defence outlays, the Russian military remains an archaic, dysfunctional, and inefficient force, and is unlikely to carry out a program of modernization that is capable of fulfilling Moscow's ambitious aims. Absent major systemic reforms reaching far beyond the defence sector, Blank asserted, Russian influence in Eurasia will continue to wane, to be replaced by a more visible Chinese presence in areas traditionally subject to Russian influence.

Volume co-editor Ashley Tellis characterized India's "very large and extremely proficient" military as capable of defending Indian territory and interests in a war with China, though not quite able to defeat Pakistan in a brief conventional war. The dramatic increases in India's defence spending over the past half dozen years, he explained, must be seen in the context of a decade of lean years for the Indian military in the 1990s. Tellis highlighted three facets of India's current modernization: 1) technological modernization, especially in air and sea power; 2) doctrinal innovation designed to enable India to field a sizable combat force 48 hours after mobilization; and 3) organizational innovations, such as an emphasis on smaller military units, that will facilitate the new emphasis on rapid response. India, Tellis added, has departed from its traditional posture of non-alignment and now has a new interest in coalition warfare, with the United States being a plausible coalition partner.

The morning's second panel explored how other Asian nations have responded to these developments in the major Asian powers. Looking at the Korean peninsula, Jonathan Pollack suggested that the ground force standoff that has long dominated peninsular security planning will decline in relevance in the years ahead. Pyongyang will increasingly focus on deterrence and longer-range strike capabilities, while Seoul will pursue deterrence without automatically assuming adversarial relations with the North. South Korea, Pollack added, will be increasingly unwilling to undertake major long-term defence investments based on a predominantly threat-based military strategy, a stance that may pose acute risks to the South Korean – U.S. alliance. In the discussion following this analysis, one participant noted that Seoul acts as if it believes that the United States needs South Korea more than Seoul needs Washington – which, if true, would mark a significant change in strategic thinking in South Korea.

Michael Swaine contended that modernization in Taiwan has been marked by inadequate funding, an absence of strategic clarity, misplaced priorities, and unaddressed vulnerabilities. Taiwan needs to be far more serious about its defence environment than it has been recently, Swaine asserted. Glaring shortcomings in Taiwan's military modernization efforts could lead to miscalculations in both China and on Taiwan, resulting in one side or the other undertaking dangerous or destabilizing actions. Nonetheless, both Taipei and Washington must continue to balance efforts to rectify Taiwan's defence deficiencies with the need to avoid an escalation of tensions with Beijing.

Turning toward the nations of Southeast Asia, Sheldon Simon of Arizona State University asserted that the region's security concerns are primarily internal, including separatism and ethnic and religious violence. Transnational threats such as piracy, terrorism, and the trafficking of contraband, people, and arms constitute the next tier of security threats in the region, while external threats from other nations are the least pressing of the security challenges Southeast Asia confronts. Simon reported that notable breakthroughs in multilateral security cooperation have taken place over the past several years, including coordinated naval patrols by Malaysia, Singapore, and Indonesia, and cooperation with the United States by several of the littoral states in anti-piracy patrols. Rising insurance rates for ocean-going commerce transiting Southeast Asian waters, Simon observed, have been an important factor pushing the region toward greater multilateral cooperation.

Kimberly Marten observed that military modernization in the five Central Asian republics has focused more on officer corps retraining and professionalization than on hardware acquisition. Regional leaders, she warned, often exaggerate the Islamist threat as a ploy to gain external support, including from the United States. Foreign defence assistance acquired in this fashion is then often used to suppress populist opposition movements and, as a consequence, to bolster authoritarian regimes while undercutting the human rights concerns of the donor nations. The opium trade originating in Afghanistan does constitute a major security concern for the region, but this threat cannot be successfully addressed by military modernization alone. The day's final panel focused more directly on the implications for U.S. national security of these developments in the modernization of Asia's militaries. Aaron Friedberg, who spent the past two years as a senior advisor to Vice President Cheney, applauded Japan's retreat from its pacifist tradition of the past 60 years, as well as the improved tone in U.S. – India relations and India's greater ability to contribute to the maintenance of a regional balance of power. Among the troubling trends he highlighted were Russian sales of advanced weaponry to China, a problematic U.S. – Russia relationship, a growing divergence in strategic perceptions between the United States and South Korea, Taiwan's failure to spend "adequately" on its own self-defence, and skillful Chinese diplomacy that is reaching out to traditional U.S. friends such as Australia, South Korea, and the Philippines.

The Brookings Institution's Michael O'Hanlon observed that for all the talk in the Pentagon of a "revolution" in thinking about American security needs, very little has actually been accomplished in this area. As one example of the continuity between the Bush administration and its predecessors, he noted that the Defence Department has still had no serious discussions with Tokyo about the U.S. Marine presence in Okinawa, notwithstanding the serious difficulties the Marine bases create for the Japanese government and for sustaining popular support for the U.S. alliance.

Robert M. Hathaway emphasized the need for American leaders tasked with managing the U.S. - China relationship to make choices among competing priorities, to realize that "we can't have it all." Even a step that is as widely supported among U.S. decision makers as Japan's movement in the direction of becoming a "normal" state is not cost-free – that is, such a Japan is going to become a less pliant partner for the United States, and could alarm not only China, but other Asian powers.

In the day's final presentation, Ashley Tellis offered three tests for American policy makers wondering if they ought to be concerned by Asia's military modernization: 1) what are the political aims of the country in question, and what is the character of the governing regime?; 2) is the modernization oriented toward denying U.S. capabilities (as much of China's is, Tellis added)?; and 3) how has the modernization impacted not only the technological base of the country's military, but its operational effectiveness?

Underlying the discussion throughout the day lay two fundamental questions: 1) do American interests in Asia require U.S. hegemony in the region?; and 2) is any enhancement of China's military capabilities, no matter how incremental, detrimental to the United States? The answers to these two queries supplied by American leaders in the years to come will go far in determining whether China's rise to power is accomplished without a repetition of the violence that accompanied the rise of Germany and Japan in the previous century.

THE GAP BETWEEN TURKISH STRATEGY AND MILITARY MODERNIZATION

Turkey finds itself caught at the intersection of three points of regional instability formed by the Balkans, the Caucasus, and the Middle East. Whereas Turkish strategists once saw themselves living in a bad neighborhood surrounded by a ring of fire with only NATO guarantees to deter Soviet adventurism, they now find their country encircled by the ashes of failed or failing states. From being on the strategic defensive since the 1940s, decision-makers in Ankara now grapple with more assertive security policies as they seek to take advantage of new opportunities and preserve Turkish interests in the face of an uncertain future.

The rise of Turkey as an independent security actor in this region has not gone unnoticed by its neighbours. Ankara's experiment with post-Kemalist foreign policies comes at a time when Turkish military modernization is on the cusp of giving Turkey capabilities that far outstrip those of any single neighbor. The Turkish armed forces are enjoying the fruition of a defence modernization program laid out in the final years of the Cold War to develop a force capable of integrated airland battle as part of the NATO alliance. As the rest of NATO took the peace dividend and downsized military establishments, Ankara continued to increase defence spending on major systems with proposals to continue the pace of spending into the next two decades. None of Turkey's neighbours - including perhaps Russia in a localized conventional sense - are likely alone to match Turkish military capabilities in the near to medium term.

The growing unpredictability of Turkish security policy, coupled with Ankara's increased military strength relative to its neighbours, contributes to regional instability. Moreover, the Turkish General Staff is now in command of a military force structure that was created to counter Soviet-era threats in the context of a wider NATO-Warsaw Pact conflict. Whether these military capabilities and organizational structures will prove flexible enough to respond to the asymmetric risks of the next century is uncertain. The gap between Turkey's ambiguous national security strategy and its proven military abilities is forcing geopolitical restructuring throughout the region.

For the West, Turkey's potential emergence as a regional hegemon is a mixed blessing. Washington has long been Ankara's most reliable international ally, but American policymakers are ill prepared to manage Turkey's growing assertiveness in foreign policy and security affairs. The tradition of military cooperation is coming into increasing conflict with the broader themes of democratization, human rights, and economic considerations that define the West's post-Cold War interests. The public rift in October 1999 within Germany's governing coalition over the decision to pursue the sale of modern battle tanks to Ankara shows that Turkey's place in Europe's future security architecture remains uncertain as part of a broader European integration. Ankara has become a less-reliable security partner at a time when Turkey's actual value as an ally is ascending.

Turkey's Uncertain Future

Much has been written about Turkey's new security environment and the obvious changes that resulted from the disintegration of the Soviet Union. The initial thinking was far from positive. Many in Turkey, including now Prime Minister Bülent Ecevit, fretted over the still-warm Soviet corpse, worrying that Turkey's strategic importance to the West had diminished with NATO's victory over the Warsaw Pact. The collapse of Yugoslavia and the invasion of Kuwait by Iraqi forces quickly forced Turkish planners to revise their estimates, however. Their country's position as a frontline state amidst areas of instability created the impression of Turkey's growing importance to America and to Europe, erasing the brief self-doubt that troubled policymakers in Ankara.

Nevertheless, Turkish leaders have been unable to translate their new sense of strategic importance into a clear formula for improved partnership with the West. Difficulties with Greece, continued tensions over Cyprus, and the European Union's indifferent response to Turkey's bid for membership have coincided with Ankara's call for a new European security architecture which recognizes the critical role played by Turkey. Washington has also proven to be a more complex partner, as common regional security interests seem to fall apart over disagreements on arms transfers, Kurdish policies, and democratization. This paradox has encouraged civilian and military leaders from across the political spectrum to experiment with new policies, suggesting Ankara's willingness to take greater unilateral risks with international relations.

Turkey's national security strategy for the next century is still a work in progress. The broad outlines of the policy are only now becoming clear. Consensus between the Turkish General Staff and the dominant political classes is still being forged. Indications suggest that Ankara is looking to move beyond the traditional Kemalist parameters of pseudo-isolationism and collective security to create a more dynamic role for Turkey in the region. The end result, however, looks to be a less-predictable actor seeking to assert greater influence over its immediate neighbours.

As late as 1997, military planners in the Turkish General Staff were still working off the National Military Strategy Concept developed in 1985 to evaluate threats to Turkey. The underlying framework of the concept was inherently defensive in its outlook, based on conventional force-on-force calçulations with nuclear considerations relegated to broader NATO or American spheres.

During the Cold War, a critical debate within NATO circles was how far Turkish forces were prepared to withdraw before an allied counteroffensive could be mounted to push back Soviet and Warsaw Pact forces. Turkish planners hoped to meet the enemy at the border and fight a structured retreat from the frontier. American planners were less hopeful, and initial estimates in the late 1950s projected a drawback into a corner of the Turkish southwest, the Iskenderun Pocket. Although the plans were modified repeatedly over time, in 1990 the General Staff still saw a multi-front defence of sovereign territory as the primary security task.

This picture did not change in the early 1990s. As late as 1997, Turkish military briefers ranked Russia, Greece, Iraq, Iran, and Syria as the top threats to security based on their perceived claims on Turkish territory and ability to project conventional forces. The former Deputy Undersecretary of the Foreign Ministry and ambassador to Washington, Sükrü Elekdag, gave a broader policy spin to these briefings when he argued for Turkey's continued need to plan on "two-and-a-half campaigns, e.g., conducting two full scale operations simultaneously... while being prepared for a `half war' that might be instigated from within the country." He argued further that interior lines of defence were no longer sufficient to allow Turkey to concentrate on one front at a time. The pace of conflict had increased to the point where the military must have the force structure to fight on at least two fronts simultaneously. Turkish policymakers saw the main threat as the disruption of territorial integrity by conventional forces projected across Turkey's borders or by terrorist forces operating in Turkey with direct support from hostile governments. Therefore, the military needed to be organized, trained, and equipped for two primary objectives. First, Turkish land and air forces were expected to blunt an armor-heavy invasion and then conduct a defence in depth in the east and the south. Second, army and gendarme troops needed to be prepared to fight a counterinsurgency with static defence and mobile reaction forces. In this strategic vision, the navy was left to coastal patrolling and initial defence of the Bosporus Strait. Although tactical mobility was clearly required, strategic mobility and deep strike capability were less critical. The conflict would be fought on Turkish soil.

Changes in Turkish foreign policy and the publication of a new defence strategy suggest that the old vision has been revised. Without repudiating its primary ties to the West and to NATO, Turkish policymakers have been softening Atatürk's claim that Turkey's future lies solely with the West. For generations of Turks, Turkey's position as a European country free from its historic baggage in the Ottoman east has been the keystone of the republic's identity. Secularist leaders, particularly in the military, had dismissed attempts to increase Turkey's role in the Muslim east as unacceptable moves by Islamist reactionaries to undermine Atatürk's pro-Western legacy. Yet, official military documents now talk of Turkey as a "country of Eurasia" obligated "to retain and enhance the ties with both the West and the East." This deviation from seven decades of orthodoxy is a significant watershed in Turkish strategic thinking. Turkish analysts argue that the change in foreign policy is a struggle between "the proponents of boldness and the advocates of caution, and that the military and the civilian bureaucrats tend to fall in the latter camp." This position posits a tension over Turkey's international orientation as a European or an Islamic state, with the establishment defending the secular Western tradition and Islamic fundamentalists and Kurdish separatists advocating more fluid perspectives.

Yet, the push toward a more activist policy has come largely from the military and is centered on the former Ottoman lands. Throughout the Cold War period Turkey maintained distant though cordial relations with its Arab and Persian neighbours. Ankara sought to distance itself from the Arab-Israeli peace process despite some affinity for Tel Aviv. In February 1996, Ankara unexpectedly signed a military training and education agreement with Israel that changed the strategic calculus in the region. The push in Turkey for this change came from Undersecretary of the Foreign Ministry Onur Öymen and the Deputy Chief of the General Staff, Çevik Bir. Although the official position in Ankara is that cooperation with Israel is in no way aimed against another country, Bir and other senior Turkish officers have publicly asserted that these two "secular, democratic countries" alone face the same strategic threats. The strategic threats enumerated by Bir, however, are not the same ones considered by Cold War planners. They drive Turkish leaders to advocate greater participation in crises in the Balkans and the Caucasus in addition to the Middle East.

Before his appointment as Chief of the General Staff in August 1998, then Land Forces Commander General Hüseyin Kivrikoglu listed these new threats to Turkey as regional and ethnic conflicts, the spread of weapons of mass destruction, religious fanaticism, drug trafficking, and international terrorism. He refrained from identifying specific countries as the origins of these threats - a noted departure from previous Turkish strategy documents - and focused instead on the effects of these challenges on the Turkish military. He argued that the military must become a "force primarily used against external and internal threats that target Turkey's territorial integrity and the republic regime." Though this does not sound different from his predecessors' call for protection of Turkey's national borders, Kivrikoglu moved beyond a mission of deterrence and strategic defence to say that the "rapid deployment of the military in distant places is of vital importance in view of the threats we face and the risks and responsibilities that we may assume." He finished by outlining a modernization program to provide strategic mobility for joint operations to strike beyond Turkey's borders.

After his promotion to chief of the General Staff, Kivrikoglu told reporters that in addition to deterrence and collective security Turkey needed to develop operational capabilities for "forward engagement" and "forward defence." The military must, in his opinion, be prepared to preempt threats to Turkish interests before they cross onto Turkish territory. The publication of the Ministry of National Defence's White Paper-Defence 1998 demonstrates how these and other positions have been distilled into a roadmap for change in the Turkish military and in Turkey's foreign policy. According to this document, Turkey's military strategy rests on four distinct points. The General Staff maintained deterrence and collective security as the first two points to highlight the continuity in national defence policy. The last two points - forward defence and military contribution to crisis management and intervention during crisis - reflect a departure from previous strategies. The crux of the latter points is for the Turkish military to identify the content of a possible conflict as soon as possible and take steps to resolve the conflict prior to its emergence as a threat to Turkey proper. Although the document softens Kivrikoglu's more troubling language of "forward engagement," it goes on to state:

"The general operation concept of the 2000s stipulates the creation of a sensor region where the aggressor is... and defeating him beyond and in the depths of the theatre. Therefore, possession of troops with overwhelming fire power and maneuver capability and... the coordinated and efficient use of target identification, detection, and warning systems as well as... command [and] control, electronic warfare, and communication information systems are important assets to this end."

Ankara has adopted a set of operational concepts wherein the military will seek to meet threats to Turkey beyond its sovereign territories. The Turkish military is not only capable, but also willing to operate outside its borders.

6

Civil-military Assistance in Stability Operations

Traditional peacekeeping during the Cold War was authorized under Chapter VI of the UN Charter and most generally comprised the "imposition of neutral and lightly armed interposition forces following a cessation of armed hostilities, and with the permission of the state on whose territory these forces are deployed, in order to discourage a renewal of military conflict and promote an environment under which the underlying dispute can be resolved". The rapid rise in civil wars and ethnic strife in the decade following the end of the Cold War and the desperate need for action to help the civilian populations who were the targets of ethnic cleansing demonstrated the need for the international community to go beyond peacekeeping and authorize peace enforcement operations under Chapter VII of the UN Charter in order to compel compliance with international resolutions and sanctions and to "maintain or restore peace and support diplomatic efforts to reach a long-term political settlement".

In the early-to-mid 1990s it became apparent that humanitarian issues were intrinsically connected to problems of peace and security. Security Council Resolution 794 (Somalia), for instance, authorized for the first time military intervention under Chapter VII " in order to establish a secure environment for humanitarian relief operations." With the number of complex emergencies rising, the United Nations developed a peacebuilding approach integrating military and humanitarian action into a series of sequential activities proceeding from observing the cease fire and assisting in humanitarian relief and refugee resettlement to contributing to economic reconstruction, social reconciliation and the restoration of essential government functions. At the heart of this approach is the simultaneous control of violence at the interpersonal and intercommunal levels, the provision of the basic needs of the suffering population, and, as needed, the planning for and monitoring of reconciliation and reconstruction efforts. It is in meeting these immediate challenges that the effective interface between armed forces and civilian aid agencies becomes centrally important, but also that the main tensions between the civilian and military peacebuilding elements arise.

Since complex emergencies frequently require a combination of traditional peacekeeping functions (e.g., the supervision and monitoring of cease-fires, disarmaments, and demobilization and the overseeing of elections) and combat-defined peace enforcement activities, peace-building or stability operations are oftentimes referred to as "third-generation" peace operations that "more closely resemble the original peace-keeping missions (in the sense that they enjoy the parties' overall consent), but also add something new in that they actively contribute to the rebuilding of state and social structures". While military forces undertook civilian tasks such as humanitarian relief and public administration by default and without a clear strategy or concrete objectives in Bosnia-Herzegovina, Kosovo, or East Timor until civilian authorities were in a position to take over humanitarian and governing responsibilities, successful peace-building in the future will depend increasingly on the quality of collaboration among military forces, UN administration and civilian aid agencies (Jeong, 2005).

Civil-Military Cooperation

Cooperation between the civilian and military elements involves integrating traditional military capabilities into a collective response to human need. At the outset, civilian and military actors share the long-term goal of promoting human security and developing the conditions for societies marked by conflict to transition back to peaceful and stable structures. Initially, civil-military relationships were formed in the field, when troops stepped in to fill gaps in civilian capabilities. In response to the growing complexity of operational requirements, states are increasingly recognizing the intensifying working relationship between military and civilian actors and are now developing their own doctrines specifying the nature of civil-military cooperation (CIMIC).

In July 2003, for instance, the North Atlantic Treaty Organization (NATO) published its own CIMIC Doctrine, which defines CIMIC as "the co-ordination and co-operation, in support of the mission, between the NATO commander and civil actors, including national population and local authorities, as well as international, national and non-governmental organizations and agencies". In essence, civil-military cooperation in stability operations includes three core functions: liaison between the military and all civilian actors in the area of operation, assistance to the civilian environment, and support to the force. For instance, during implementation of the General Framework Agreement for Peace (GFAP) in Bosnia and Herzegovina, CIMIC personnel coordinated with the Implementation Force (IFOR) for increased security presence when cargo of a strategic nature (e.g., electrical transformers and hydroelectric turbines) was transported through contested territory and worked closely with a number of civilian agencies to install temporary power lines, facilitate the repair and reconstruction of roads and bridges, and perform periodic joint environmental inspections of the local water supply.

Generally, CIMIC expands tasks that the U.S. military considers "Civil Affairs (CA) activities" which refer primarily to "support of the civilian environment." CA encompasses activities undertaken to establish and maintain relations between military forces and civil authorities as well as the general population. While CIMIC and CA activities oftentimes overlap on the ground, there is a clear doctrinal difference in scope. CIMIC focuses on humanitarian need and provides guidance for how to interact with civilian actors (civil authorities, local populations, international organizations, and non-governmental organizations) in order to effectively complete the objectives of a humanitarian mission. CA, by contrast, focuses on military needs and provides suggestions for how to gain the support of civilians for the military mission. NATO identifies CIMIC as the interface intended to primarily improve coordination and reduce overlap and duplication of efforts between civilian organizations and authorities in order to meet humanitarian needs more effectively. By contrast, CA, as described in the U.S. Department of Defence Doctrine for Civil Affairs, seeks to influence the civilian environment in support of the armed forces. Despite these noticeable distinctions between CA and CIMIC, the two approaches share sufficient common ground to be compatible.

CIMIC in Practice: Afghanistan

Although the distance that the military had traditionally maintained to civilian aid agencies was beginning to shrink considerably during the Balkan missions, some observers now believe that the relationship established in Afghanistan is creating a precedent for the future of civil-military cooperation. It was clear from the initial planning stages of the Afghanistan operation that CIMIC would play a central role in the coalition's efforts to "win the hearts and minds" of the local population. To illustrate the importance of CIMIC to the perceived success of the mission, a number of humanitarian agencies were invited to participate in the Coalition Governing Council based at the U.S. Central Command (CENTCOM) in Tampa, Florida. Shortly after the fall of the Taliban regime, the coalition established a Joint Civil-Military Operations Task Force (CJCMOTF) to oversee CIMIC on the ground.

Under the auspices of the CJCMOTF, the coalition deployed a number of Coalition Humanitarian Cells (CHLCs) in key urban centers across the country whose main functions included: "to 'win the hearts and minds' among the Afghan population; to secure the support of local communities by showing 'the benign face of the Coalition;' to jumpstart reconstruction efforts; and to gain positive publicity for the war effort in the United States". Initial "quick impact" projects included drilling wells, constructing schools and health clinics, and repairing roads and bridges. "Indeed," Fields recalls her experience on the ground, "it appeared as if the CJCMOTF was a 'military NGO.'" From the outset, NGOs objected to military involvement in many of these projects as they saw a duplication of their own efforts and a threat to NGO staff by blurring the lines between military and civilian actors. Fields explains, "The relief community saw these projects as outside the purview of the military, particularly a military that was still fighting in certain parts of the country. They took exception to the projects themselves, as well as to the oversight of these projects by soldiers in civilian clothes." Demonstrating their concern, NGOs rejected invitations to attend weekly CJCMOTF coordination meetings (Sedra, 2004).

By early 2003, the Coalition established Provincial Reconstruction Teams (PRTs) based on the experiences of U.S. civil affairs teams in an effort to expand the influence of the then still transitional Karzai government outside of Kabul and to help accelerate the process of national reconstruction. Perceived as integrated civil-military units, the PRTs operational assignments went far beyond any *ad hoc* protection force charged with the provision of a secure environment in which civil reconstruction projects can be completed. The PRTs were supposed to "extend the influence of the central government outside the capital; provide a security umbrella for [non-governmental humanitarian agencies] to operate; facilitate information sharing; and carry out small-scale reconstruction projects based on concise needs assessments and local consultations". Teams operating under military command structures ranged from 50-100 personnel and comprised of civil affairs soldiers, special forces, and regular army units as well as representatives from the United States Agency for International Development (USAID) and the Departments of State and Agriculture. Initially, American PRTs conducted various projects (e.g., school construction) on their own and some soldiers even started out working in civilian dress. Throughout

2003, the PRT concept was gradually internationalized with Great Britain, New Zealand and Germany establishing PRTs in different areas and NATO assuming command of International Security Assistance Force in August 2003.

From the outset, the PRT concept was criticized by members of the relief community for its lack of military strength to confront insecurity, inadequate predeployment consultation with NGOs and local stakeholders, ambiguous mandate and legal framework, lack of institutional memory due to frequent personnel rotation schedules, and potential for compromising the role of humanitarian agencies through the implementation of aid projects (Sedra, 2004). More specifically, many NGOs felt that PRTs constituted a security risk foı aid workers by making them a "soft target" for insurgents. Following the shooting death of five of its employees by anti-government militants, Médicins Sans Frontieres (MSF) suspended its operations in Afghanistan in the summer of 2004 after having worked in the country for over 24 years. MSF attributed its decision to the proliferation of Provincial Reconstruction Teams (PRTs) which it claimed had blurred the lines between civilian and military spheres and placed its staff at undo risk. According to MSF, "PRT actions had effectively curtailed 'humanitarian space' within which MSF and other humanitarian organizations could operate".

Organizational Structures and Operational Differences

The organizational structures of peacekeeping forces and NGOs are typically polar opposites. Command structures in the military are centralized and vertical with clear and well-defined lines of authority flowing hierarchically from top to bottom. The chain of command is typically structured so that it can respond quickly and promote fast and efficient decision-making. Decisions typically include finite deadlines and mission specific rules of engagement that guide the entire operational structure from senior decision-makers to the behavior of soldiers on the ground. By contrast, the organizational structure of most NGOs is horizontal and fluid based on a consensus-approach and allowing for considerable decision authority left to field operatives. Relief and development agencies commonly promote participatory and collaborative working relationships that presuppose informal management and the ability to quickly adjust objectives and activities to sudden changes in civilian needs. Overall, Jeong finds, "the efficiency of small NGOs depends on a minimum administrative overhead without the necessity of a formal management structure. In the areas of development and civil society building, hierarchical structures with links to central headquarters are less effective at developing appropriate local strategies."

Humanitarian agencies, especially smaller ones, in part because of constraints of size and resources, do not usually strive for "unity of command" but rather for what Rubinstein (2003) has termed "camaraderie of command." Instead of the common *modus operandi* of highly bureaucratized organizations that assign well-defined tasks and responsibilities to individuals, the more fluid structures of many NGOs require all to "contribute their efforts and expertise whenever and wherever these are needed, regardless of the structural definition of their position".

In addition, observers point to organizational differences in terms of resource availability and usage and accountability and transparency. The military's ability to mobilize massive resources and deploy significant numbers of personnel to anywhere virtually overnight has become the envy of many humanitarian organizations that often experience difficulty finding the necessary number of qualified staff to deploy. In their work, humanitarians are widely accountable to donors, private constituents, and their beneficiaries and, therefore, tend to favour transparency even in relation to belligerents. For the military, transparency is obviously limited by national security interests and accountability is more limited to their respective defence ministries and parliaments. Minear et al. (2000), for instance, recount an incident during the Kosovo operation, where Saudi Arabian peacekeepers had opened a hospital for treatment of civilians but had, on grounds of military secrecy, refused to share epidemiological data with health care professionals from civilian aid agencies.

Operating Principles and Normative Foundations

The normative foundations underlying stability operations are reflected above all in the laws of war, especially the 1949 Geneva Convention and its Two Additional Protocols of 1977, representing the international community's attempts to humanize war. The International Red Cross (ICRC) specifies that: "Measures are humanitarian if they meet the principles of neutrality, impartiality and independence. Aid measures that do not do this are not humanitarian, regardless of any well-meaning intentions and their effectiveness". In theory, humanitarian aid is supposed to reach all victims of crises and disasters and is aimed at saving lives and mitigating human suffering. As such, it is to be administered impartially and unconditionally without discrimination on the grounds of race, religion, sex, age, nationality or political affiliation. It is also to be administered neutrally without any political agenda. Impartiality and neutrality are indispensable for ensuring access by aid organizations to the "victims" on all sides of the conflict. Given this very general understanding of these principles, the scope and nature of legitimate action remains open-ended and at times ill defined, thereby complicating peacebuilding efforts, especially in situations where relief workers operate without permission of local or national authorities.

Traditionally, the military has been designed for pursuit of national political interests, to accomplish governmental objectives through the use of force. As such, military action is always political in nature. Military missions are legitimized through the political process, but ideally also by reference to international law and broad-based international support. As a result, legitimacy is much more confined. For instance, peace operations authorized by the United Nations Security Council clearly specify the scope of the mandate and the nature of legitimate action (e.g., the supply of food, medicines, shelter, and health care for disaster victims). The rules of engagement provided to forces on the ground operationalize the mandate further and very specifically instruct soldiers on appropriate and inappropriate courses of action.

Impartiality is also a fundamental organizing principle for the military in providing humanitarian assistance. For peacekeepers, the Handbook on United Nations Peacekeeping Operations specifies, "impartiality may mean that all parties to a conflict are treated in the same way based on international law and Security Council resolutions and that sanctions may be imposed or enforcement action taken against spoilers. For humanitarian staff, however, impartiality means that emergency life-saving assistance and protection be provided to the needy civilian population, regardless of politics." Tactically, the Handbook explains further, "peacekeepers may, on occasion, need to keep a particular faction at arm's length or under sanction. At the same time, it may be tactically important for humanitarian staff to maintain close dialogue with the same faction to ensure access to civilians under their control. Strategically, in places of active conflict or where access is contested, it is critical for humanitarian workers to be able to reach beneficiaries regardless of how the peace process evolves".

This brief description of the cultural, organizational, and operational differences elucidates the dilemma inherent in stability operations: Effective peacebuilding and post-conflict reconstruction aimed at building a stable and lasting peace requires the cooperation between civilian and military actors. Yet, the effectiveness of humanitarian efforts hinge largely on the ability of the civilian element to remain impartial, neutral, and independent, while the military component is politicized, relying on the consent of the parties involved. Gourlay (2000, p. 35) conjectures that "when levels of consent among the local population run low or the military is perceived as a party to a conflict, civil-military relationships become strained and civilian humanitarians distance themselves from the military." During NATO's military action in Kosovo, for instance, virtually the entire humanitarian community left the battlefield as the air campaign began, and some attempted to actively distance themselves from the political context of the NATO operation. Médicins Sans Frontièrs, for instance, decided not to accept funding from NATO states.

Effective peacebuilding requires a unity of effort and a coherent response from civilian and military actors alike. Nevertheless, irrespective of how long a conflict endures the civilian population must be provided basic protection including humanitarian aid. Clearly, stability operations in response to complex emergencies present significant challenges and humanitarian and peacebuilding efforts may at times be at odds. Effective peacebuilding becomes a management challenge on the ground that requires civilian and military, as well as local and international actors to work together, anticipate differences that may arise, attempt to avoid conflicting approaches, communicate clearly, share information and undertake common analysis, and, in a best-case scenario, agree on a strategy. How can this be accomplished?

The Dilemmas

Recognizing the potential of CIMIC for undermining the neutrality and independence of humanitarian organizations and NGOs, the ICRC began already in the early 1990s to advocate the concept of "humanitarian space" which describes the ability of humanitarian agencies to "work independently and impartially without fear of attack in pursuit of the humanitarian imperative. This means they are free to assist populations in need, and are not constrained by political or physical barriers to their work". In theory at least, the military becomes involved in humanitarian operations only *in extremis*, "where people are dying, or at risk of dying, and only the military can safe them". In practice, however, NGOs are especially concerned with military forces undertaking assistance work as part of their strategy to "win the hearts and minds" of the local population. The military objectives behind this strategy include enhanced force protection and information gathering as a result of gaining the people's trust. The military's "hearts and minds" approach can easily result in a confusion of the role of humanitarian agencies and military forces on the ground. The problem, as Sedra observes, is that "[w]hile the military has emphasized the need for 'complementarity' in this new situation, humanitarian groups have been wary of its impact on their ability to remain impartial, neutral, and independent." Military encroachment on humanitarian space is viewed critically not only by civilian relief providers.

Peacebuilding as a core operational responsibility is also contentious within the military establishment. While peace operations have traditionally been perceived as less honourable and prestigious or as career stoppers and military professionals had been significantly less committed to participating in Operations Other Than War (OOTW) than in combat, both the nature of the missions and the perceptions of what it means to be a soldier are changing. Unlike most Cold War missions, which were either combat or non-combat in nature, peacebuilding or stability operations cannot be classified easily. They typically require military forces to simultaneously fulfil combat and non-combat functions and coordinate their efforts with partner militaries and a host of civilian relief organizations.

As peacebuilding gains operational importance, a growing number of military leaders seem to accept the military's emerging dual responsibility: to act as a fighting force and to contribute to humanitarian relief efforts, especially as the "Cold War" generation of officers is being replaced by a generation of officers who spent their formative years deployed in the complex emergencies of the Balkans, Somalia, Sierra Leone, or Afghanistan. Confirming this trend, Tomforde found in a recent study that "younger soldiers define their role more in light of peacekeeping missions and therefore share the view that 'a real soldier' needs to have been deployed at least once." Despite growing acceptance of widening operational needs, problems persist in the coordination of efforts between military forces and civilian relief agencies and a number of factors continuously hinder effective operational coordination.

Cultural and Perceptional Differences

Conducting interviews with more than 200 military and humanitarian aid officials with experience on the ground in the Kosovo theatre, Minear and colleagues (2000) found major differences in institutional cultures. Generally, they argued,

Western militaries are paid, trained and equipped to "use organized and regulated violence to accomplish objectives set by democratic governments". The military places high value on command-and control, clear lines of authority, discipline, and accountability and prioritizes logistics, i.e., "guaranteed functioning under the most adverse circumstances, with the necessary 'force protection' to carry out tasks". The military's institutional culture is characterized by considerable investments in human resources management, including extensive training at all levels, redundancy of staff, lessons-learned exercises, and, where possible, well rehearsed responses in the field. By contrast, humanitarian organizations tend to be less hierarchical, place higher priority on process, i.e. how objectives are accomplished, and generally view redundancy as needless duplication of efforts. Moreover, relief workers tend see themselves as nonviolent people who have dedicated part of their lives to assist the less fortunate whose most formidable task oftentimes consists in building consensus among conflicting parties without favouring one side or the other.

These cultural differences contribute not only to discrepant mutual expectations, but, at times, also to negative perceptions of members of the other group. Minear et al. (2000) report that military officials were surprised by the small number of relief workers assigned to complete particular humanitarian tasks, while aid workers wanted to utilize what they considered the "idle capacity" of military contingents deployed as a necessary reserve for unexpected emergencies. Minear and colleagues also criticize a lack of understanding between institutions at the operational level: "Humanitarians insist on distinctions between and among themselves. They are critical of the military for failing to understand that OCHA [Office for the Coordination of Humanitarian Affairs (UN)] is not an operational agency, that the World Food Programme is not an NGO, the GTZ [*Deutsche Gesellschaft für Technische Zusammenarbeit* (German Society for Technical Cooperation)] is a bilateral aid agency, and that the ICRC is none of the above. Yet distinctions that are equally important for the military—for example, between ARRC [Allied Command Europe Rapid Reaction Corps] and AFOR [Albanian

Force (NATO)]—are often lost on humanitarians." Earlier, Aall (1996) had already observed that NGOs felt uneasy working with military forces, especially if those forces served non-democratic governments with "unsavory human rights records." Moreover, Weiss' (1999) research and recent events in Iraq confirm that the more closely civilian agencies are associated with an unpopular military force, the less room for maneuver the agency has and the more problematic and contentious CIMIC on the ground becomes. Soldiers, on the other hand, oftentimes regarded NGOs as "undisciplined and their operations as uncoordinated and disjointed".

In Somalia (UNOSOM II), for example, the military expected civilian agencies to support its objective of enforcing order, while the civilian agencies wanted the military to supplement their efforts of delivering aid (Jeong, 2005). Given its concern with "mission creep," the military tends to favour conditions where it can go in, provide technical assistance or logistics support, and then get out quickly. This can be problematic as this approach rarely considers the long-term management implications of military infrastructure projects for the civilian population. For instance, in Somalia, the U.S. military deployed its own engineers and support troops to rebuild roads and other infrastructure at a time when Somalis desperately needed jobs. But, the military was not interested in hiring Somalis because it wanted to complete the mission quickly and feared that involving "untrained" locals would unnecessarily prolong the reconstruction efforts. Similarly, Mockaitis (2004, p. 17) recalls an incident in Kosovo where an American officer forced a solution over what color to paint a youth center, "leaving the NGO to spend the next month sorting out the mess." He concludes that the strong desire on the side of military actors to solve problems often creates more problems and that "the line between 'can do' and 'bull in a China shop' is small indeed." These examples confirm the conclusion that the military's approach is focused on short-term, non-participatory, and decisive action and primarily informed by security rather than by the long-term development considerations that shape the operational activities of many civilian activities.

Military units, by their very nature, are trained to respond to and operate in a "low context culture" relying on directives, specific orders, and standard operating procedures that are communicated clearly down the hierarchy. This stands in stark contrast to the "high context" cultural and operational requirements of complex emergencies where nonverbal signals, family or tribal status, age, gender, or ethnic differences, or social roles and expectations carry a lot of meaning. The concepts of low and high cultures were first articulated by anthropologist Edward Hall (1976) in his theory of cultural differences which assumes a strong linkage between culture and communication. Interactions and communication in a given culture are determined by the social context in that culture, i.e., the network of social expectations that shape a person's behavior.

Effective peacebuilding requires a thorough intercultural understanding and an enduring commitment that ranges from a stabilization of the post-conflict situation and the normalization of relations between adversaries through confidence building measures to the creation of a stable political order and sustainable democratic relations (Jeong, 2005). International organizations and NGOs whose mandate includes conflict resolution, reconciliation, reconstruction, and nation building typically take a "high-context" long-term approach to peacebuilding in order to establish "structures which will tend to strengthen and solidify peace in order to avoid relapse into conflict".

In general, most relief and stability operations are characterized by an *ad hoc* and oftentimes improvised response to an immediate humanitarian need. There is typically little time for organized advanced planning and coordination, especially in terms of bringing together civilian and military actors, so the need arises for improved a priori coordination and preparation. Despite the fundamental differences in structure and approach to peacebuilding between civilian and military actors, there is also clear evidence that training, institutional socialization, and shared experiences through collaboration on the ground can help to bring these actors together and facilitate effective and meaningful cooperation. One strategic approach to civil-military cooperation in stability operations is to carefully create a division of labor based on the comparative advantages of civilian and military elements. For the military, these include the ability to provide security, lift and other logistic capacity, a strong sense of discipline, and the ability to get things done. The comparative advantage of humanitarian organizations are in their technical expertise, experience in working together with other civilian actors, knowledge of the region and established relationships with the local community, and a longer-term commitment to the people and their institutions.

Utilizing a comparative advantage approach, the purpose of military action during stability operations is to complement rather than compete with the work of humanitarian relief organizations. More specifically and in order of priority, Gourlay (2000) suggests the military should first and foremost foster a climate of security for the civilian population and humanitarian organizations. This would include controlling violence generated by military opposition or between organized military formations—but not controlling riots and civilian disturbances for which peacekeepers are not well suited— and providing protection for the relief effort. Second, military contingents should support the work of civilian humanitarian agencies by providing technical or logistical support, assistance on the reconstruction of basic infrastructure (water, power, roads), and security-related support tasks such as demobilization and demining. Finally, and only in rare circumstances should the military provide direct assistance to those in need. As the analysis has demonstrated, this is the most contested area as it runs the risk of politicizing and militarizing humanitarianism. However, it can also be a very effective measure to improve the popularity of the military and garner support of the local population, thereby aiding the achievement of the mission objectives.

Regardless, in order to avoid jeopardizing the humanitarian mission objectives, attempts should be made to minimize politicization of the humanitarian effort. This could be accomplished in some missions by a national division between providers of relief and humanitarian services and those engaged in the use of force. Of course, the more complex the emergency and the more extensive the relief support from the international community, the less viable this suggestion becomes. Alternatively, the deployment of a standing rapid reaction or peacebuilding force that does not rely on emergency- or crisis-specific contributions from states and that operates under international command—such as the UN Stand-by Forces High Readiness Brigade (SHIRBIRG)—could also de-politicize CIMIC in complex emergencies.

In 1996, Aall (1996) concluded her analysis of civil-military interaction in peacebuilding with the recommendation that humanitarian operations should form a key part of training of the armed forces. In November 2005, recognizing the growing importance of peacebuilding missions, the U.S. Department of Defence issued Directive 3000.05 elevating stability operations to "core U.S. military missions" and giving it "priority comparable to combat operations." Calling for the incorporation of stability operations into "military training, exercises, and planning, including intelligence campaign plans and intelligence support plans", the directive specifies the need to identify stability operations capabilities and assess their development; develop stability operations joint doctrine in consultation with relevant U.S. departments and agencies, foreign governments and security forces, international organizations, NGOs, and members of the private sector; provide annual training guidance specific to stability operations capabilities; and develop curricula at joint military education and individual training venues for the conduct and support of stability operations.

As stability operations increase in number and complexity, it is important for militaries and humanitarians alike to develop a joint understanding of their roles and functions and to improve interagency and inter-force cooperation before and during operational deployments. A first step in achieving this at the military level would be for NATO members to adopt NATO's CIMIC doctrine and to foster a common understanding about capabilities, limitations, roles, and missions of CIMIC units and personnel during the operational phase of peacebuilding and reconstruction missions. Effective peacebuilding requires sharing strategic and operational responsibility among participating forces. Closer examination of the KFOR mission which divided Kosovo into five multinational brigade (MNB) areas, each under command of a different lead nation, may provide lessons for best practices in multinational stability operations with respect to the internal operations of the armed forces, interaction with local populations and among international organizations, NGOs, and other militaries and in terms of prioritizing among relevant peacebuilding activities.

Socialization and training would not only help civilian and military actors alike to prepare for their respective responsibility, but would also sensitize members of each community to each other and build the skills for effective and quick improvisation on the ground, thereby simultaneously building mutual respect for and more effective utilization of "humanitarian" and "military space".

Improved cooperation and coordination among the actors can help to also overcome mission-impeding negative perceptions of the other side. Specifically, cooperation should include cultural sensitivity training intended to foster greater understanding for the differing organizational structures and cultures. This could be achieved, for instance, through internship programs and staff exchanges and the creation of common training and guidepost manuals describing the roles and functions, the values and capabilities, and the organizational structure and chain of command of multinational or UN forces, including details on military culture, fundamental principles of peacekeeping operations, mission responsibilities, rules on the use of force, and applicability of international law to UN troops. The manuals should contain similar descriptions for NGOs including details on varying operational and organizational structures, chain of command, decision-making procedures, culture and ideology, specializations, fundamental principles, operational responsibilities.

Apart from recommendations pertaining to the planning and pre-operation phases, it is also important to improve coordination mechanisms in the field. Core operational CIMIC tasks include communication, interagency coordination, information exchange, and outcomes assessment. Implied in these core functions is, of course, a focus on empowering local and international humanitarian support agencies so they can facilitate a complete transition of responsibility to civilian authorities and organizations.

Preparation for a successful transition is perhaps the most crucial objective of effective peacebuilding. Aiding this process necessitates civil affairs training at all levels encouraging a broad based understanding of the CIMIC purpose and of mission-specific requirements. Improving operational decision-making involves decentralizing command and control and granting officers in charge on the ground more authority and responsibility to make *ad hoc* decisions. Effective peacebuilding, the experiences in the former Yugoslavia and in Afghanistan and Iraq demonstrate, demands a "high context" approach from civilian and military actors alike. This, in turn, requires extensive knowledge and understanding of the emergency or conflict context and continuity of effort. Depending on the mandate and structure of a stability operation, different mechanism may ensure optimal coordination on the ground, but a joint operations center or civil-military coordination cell could provide valuable logistics and coordination support for developing contingency plans and procedures for distribution of aid, separation of the conflicting parties, return of refugees and other pressing decisions.

A number of observers have suggested that the presence of units of civilians or reservists with civilian skills made collaboration easier, as it helped bridge the cultural gaps between the military and civilian relief providers and also to the local population. Due to their transferable civilian skills, reservists may indeed be better prepared for undertaking CIMIC duties than combat-trained full-time professional soldiers. In addition, to address the issue of lack of institutional memory as a result of frequent personnel rotation schedules, it may be beneficial to extend military deployments to more than the typical 6-12 months duration and to limit rotations to ensure consistency and continuity and build trust with NGOs and locals.

The career patterns of the U.S. military were a problem. For family reasons, and to keep moving in rank, American soldiers rotate out of Iraq at the end of a year. They may be sent back to Iraq, but probably on a different assignment in a different part of the country. The advisor who has been building contacts in a village or with a police unit is gone, and a fresh, non-Arabic-speaking face shows up.

Counterinsurgency manuals usually emphasize the need for long-term personal relations. Obviously, it is impractical to advocate that entire units remain in place for extended periods of time—especially if they are composed largely of reservists who may resist longer-term assignments—but it might be possible to specifically train civilians alongside the military to function as CIMIC liaisons and ask them to remain in place for extended periods to provide continuity and operational consistency. This could also create an important stability interface in the relationship between the peacekeepers and the local population and between military and civilian aid providers.

More specific recommendations pertain to the use of civil-military reconstruction teams (CMRTs), especially as this might help enhance the security of relief workers and improve the effectiveness of CIMIC in post-conflict reconstruction. The experiences in Kosovo and Afghanistan have demonstrated the importance and effectiveness of Provincial Reconstruction Teams, but the discussion has also revealed the shortcomings of this concept. To avoid a blurring of the lines, CMRTs should implement humanitarian assistance only in emergency situations. Should CMRTs, however, be required to engage in non-security activities, their focus should be on rehabilitation of government infrastructure, capacity-building at the local level, and security sector reform rather than on initiatives that infringe on or duplicate traditional humanitarian work such as the provision of health care or education. Military forces ought to recognize the need to clearly demarcate themselves from civilian actors. As such, military personnel should at all times wear uniforms and travel in clearly marked vehicles. All CMRT personnel should receive extensive CIMIC training prior to deployment (including clearly articulated mandates and objectives) that sensitizes them to area and culture specific mission objectives and, more generally, to the dangers confronted by civilian aid workers when the lines between civilian and military spheres become blurred.

Effective CIMIC must be based upon regular and frequent consultations among government stakeholders, military officials, local communities, intergovernmental institutions, and IGOs and NGOs. Some observers have even argued that reconstruction teams should be "owned" by local communities and the central government so the local population will have decisive influence over the design and direction of the operation (Sedra, 2004). Effective CIMIC should be civilian-lead—most PRTs in Afghanistan are currently military-lead—in order to provide greater operational and policy coherence by establishing a single focal point for coordination and reinforce the democratic principle of civilian control over military forces.

Finally, effective CIMIC should include plans for developing a viable exit strategy. The greatest difficulty of CIMIC operations, Gourlay (2000, p. 43) acknowledged, "relates to the implementation of these exit strategies in the absence of the construction of alternative civilian structures." The ultimate goal of post-conflict reconstruction is the transfer of political authority to indigenous authorities. Effective CIMIC in stability operations must take into account the political context of the mission and aim at creating acceptable, legitimate, representative, just, and stable institutions that bring about and can sustain a peaceful political transition.

Contemporary peacebuilding is inherently political, often rendering a clear demarcation between humanitarian and political activities neither possible nor fruitful. While separating military and civilian elements in stability operations may be impossible, careful training sensitizing civilian and military relief providers to the cultural, organizational, operational, and normative differences will be an important step in enhancing interagency coordination to achieve the shared mission objectives that inform peacebuilding and post-conflict reconstruction.

THE MILITARY DIFFICULTY ASSOCIATED WITH SSTR OPERATIONS

If a national government is weak, corrupt, incompetent, or in the absence of any governing authority, then a triggering shock can seriously exacerbate the already difficult situation, producing widespread suffering, growing popular grievance, and often civil unrest, all of which can be intensified by several interrelated factors: the absence of key government functions, widespread lawlessness, poor economic performance, pronounced economic disparities, and in some cases, a serious external threat.

Once such difficult conditions emerge, the drivers of instability and conflict tend to reinforce one another, creating a degenerating cycle in which conditions continue to deteriorate, and the feelings of insecurity and the grievances of the local population intensify. Without a countervailing force to break this cycle, these developments can eventually destabilize the interlinked political, economic and social systems that make up the fabric of a society. Within this setting, the Joint Force must be able to establish a safe, secure environment and simultaneously work with interagency, coalition, multinational, and host nation partners to support the establishment of a new domestic order.

The Answer - The Central Idea

During SSTR operations, the primary focus of U.S. policy carried out by U.S. military forces, civilian government agencies, and, in many cases, multinational partners, will be on helping a severely stressed government avoid failure or recover from a devastating natural disaster, or on assisting an emerging host nation government in building a "new domestic order" following internal collapse or defeat in war. The new domestic order refers to a series of new patterns of organization and process within the security, economic and political systems, which are significantly different than the previous character of these systems.

Whether responding to a devastating natural disaster or assisting in rebuilding a new domestic order, U.S. military efforts in SSTR operations will be focused on effectively combining the efforts of the U.S. and coalition militaries with those of USG agencies and multi-national partners to provide direct assistance to stabilize the situation and build self- sufficient host nation capability and capacity in several key areas. These efforts, which are called "major mission elements (MMEs)" or "lines of operation" are executed in a concurrent manner and are integrated and tailored to the specific situation. Additionally, most of the MMEs represent desired end states within the overall SSTR operation. The six MMEs are:

- Establish and maintain a safe, secure environment;
- Deliver humanitarian assistance;
- Reconstruct critical infrastructure and restore essential services;
- Support economic development;
- Establish representative, effective governance and the rule of law; and
- Conduct strategic communication.

Throughout the conduct of SSTR operations, the Joint Force will implement a continuous learning process that incorporates lessons learned into ongoing and future operations. This continuous learning process will be conducted through constant observation of tactics, techniques, and procedures (TTPs); assessment of best practices; understanding how to implement best practices; and adapting TTPs.

In major combat operations (MCO) fought by the United States for objectives short of forcibly changing an adversary regime, some combination of the major mission elements may be carried out to achieve stabilization, security, transition, and reconstruction in territories annexed from the defeated adversary. These MMEs may also be drawn upon to help care for refugees displaced by the war and to directly assist the recovery of partner nations in the region, which suffered serious damage during the conflict. Under a less challenging security environment associated with helping a government cope with the consequences of a devastating natural disaster, the U.S. military will coordinate its support of humanitarian assistance, and, in some cases, reconstruction efforts with those of the United States Agency for International Development (USAID) and other parts of the Department of State, including the Office of the Coordinator for Reconstruction and Stabilization, and the host nation. In addition, the U.S. military will often coordinate with multinational relief organizations. These efforts will generally focus on rapidly providing food, clean water, shelter, and emergency medical treatment to ease the suffering of disaster victims when their needs are most acute and will, if necessary, help to restore order in the disaster area. U.S. military personnel may also provide support to initial rebuilding efforts in the affected area.

During the planning and conduct of military support to SSTR operations, it is imperative to achieve unity of effort, through what the *Capstone Concept for Joint Operations* labels "unified action," in order to successfully integrate efforts across the "seams" of the wide range of U.S. and multinational military and civilian organizations involved in the many aspects of the operation. With respect to this *Military Support to SSTR Operations JOC*, unified action involves the successful integration and synchronization of the multidimensional efforts of the U.S. military, U.S. Government agencies, coalition partners, as well as multinational and private sector actors, along with host nation agencies in pursuit of success in all of the MMEs.

Unforeseen event Planning & Preparation

The objective of the planning and preparation stage of SSTR operations is to harmonize the many diverse civilian and military efforts within a comprehensive, integrated strategy. While integrated civil-military SSTR planning is crucial, certain pre-crisis military security cooperation activities can help create the conditions for the successful conduct of SSTR operations; or they can prevent the emergence of a situation that triggers the conduct of a future SSTR operation. SSTR-related security cooperation activities are those activities that (1) help build SSTR-related capabilities of partner countries in ways that directly support U.S. efforts with regard to the potential conduct of SSTR operations and (2) assist a fragile, stressed government or region to avoid becoming unstable.

The objective of the effort to conduct strategic communication is to understand and engage key local and foreign audiences in order to create, strengthen, or preserve conditions favorable to achievement of overall SSTR goals and objectives. Throughout the operation, the three primary supporting capabilities of strategic communication—public affairs, information operations, and defence support to public diplomacy, must be continually coordinated and synchronized, both horizontally and vertically. Thus, strategic communication involves unified action by military, civil, and coalition entities operating from the national strategic to the tactical unit level.

Capabilities

The effective conduct of SSTR operations requires a range of functional and operational capabilities across the Joint Force, U.S. Government departments and agencies, and multinational organizations. Each functional and operational capability is made up of a series of critical and enabling capabilities. Critical capabilities focus on the primary abilities that allow the force to accomplish a desired effect. Enabling capabilities support critical capabilities and allow a force to accomplish an important task that underpins the accomplishment of a desired effect. Due to the multiple foci of the various SSTR mission elements, many required capabilities may reside outside of DOD. This JOC identifies four SSTR functional capabilities and six operational capabilities.

Functional capabilities are those capabilities that allow the Joint Force to perform tasks that occur across all aspects of SSTR operations; thus, functional capabilities are required to successfully carry out each of the major mission elements throughout the campaign, e.g. creating shared situational awareness among diverse stakeholders. The four functional capabilities are:

- U.S. Government institutional agility: the ability of U.S. government institutions to distribute funds, goods, and services rapidly and efficiently under challenging circumstances to successfully conduct SSTR operations.
- Command, control, and coordination: the ability to exercise authority and direction over assigned and attached forces in the accomplishment of SSTR missions; and the ability to effectively coordinate and integrate efforts between elements of DOD, engaged U.S. Government agencies, intergovernmental organizations, nongovernmental organizations, and the private sector in order to accomplish SSTR objectives.
- Battlespace awareness/understanding: the ability to develop situational awareness and understanding and to produce intelligence through persistent and pervasive observation of all domains.
- Joint Force generation and management: the ability to man, equip, and organize resources and to develop Joint Force skills necessary to ensure the Joint Force Commander can fulfil SSTR objectives

Operational capabilities focus on capabilities associated with accomplishing a desired end state (i.e. major mission element) within a SSTR operation, e.g., delivering supplies of food and medicine, rebuilding a power generation and distribution system. The six operational capabilities are:

- Creating a safe, secure environment. The ability to provide sufficient security in order to allow the conduct of large-scale civilian and host nation-led reconstruction and activities.

- Delivering humanitarian assistance/disaster relief. The ability to provide the immediate provision of basic necessities (e.g., water, food, sanitation, public health, medical care) in order to relieve human suffering.
- Reconstituting critical infrastructure and essential services. The ability to rebuild and/or improve strategically important institutions and essential services.
- Supporting economic development. The ability to assist in the early recovery of local and national economic activity and lay the foundation for sustained economic growth.
- Establishing representative, effective government and the rule of law. The ability to engage in early restoration of local governance activities, e.g., restoring city/regional councils, developing transparent reconciliation processes, restoring or possibly reforming the internal security and judicial systems, and resolving property claims and disputes.
- Conduct strategic communication. The ability to engage key local and foreign audiences in order to create, strengthen, or preserve conditions favorable to achievement of overall SSTR goals and objectives.

Establish and Maintaining a Safe, Secure Environment

The objective of the efforts to establish and maintain a safe, secure environment is to create a situation where the security of the people, property, and livelihoods within the country is sufficient to allow the general populace to routinely go about its business.

This includes freedom from undue external threats that divert attention and limited resources from internal security efforts. A secure environment will also facilitate the conduct of large scale, civilian-led reconstruction efforts. Ultimately, however, the ability of the existing or new host nation government to maintain a safe, secure environment—both internally and with regard to external security threats—will be a crucial factor in its gaining political legitimacy and widespread popular support.

Capacity and Reducing the Drivers of Instability and Conflict

The host government needs to develop its indigenous security, and economic and political capabilities in order to successfully reduce the drivers of internal instability and conflict within the context of the "new domestic order" it seeks to build. Building this new capacity is critical to enabling host nation leaders at all levels to garner the popular support they will need to be able to carry out comprehensive nation building.

The lion's share of the international assistance to these host nation efforts across the MMEs, including security sector reform, will be undertaken by civilian organizations in a permissive environment and by military organizations in a contested environment. Therefore, it is essential that military organizations develop the capability to support nation building in an insecure environment and that the USG acquire adequate numbers of deployable civil agency capabilities to sustain on-the-scene nation building assistance over a period of years.

Risks and Alleviation

There are several risks associated with conducting SSTR operations that could significantly hinder the conduct of or even halt such operations. These risks include:

- The American public and its elected representatives will not allow the United States to get involved in a major SSTR operation, or should such involvement be permitted, will prove unwilling to sustain their support for the conduct of a lengthy, costly SSTR campaign. (high risk) The recommended mitigation strategy focuses on having DOD and its IA partners develop the rapidly deployable and sustainable capabilities that will be needed to rapidly initiate effective operations within and across the MMEs of a major SSTR operation. These capabilities will include strategic communication strategies and means that complement other SSTR operations. SSTR strategic communication strategies must include a strong focus on keeping the American public accurately informed prior to and during the course of the SSTR operation.

- The U.S. interagency community will not aevelop sufficient amounts of the kinds of deployable civilian capabilities needed to conduct an extended SSTR campaign. (high risk) The recommended mitigation strategy involves working with the National Security Council, as well as other applicable U.S. departments and agencies, and with the Congress to gain the support needed to build SSTR-related civilian capabilities in the interagency.
- DOD force structure and force management policies will not facilitate the recruitment, development, rotation, and sustainment of sufficient military personnel for extended duration and manpower intensive SSTR operations. (medium risk) The recommended mitigation strategy involves the development and experimentation of innovative concepts that would enable the Joint Force to conduct SSTR operations without a dramatic increase in manpower, e.g., the development of niche and surge capabilities within the Total Force, longer tours to maintain force structure, and on-the-ground expertise.
- In the coming years, the U.S. military will abandon the very significant new approaches that have recently been implemented to prepare American military forces to effectively conduct multi-dimensional SSTR operations. (low risk) The recommended mitigation strategy is to ensure that U.S. military personnel are taught at all levels during their training and Professional Military Education (PME) to understand the importance of SSTR operations for U.S. national security and to recognize these operations as one of their most important and challenging missions.
- Multiple external actors, including the U.S. military and interagency elements, will prove unable to integrate their

efforts across the SSTR operation's multidimensional mission elements with those of the existing or new host nation government during a high end SSTR operation and thus the operation will not succeed in creating the new domestic order or a viable peace. (low risk) The recommended mitigation strategy is to give priority to developing and exercising integration mechanisms for the planning and conduct of SSTR operations.

Campaign structure for SSTR Operations

The *Capstone Concept for Joint Operations* establishes a new framework, which emphasizes that a campaign within theatre conflicts generally consists of six simultaneous lines of effort—*shape, deter, seize the initiative, dominate, stabilize,* and e*nable civil authority.*

The CCJO campaign framework provides a means to plan, execute, and assess campaigns in an integrated manner. The simultaneous execution of activities within each line of effort reinforces the need to continuously consider activities across all lines of effort during planning and execution. This approach also captures the varying levels of activity within each line of effort over time that may be required to achieve priority objectives.

This *JOC* posits that the more challenging types of SSTR operations are those that seek to build a new domestic order in a defeated or failed state and are carried out in a contested security environment. In such circumstances, the Joint Force Commander will be required to simultaneously conduct a military campaign with multiple lines of effort, including conventional and irregular offensive and defensive operations, while providing support to USG and coalition agencies undertaking SSTR efforts. It is precisely the challenge of integrating military full spectrum operations with the SSTR efforts of other USG agencies and often multinational partners that requires us to develop innovative ways and means for the Joint Force to conduct major combat and SSTR operations simultaneously.

DEFINING MILITARY MAINTAIN TO SSTR OPERATIONS

Using the CCJO as a guiding framework, this *Military Support to Stabilization, Security, Transition, and Reconstruction Operations JOC* focuses on the full range of military support that the future Joint Force might provide in foreign countries across the continuum from peace to crisis and conflict in order to assist a state or region that is under severe stress or has collapsed due to either a natural or man-made disaster. SSTR operations are highly integrated interagency operations that involve a carefully coordinated deployment of military and civilian, public and private, U.S. and international assets. Accordingly, this JOC adheres to National Security Presidential Directive (NSPD) 44 - *Management of Interagency Efforts Concerning Reconstruction and Stabilization* by recognizing that the Secretary of State is the designated lead of U.S. Government (USG) efforts to prepare, plan for, and conduct SSTR activities. Therefore, the U.S. military will conduct SSTR operations in support of a broader USG effort to advance U.S. interests by restoring an existing government or establishing a new social, economic, and political domestic order in the short-term, and in the longer term, by establishing conditions for a sustainable peace.

The central elements of SSTR operations that are conducted to assist a state or region under serious stress are: stabilization, security, transition, and reconstruction. Stabilization involves activities undertaken to manage underlying tensions, to prevent or halt the deterioration of security, economic, and/or political systems, to create stability in the host nation or region, and to establish the preconditions for reconstruction efforts. Security involves the establishment of a safe and secure environment for the local populace, host nation military and civilian organizations as well as USG and coalition agencies, which are conducting SSTR operations. Transition describes the process of shifting the lead responsibility and authority for helping provide or foster security, essential services, humanitarian assistance, economic development, and political governance from the intervening military and civilian agencies to the host nation.

Transitions are event driven and will occur within the major mission elements (MMEs) at that point when the entity assuming the lead responsibility has the capability and capacity to carry out the relevant activities. Finally, Reconstruction is the process of rebuilding degraded, damaged, or destroyed political, socio-economic, and physical infrastructure of a country or territory to create the foundation for longer-term development.

This *Military Support to SSTR Operations JOC* addresses how future military operations will be conducted both in response to a crisis and addresses selected routine, military theatre security cooperation in order to:

- Assist an existing or new host nation government in providing security, essential public services, economic development, and governance following the significant degradation or collapse of the government's capabilities due to internal failure or as a consequence of the destruction and dislocation of a war ;
- Provide support to stabilize and administer occupied territory and care for refugees in major combat operations fought for limited objectives that fall short of forcibly changing the adversary regime;
- Support a fragile national government that is faltering due to serious internal challenges, which include civil unrest, insurgency, terrorism and factional conflict;
- Assist a stable government that has been struck by a devastating natural disaster;
- Provide limited security cooperation assistance to a state that is facing modest internal challenges; and
- Provide military assistance and training to partner nations in order to build their capability and capacity to conduct SSTR operations at home or abroad.

The circumstances under which the United States might become involved in SSTR operations can vary greatly. In some cases, the United States will be asked by a nation under stress to provide assistance, or the United States may also elect to conduct SSTR operations without an invitation from the local government. The decision to participate in SSTR operations will be made by the President, in consultation with the Secretaries of State and Defence. Once the decision is made to conduct SSTR operations, the United States can participate in either a leading or supporting role and, in some cases, in the context of a mandate from the United Nations Security Council. If it is the lead country, the United States will generally assume responsibility for planning and coordinating most of the activities within the operation; whereas in a supporting role, the United States will offer limited, targeted assistance to the host nation or international organization(s) conducting the operation.

Reason

The purpose of the *Military Support to Stabilization, Security, Transition, and Reconstruction (SSTR) Operations Joint Operating Concept* [hereafter cited as the *Military Support to SSTR Operations JOC*] is to describe how the future Joint Force Commander (JFC) will provide military support for stabilization, security, transition, and reconstruction operations within a military campaign in pursuit of national strategic objectives in the 2014-2026 time frame. This joint operating concept posits an operational level solution for a very challenging future military problem: how the Joint Force can more effectively prepare for and conduct SSTR operations to assist governments or regions under serious stress. Additionally, this JOC identifies the operational capabilities required for achieving military campaign objectives and effects in support of national strategic end- states.

Additionally, this *Military Support to SSTR Operations JOC* will provide the basis for experimentation and exercises addressing the conduct of such operations. It will influence subsequent concept development regarding military support to SSTR operations and will provide a basis for force development guidance that could result in doctrine, organization, training, materiel, leader development and education, and personnel and facilities (DOTMLPF) changes associated with the development of the enhanced capabilities needed to successfully conduct future SSTR operations.

Scope

The *Capstone Concept for Joint Operations* (CCJO) establishes the foundation for the military support to SSTR operations. It emphasizes that the Joint Force must be capable of successfully conducting stability operations prior to, during, and after combat operations or as a stand-alone mission. The CCJO defines stability operations as inherently interagency operations. In carrying out these integrated operations, the Joint Force may be required to establish a safe, secure environment and initiate reconstruction efforts to facilitate transition to civilian control. The Joint Force may also be required to provide security, initial humanitarian assistance, limited governance, restoration of essential public services, and similar types of assistance typically required in reconstruction efforts.

A Broader View of "constancy Operations"

The scope of this JOC is a sub-set of the broader view of stability operations outlined DOD Directive (DODD) 3000.05, *Military Support to Stability, Security, Transition, and Reconstruction Operations*. DODD 3000.05 defines stability operations as "military and civilian activities conducted across the spectrum from peace to conflict to establish or maintain order in states and regions." The directive goes on to define military support to stability, security, transition and reconstruction (SSTR) as "DOD activities that support USG plans for stabilization, security, reconstruction, and transition operations, which lead to sustainable peace while advancing U.S. interests." While the scope of this JOC is more limited than DODD 3000.05, the activities described in this JOC are consistent with and support the directive.

Some U.S. military publications, including Joint Publication (JP) 3.0, *Joint Operations,* and Army Field Manual (FM) 3-0, *Operations* have defined "stability operations" much more broadly than the SSTR operations addressed in this joint operating concept. These publications emphasize that any major military operation abroad will almost certainly involve the full spectrum of operations, that is, the simultaneous conduct of offensive, defensive, and stability operations. Such conduct of full spectrum operations is distinct from phasing. Commanders combine the three types of operations according to the situation throughout the campaign.

The relative emphasis the JFC places among these three types of operations will vary across the continuum of military operations and will also vary significantly within operations of the same type based on the USG desired strategic end state, military campaign objectives and desired effects and the specific situation. A major combat operation, for example, will require the simultaneous conduct of offensive, defensive, and stability operations. According to this paradigm, any ongoing SSTR operation will also likely involve a mix of offensive, defensive, and stability operations, with the precise mix among these three operations during a given time period varying substantially within the overall area of operations. The more expansive definition of stability operations includes all of the military actions undertaken to support governments under serious stress that are identified above and discussed within this *Military Support to SSTR Operations JOC*. However, the broader stability operations category also includes the full range of American military engagement and security cooperation activities undertaken in peacetime to shape the international security environment in ways that protect and advance U.S. national interests.

While a wide variety of theatre security cooperation activities could play a significant role in creating more favorable conditions for the conduct of a particular SSTR operation, the *Military Support to SSTR Operations JOC* does not include the full spectrum of shaping/security cooperation activities as elements of SSTR operations. This JOC does, however, encompass those theatre security cooperation activities that *directly* lay the foundation for conduct of military support to SSTR operations or seek to prevent the destabilization of a particular state or region. These activities include:

- Helping partner militaries improve their SSTR related capabilities for employment internally or abroad;

- Conducting multinational experiments to enhance collective planning and execution of SSTR operations; as well as
- Military assistance activities, which are undertaken to help beleaguered states address internal instability challenges and thus avert failure that could trigger a responsive SSTR operation.

The *Military Support to SSTR Operations JOC* also recognizes that many other types of theatre security cooperation activities could help support the successful conduct of a specific SSTR operation. For example, routine security cooperation, including security assistance programs, bilateral and multinational exercises, military-to-military consultations and the like, that help build positive political and defence relationships with individual states can prove very useful when the U.S. Government needs to conclude transit, staging, or basing arrangements that are critical to conducting a specific SSTR operation.

While routine security cooperation activities certainly can bear fruit during the mounting of a major U.S. crisis response like SSTR operations, they are undertaken in pursuit of broader U.S. national security objectives, that is, in support of the "assure, dissuade, deter, and defeat" aspects of the *National Defence Strategy*. Consequently, this *Military Support to SSTR Operations JOC* does not encompass the full range of shaping and security cooperation activities.

7

Defence Diplomacy

INTRODUCTION

The aftermath of the Cold War and the tragic events of 9/11 have forced western nations to re-examine the principles according to which they manage the international environment. The conflicts in the Balkans during the 1990s taught that ethnic hatred can still be a far stronger motivator than reason. 9/11 taught North America that its once-vaunted security is far more vulnerable than it had thought. In addition, the world has also had to come to grips with a variety of so-called "non-traditional" security threats, including environmental degradation, global warming, potential pandemics, failed states, transnational crime, etc.

When George F. Kennan penned "the Long Telegram" in 1946(1) outlining his views on how best to meet the growing Soviet threat, he realized that military might, although essential, would not in itself prove sufficient. While Moscow was "impervious to the logic of reason" but "highly sensitive to the logic of force," in the long run the principal tools required were to be economic, political, cultural and diplomatic. In order to be effective, the strategy of "containment" would have to comprise much more than military superiority.

Kennan proved the major architect of U.S. foreign policy during the Cold War. It was because of his profound understanding of the complexity of the strategic environment, and the views of others like him, that the post-World War II period saw the development and growth of a variety of multilateral institutions. Along with a strong military, these institutions helped the West confront the moral and strategic challenges of the Cold War.

THE FINANCIAL COSTS OF PEACEKEEPING

Preventive diplomacy should always be the chosen option for resolving a crisis. However, if diplomacy is insufficient, a peacekeeping operation is the next best option. Peacekeeping presents a range of different problems, the first of which is finding the necessary funds to finance the operation. As a consequence of growing scepticism with regard to the effectiveness of peacekeeping operations, the UN has been forced to reduce its peacekeeping budget. This marks an unfortunate reversal of an earlier trend. The UN's peacekeeping budget increased from $379 million in 1990 to a high of $3,5 billion in 1994. However, 1995 saw a decrease to $3,2 billion, while 1996 recorded the lowest expenditure in five years at $1,3 billion. In addition, the number of UN peacekeepers have also shown a marked decrease from 65 000 in 1995 to 25 600 at the end of 1996. The number of peacekeeping missions have decreased from 22 in 1994 to only 16. The UN's new Secretary-General, Kofi Annan, has suggested that "peacekeeping as a primary activity of the United Nations will not end." However, the negative trend in peacekeeping missions, deployment and spending suggests that a number of critical issues need to be reviewed before a new wave of hopefully more successful peacekeeping initiatives can be undertaken.

The cash crisis for the UN, with a budget deficit of $2,3 billion in unpaid dues, undermines the ability of the organisation to continue as the world's leading peacekeeper. Moreover, the UN cannot settle the $1 billion debt owed to 81 member states which provided troops and equipment for operations during 1996. Understandably, member states are more and more reluctant to participate in UN operations because of the high costs involved. At the end of 1996, the UN owed Pakistan $67 million and India $58 million for their contributions to peacekeeping.

Former UN Secretary-General Boutros-Ghali confirmed that some member states refused to take part in future operations until they were paid. Boutros-Ghali summarised the problem before the UN Security Council in 1996 saying, "You give me a mandate for a peacekeeping mission. But you don't give me the troops and the money I need to implement that mandate."

The UN plan to establish a standby force intended to accelerate the deployment of forces to trouble spots, has only met with five positive responses from its 185 members. The standby agreement is designed to ensure the rapid deployment of a significant number of troops to fill the three to six-month gap between the UN authorisation of a peacekeeping mission and full deployment. The North Atlantic Treaty Organisation's (NATO) take-over of the UN's peacekeeping operation in Bosnia suggests that peacekeeping may move increasingly towards control by regional organisations which have the ability to finance such operations.

The most costly UN peacekeeping operation was that of Somalia which totalled $1,6 billion. The Somali experience has provided an important lesson for all potential African peacekeeping missions. Major operational challenges in Somalia were posed by problems relating to geography, transportation and the complex political system.

The colonial division of Africa has ensured that peacekeepers on the continent will always face major political complexities. Africa's artificial political borders, combined with decades of colonial manipulation and economic exploitation, guarantee that the continent's political jigsaw will provide serious and expensive challenges for peacekeepers. The lack of infrastructural development and the political intractability of most African conflicts confirm that the financial cost for peacekeeping on this continent will always be high.

The British experience in Bosnia supports the contention that peacekeeping operations tend to cost more than originally planned. The cost of the British contribution to NATO's Implementation Force (IFOR) in 1996 amounted to £300 million.

This was above and beyond the cost of sustaining the deployed forces in home bases. During the 1995/96 financial year the cost of involvement was carried by the Ministry of Defence. Over the period 1992-1995 of the United Nations Protection Force's (UNPROFOR) deployment, the Ministry of Defence was reimbursed by the Foreign and Commonwealth Office (FCO). The FCO then began to lobby the UN to recover the costs of the British military participation. The Ministry of Defence expressed a concern that IFOR expenditures should not undermine defence expenditure as a whole. Moreover, it was pointed out that it was extremely difficult to predict how much would be spent on peacekeeping. The Ministry's suggested solution to the problem was to include a "substantial contingency element" within the defence budget earmarked for peacekeeping which would be returned to the Treasury if not used. The British deployment in Bosnia also highlighted the need for a substantial logistic operation. Planning for the mission assumed that participants would provide their own "national stove-pipes" to support their forces. The British supply operation makes extensive use of the port of Split in Croatia. The Royal Logistics Corps (RLC) has been under pressure to meet approximately 1000 daily requests for supplies. The logistics system is based on the concept of 'just in time' thus supplies have to be flown in daily. The costs of the operation are extremely high and require a complex transportation and communication system.

In March this year, the US Department of Defence indicated that a further $2,1 billion was required to pay for peacekeeping operations in Bosnia. Secretary of Defence William Cohen indicated that if the funds were not made available, the military would be forced to scale back on training and other programmes. Under rules set up by the Republican-controlled Congress, money for any emergency must be offset by cuts in existing defence programmes to avoid adding to the national debt. Funds earmarked for long term procurement and weapons purchasing programmes are likely to be used to pay for the Bosnia operation. In 1992, former Secretary of Defence Les Aspin proposed the establishment of a separate fund of $300 million (Contributions for International Peacekeeping and Peace Enforcement Activities fund) intended to assist other countries to participate in peacekeeping and to minimise budgetary problems for the US. The proposal was rejected as "yet another raid" on the Pentagon budget.

At the first meeting of the Chiefs of Staff of the Member States of the Central Organ of the OAU held in Addis Ababa during early June 1996, the issue of peacekeeping and methods to finance these operations were raised but not discussed in any detail. A wide range of other issues were dealt with and some excellent proposals were laid on the table, but funding received only minor coverage. The official report on the meeting indicated that financing peacekeeping operations was "of a policy nature and should, therefore, be left to the policy makers." Some participants suggested that the UN should be responsible for funding. It was concluded that this issue, as well as logistic problems, would be dealt with by the proposed group of experts to be called the Budget and Logistics Committee. At the same time, there was general acceptance that African states, individually or collectively, would have extreme difficulty in providing the necessary resources for any major peacekeeping operation.

Funding for peacekeeping is a critical issue for any government. The potential costs of such operations and the massive logistic commitment for long distance operations are key factors in any decision-making process. Developing countries, South Africa included, cannot rush into any peacekeeping venture without careful consideration of the financial implications. South African involvement in a Somalia type operation could consume between one third and one half of the nation's annual defence budget. The solution for the financial crisis with Africa's peacekeeping may lie in the establishment of a peacekeeping bank, set up by donors from the developed world, who could lend or grant money to peacekeeping participants. The peacekeeping bank would be advised by military experts as to the feasibility of any operation and would require reasonable guarantees of success before making loans or donations. The successful peacekeeper would be rewarded with lower interest rate payments or the conversion of loans into grants.

A NEW DISCOURSE

Today, the world faces equally serious challenges and has begun to develop "appropriate" mechanisms and concepts for dealing with them. Just as Kennan and his generation of visionaries understood, our generation too will need to use a mixture of military and civilian means. Indeed, we have adopted a discourse informed by a broader and more subtle set of concepts than previously possible. We speak of human security, capacity building, the sanctity of the individual, multilateralism, and the need to hold the authority of states themselves accountable.

It is no longer accepted that the pursuit of genuine security for human beings, as individuals, is necessarily subversive of the foundations of international society. Intervention in the behaviour of states to protect individuals is now deemed an accepted principle of international relations. In fact, Rwanda has taught that it can, at times, be an obligation. These views entail far more than the musings of disaffected intellectuals and idealists. They are attempts to come to terms with a reality that is not fully comprehended or accepted. What is certain is that today "security" means coming to terms with forms of domination and insecurities that had long been ignored or sacrificed on the altar of "realpolitik."

The primacy of the state in strategic thinking permitted a gap to develop between the meaning of the term security as applied to individuals and its meaning for the state. For security to make sense at the international level, it must make sense at the basic level of the individual human being. Thus, attempts to understand the complexities of security threats need to look not only to the perceptions and histories of statesmen and diplomats; they also need to take into account the experiences of those rendered insecure by the present world order. While developed nations continue to speak of the importance of foreign aid, they now also accept the fact that the principle of state sovereignty can be breached in order to save those victimized by the state and its agents. Human security, first and foremost, entails physical security-the basic security of the individual. Without such security, foreign aid remains little more than a cheap meal on the road to continuing despair.

The language of realpolitik is slowly giving way to the more nuanced and humanitarian principles of "soft" power and human security. This new lexicon has enabled the West to widen its horizons and to put on the table security concerns formerly relegated to subsidiary, if any, relevance. It is, in part, because of this rethinking that we can seriously ponder the implications of a variety of so-called non-traditional threats for our long-term "common security" interests.

Needless to say, attempts to deal with the dislocations of the post-Cold War era have not been particularly successful. When looking at the failures of Rwanda and Somalia, the continuing struggle in Afghanistan, failed states like Haiti, and the fiasco in Iraq, western nations are led to wonder whether events have run ahead of our understanding or whether we simply lack the institutional capabilities for dealing with them. If our understanding is such that we cannot really grasp what is transpiring, then our ability either to construct or to restructure relevant institutions will be seriously hampered.

A NEW MISSION

Defence diplomacy is one of the organizing principles used to help the West come to terms with the new international security environment. It has become an increasingly important component of the "whole of government" approach, and in the United Kingdom defence diplomacy has been made one of the military's eight "defence missions." The United Kingdom began work on security sector reform in 2000. Early in the process, planners realized that new policy frameworks would be required if Britain's efforts in conflict prevention were to be effective. While relevant ministries drew up policy papers, it soon became clear that a joint approach to security sector reform required a common policy framework. The government went on to set up a security sector reform policy committee and an informal interdepartmental strategy was then developed.

Planners also created two interdepartmental funding pools, the Global Conflict Prevention Pool and the Africa Conflict Prevention Pool, in order to improve the United Kingdom's conflict prevention policy and effectiveness through joint analysis, long-term strategies, and improved coordination with international partners. Much of the U.K. security sector reform work is financed through these two pools, which receive both overseas development assistance (ODA) and non-ODA funds for programs based on agreed Ministry of Defence (MOD), Department for International Development (DFID) and Foreign and Commonwealth Office (FCO) strategies. In order to promote stronger adherence to the common framework, the U.K. Treasury contributes additional resources to the pools beyond those committed by the foregoing ministries. The Netherlands has also established a "Stability Fund" in order to provide for coherence through pooled funding, as well as an integrated policy-driven approach to security and development issues.

The consensus seems to be that U.K. interventions have proven more effective when based on a shared analysis of a conflict and a joint response. Such an approach also makes for a better synergy between government policy and operations. The conflict prevention pool approach has also been helpful in giving the Treasury a better understanding of the issues faced by the departments on the ground. Both pools have a peacekeeping and a program component. The peacekeeping component covers the United Kingdom's assessed and voluntary contributions to international peacekeeping and related operations. The program component is further subdivided into country or regional strategies and thematic strategies, like security sector reform. A parliamentary vote decides the settlement figure given to pools, which incorporates an extra top-up amount to encourage interdepartmental collaboration.

Money contributed to the Global Pool by the four departments is managed by the FCO, and funding for the Africa Pool is managed by the DFID. Once activities are agreed upon, they are examined by the DFID for ODA eligibility. The strength of this approach lies in the fact that "distinct roles remain for development and security sectors, [while] working under one overarching security system reform policy in a coherent way with relevant departments." Also, under such a scheme, development agencies can better comprehend and have an increased impact on security-related issues when they are vital for development goals. It is important that development agencies establish effective partnerships with their defence and security counterparts, especially when operating in areas where their effectiveness might be restricted because of security issues.

It is then easy to see how defence diplomacy fits into the overall policy framework. Its basic aim is "to provide forces to meet the varied activities undertaken by the MOD to dispel hostility, build and maintain trust and assist in the development of democratically accountable armed forces, thereby making a significant contribution to conflict prevention and resolution." Included in the mission are a number of military tasks, e.g.:

- arms control, non-proliferation, and confidence and security building measures;
- outreach (advice and assistance to countries);
- other defence diplomacy activities.

Recognizing the importance of security sector reform and defence diplomacy, the United Kingdom also established what is called the Defence Advisory Team (DAT) in 2001. Today the DAT provides advice and assistance on governance and civil military relations, defence reviews, defence organization, force structures, procurement and logistics, and change management, financial and human resource management and development in the defence sector. Since the DAT's inception, the U.K. government has significantly increased its funding.

The British approach to security reform and defence diplomacy might prove a useful model for Canadian policy makers. The integrated policy framework and pooled funds provide an important degree of flexibility and efficiency when addressing security concerns. The type of approach envisaged would, of course, require both cooperation and coordination among several government departments and agencies, including the Canadian International Development Agency, the Department of National Defence, Foreign Affairs Canada, Finance, and the Privy Council Office. Given Canada's ongoing commitment to peacekeeping and the 3D approach (Defence, Diplomacy, and Development), policy makers might do well to look at the British model as a way of organizing our "whole of government" approach to security matters.

CASUALTY TOLERANCE

A clear estimate of the number of casualties which would be acceptable is essential for any military operation, peacekeeping included. The Vietnam war indicated the limits of public support in the face of mounting casualties. Between 1961 and 1973, 47 244 American troops were killed and over 300 000 wounded. The unacceptable losses had a major impact on decision-makers and popular support for the war in general. The US Government discovered that public and congressional support for any military operation was essential. Colonel Harry Summers addresses this issue in his recent book The New World Strategy, and concludes that, "[i]f the war in Vietnam proved nothing else, it proved the American people could not be excluded from the strategic equation." In 1984, US Secretary of Defence Caspar Weinberger outlined the Weinberger Doctrine, emphasising that "before the US commits combat forces abroad, there must be some reasonable assurance we will have the support of the American people and their elected representatives in the Congress." High casualties will erode public support and are therefore important in the decision-making process. This factor, the so-called 'sixth test' of the Weinberger Doctrine is applicable to any democratic country considering the deployment of military force for peacekeeping.

The number of casualties any government can tolerate in a peacekeeping operation is a key issue that has to be decided before any deployment commences. A negative public response to high casualties in a peacekeeping operation, not considered to be of major importance, could obviously have very serious ramifications. High casualties could have long term effects on a nation's willingness to participate in future operations. The UN experience in Somalia illustrates the importance of the casualty tolerance issue. The first announcement of US casualties in Somalia led to popular calls for an immediate withdrawal from UNOSOM II. Following the death of the first four US soldiers, Senator Robert Byrd suggested that the "operation was crumbling" and that it was "not worth American lives lost and injuries sustained."

The US public began to apply very strict limits on the number of casualties acceptable in a far-off peacekeeping operation which had no clear place on the national interest agenda. On 5 June 1993, twenty-four Pakistani soldiers were killed in an ambush set up by supporters of Mohammed Aideed. The following day the UN Security Council passed Resolution 837, demanding the immediate apprehension of those responsible for the attack. Consequently, US forces were mobilised in a manhunt for Aideed. A few weeks later, a major clash occurred with Aideed's forces, leaving 18 American troops dead and 75 wounded. This event clearly surpassed the US casualty tolerance level and President Clinton immediately announced the phased withdrawal of US troops. American forces in Somalia were confined to force protection missions until the completion of the phased withdrawal. By all accounts, the US' failure to capture Aideed was caused by "inaccurate and untimely intelligence."

With the rise in casualties sustained by UN peacekeeping forces world-wide, most countries have become increasingly reluctant to commit forces. For any democratic government it is extremely difficult to justify casualties in peacekeeping operations where clear and compelling national interests cannot be identified. Lack of public support will thus always be a limiting factor in peacekeeping operations.

The Somali experience turned into the US' "peacekeeping Vietnam"-the US remains extremely reluctant to become directly involved in any African peacekeeping operation. Instead, the emphasis has shifted to efforts to sell the idea of an 'African

Crisis Response Force' (ACRF-subsequently renamed the African Crisis Response Initiative (ACRI)). The ACRI has been clearly designed to promote African peacekeeping without endangering the lives of US troops. The plan contains an emphasis on humanitarian support based on the US strategic airlift, in conjunction with extensive diplomatic initiatives involving the UN, OAU and regional stakeholders.

The solution to potentially unacceptable casualties in peacekeeping could possibly be found in the provision of high quality body armour for participating forces, combined with the necessary equipment and skills to do the job. In addition, the US experience in Haiti provides some guidelines for reducing peace operation casualties. Long before the US XVIII Airborne Corps landed in Haiti, the US Army's 4th Psychological Operations (PSYOPS) Group at Ft. Bragg had analysed and divided Haiti's population into twenty different target groups to be provided with appropriate information and warning of the impending US involvement. Thousands of leaflets were distributed, supported by extensive radio broadcasts. Prior to the US intervention, the Pentagon expected widespread conflict and unrest leading to unacceptably high casualties. However, only one US soldier was killed and the overall campaign was successful. According to the mission commander, "there (was) no question that PSYOPS helped save lives."

CHANGING HISTORY-PEACE BUILDING IN NORTHERN IRELAND

On Good Friday, April the 10th, Northern Ireland politicians stumbled out from the portals of Stormont into the breaking daylight. Many of them were not far from tears. All were obviously exhausted by the roller coaster of adrenaline and the lack of sleep they had incurred during the last few days and nights of the talks, as deals were crafted, walk-outs were threatened and averted, and the apparently insuperable barriers on decommissioning and other issues were overcome. Both the British and Irish Prime Ministers had been called upon to provide support in the last few days and even President Clinton had assisted by encouraging telephone calls. The waiting populace held their breath alternating between despair and hope.

The hope was justified-the miracle happened, the Belfast Agreement was reached. After thirty years of a bloody civil war, Northern Ireland's political parties finally achieved consensus on the principles, and in some cases the practice, necessary to govern a society divided on constitutional, political, and cultural perspectives. Six weeks later, by a vote of over 71%, and despite the best efforts of fundamentalist nationalists and unionists, the deal was endorsed by the peoples of the island of Ireland, North and South. The road to peace appeared to have been secured.

What had brought Northern Ireland to this particular turning point? What had been the major developments in eventually securing the peace? While obviously the debates about such developments will continue for some decades, the following would appear to have been the most important in creating a positive context for a political solution.

A. Community Development/Community Relations work within and between communities which opened up new possibilities for dialogue and co-operation between them.

When civil violence broke out in 1969 in Northern Ireland and particularly in the aftermath of the riots in Belfast and Derry/Londonderry in August 1969, the British Labour Home Secretary, James Callaghan announced the establishment of a Ministry for Community Relations and a Community Relations Commission which was charged with the promotion of policies which would improve community relations2.

The Commission decided to adopt as its main strategy the initiation of local community development programmes across Northern Ireland, based on the belief that communities which lacked self-confidence were more likely to relate aggressively to one another. Furthermore, it believed that the problem, particularly for people in more socially marginalized communities, of relating to the structures of power, contributed to feelings of helplessness and resentment which in turn contributed to community tensions. (Hayes) The Commission survived until the Sunningdale Agreement in April 1974, which set up a new power sharing assembly for Northern Ireland. In one of its first actions, the power sharing assembly abolished the Community Relations Commission on the basis that henceforth the politicians themselves would be responsible for community development and community relations issues. Ironically, the new assembly itself only lasted five months due to disagreement among the politicians about the remit of cross-border bodies which had been set up as part of the Agreement, and a loyalist workers strike which paralysed Northern Ireland.

However, the process of community development remained an important method of facilitating communication within communities, and between government and communities, and this process continued to underpin many programmes subsequently initiated and funded in the last two decades.

Over a decade later, in 1985, the Standing Advisory Commission on Human Rights commissioned a report on the current state of community relations work, and its potential for future development. (Frazer & Fitzduff) This report on the under resourced, underdeveloped and unstrategic nature of much of the work, suggested a theoretical framework for its development, and suggested some practical structures that should be considered if the government intended to take the work seriously. It suggested the creation of a specialist community relations unit within government and the creation of an independent community relations body which would address issues of policy, training, and funding community relations work. In 1987, the Central Community Relations Unit (CCRU) was set up, which was located at the heart of government and in 1990, the independent body, the Community Relations Council (CRC) was established.

COMMUNITY RELATIONS 1990-98

In drawing up its initial strategic plan the CRC decided not to concentrate on developing more 'reconciliation' groups, but expanded its remit to include bodies who had not previously been working actively at peace-building e.g. business, church and sports groups, health and education boards, etc and many groups from the voluntary and community sector. It also worked closely with the Trade Unions who had, since the late 1980's, been developing anti-intimidation and anti-sectarian programmes for the workplace.

Subsequently there was a significant expansion of the number of groups working at peace-building much of which growth was facilitated by a hugely increased financial investment in such work 3 so that by 1998 the number of civic groups engaging in contact work, and developing programmes and training to address issues of human rights, cultural diversity, co-operation on social and economic issues, single identity work, neutral venue work, anti sectarian work, anti-intimidation work as well as political dialogue and mediation work had increased significantly i.e. from 40 in 1986 to 140 in 1996.

As the theoretical framework for such a focus expanded the work also began to engage a much wider spectrum of people, including those who had previously been cynical of the 'peace and doves' stereotype attached to the work. (Fitzduff) It therefore became more possible to build a coalition of people and organisations addressing both the 'softer' issues such as understanding and co-operation, as well as the 'harder' issues of inequality, rights, policing and political and constitutional differences.

In addition, the programme begun in the 70's of more substantially resourcing community development began to pay significant political dividends. Such work, in the absence of local democracy, had provided for community participation in governmental consultation processes, about social, economic and political issues. By the 1990's, however, it had also helped to generate a new breed of 'community' politicians who developed loyalist, republican and feminist thinking in a way which significantly enriched the political mix of parties who were eventually able to sign the Belfast Agreement.

Parties such as the PUP, the NIWC and Sinn Fein all have considerable experience at community and social politics. 5 Such work also provided them with fruitful contacts gained from their collective experience in addressing local social issues together, and such experience should augur well for the social and economic tasks that face them as representatives in the new Assembly.

External assistance offered by the European Union was also of significance. When the ceasefires were declared in 1994, the EU decided to help to underpin the peace by allocating £250,000,000 to help build up the economy and establish peace. Such funds have been useful, as their criteria for distribution included in many cases the need for communities to work together on funding decisions. Such processes ensure that communities can no longer continue to be unaware of each other's social and economic needs, and have in many cases provided very useful training for future collaborative government at both local and regional level.

Political Dialogue and Development work which focused on work with politicians and others on political divisions and political options.

Given the small size of Northern Ireland-less than 3 hours drive from end to end-it is hard to imagine just how difficult it is to facilitate and promote political dialogue. This is partly because of the culture of silence which is adhered to between the communities where raising any issues of cultural or political difference is seen to be either impolite or dangerous, depending upon the circumstances. For politicians, who exemplify community differences, being seen to have any meetings outside of the context of formal dialogue-which dialogue is usually characterised by hostility is almost impossible. And for much of the conflict, it was almost impossible for the government, and most political parties to have any dialogue at all with Sinn Fein, because of their perceived association with the IRA and paramilitary violence. In such circumstances, much ingenuity was needed on the part of many groups to facilitate political dialogue and to eventually achieve sufficient consensus between the parties to move into inclusive dialogue. Primary among these dialogues processes were those conducted by the Quakers and others with and between politicians, particularly during the early nineties and which kept open dialogue through processes of shuttle mediation.

In addition, some academics were extremely useful in organising workshops for politicians and others, often outside of Ireland, in places like Washington or South Africa, where it was easier to meet than at home. Often such conferences gave the participants opportunities to address wider perspectives and possibilities for conflict resolution, as well as providing opportunities for relationships to form between the politicians-which relationships could never have formed in the socially and politically constricting circumstances of Northern Ireland.

Another particularly useful initiative was that by a small group of Protestant clergy who opened a confidential process of dialogue with Sinn Fein, at a time when such processes were viewed with deep opprobrium by most political parties, and who provided a useful context within which Sinn Fein could address the reality of their perceptions of the hopes and fears of the Protestant/Unionist community. Other groups such as the Glencree Centre for Reconciliation, just outside of Dublin, also involved itself in workshops with politicians, particularly following the ceasefires of 1994. And community workers themselves-some of whom were ex-republican and loyalist prisoners-eventually began to find many creative ways, despite the danger to them from their own and their opposing community, to involve themselves in processes of dialogue and relationship building through their common social and community concerns.

What was important about all of the above processes was that they were almost all conducted in confidence and thus provided a safer context within which politicians fears and hopes could be constructively addressed. Such dialogue processes-in addition to those eventually developed by the Government and between political parties-were to prove invaluable in accumulating the possibilities, and the beginning of enough understanding and trust on the part of at least some politicians, to enable the peace process to truly begin.

What was also useful was the eventual emergence of a party that was not dedicated to a particular political position-but to the dialogue process itself. This was the Northern Ireland Women's Coalition which was formed just six weeks before the election to the Northern Ireland Forum for Political Dialogue in 1996.

It was formed in response to the dismay felt by many women in Northern Ireland at the lack of response by existing political parties to the need to include women in Northern Ireland politics. The party included nationalists and unionists, and was jointly chaired by two women from both perspectives. Its members came from all classes of life e.g. community workers, professionals, academics, nuns, trade unionists, etc. and they fought the elections on a cross-community approach. They secured a place at the negotiating table, focusing on principles of equality and inclusion. Although originally treated with sexism and hostility by many parties, particularly the unionist parties, they were eventually able to play very useful part by facilitating discussions between the parties-often using a shuttle-mediation approach-on difficult issues like the release of prisoners and decommissioning.

Another newcomer to the peace process was the business community who began to develop their approach to the ending of violence in the early nineties. Whereas before they had been content to complain about the effect of the violence on business from the sidelines, they now began to coalesce with the Trade Unions to see if a more strategic approach could be put into place which would put pressure on both republican and loyalist paramilitaries to end their campaign, and to pressurise the politicians in getting down to the business of building an agreement. Groups like the Chamber of Commerce, the Institute of Directors, the Confederation of British Industry, and all the major trade unions joined together and began to make statements urging the need to end the war, and the need for serious political negotiation. In addition, they involved themselves in dialogue with all the political parties, including Sinn Fein, even before the ceasefires were announced in 1994. Their influence was very salutary, particularly on the Unionist political parties, who began to feel the need to respond to the pressure from them to enter into serious political dialogue.

During the nineties, the United States was also of substantial assistance in helping to develop and secure dialogue and peace. The US had gradually developed a perspective which was able to take account of the needs and fears of Unionists as well as nationalists, and-spurred by the interests of the huge Irish vote in the USA-they began to focus on ways of ending the violence. People like Congressman Bruce Morrison, and business men like Bill Flynn and Charles Feeney visited Ireland to persuade the IRA of the need to end the military campaign, and to engage with the unionist community.

Clinton granted a visa to Gerry Adams to enter the US in 1994 while the IRA was still bombing cities and killing people, in the hope that it would assist his alleged quest for a solution. Although such activities were initially viewed with suspicion by many within the British Government, many subsequently came to appreciate the assistance which such interventions were able to offer. Such assistance was particularly exemplified by the assistance of Senator George Mitchell who acted as Chair of the talks process for almost two years and whose efforts were invaluable to its success. Equality work which ensured equal access to power and resources for Catholics as well as Protestants and economic development to assist this.

The outbreak of civil violence in 1969 in Northern Ireland which cost over three and a half thousand lives was significantly attributable to the failure of policies of equity in Northern Ireland since its inception as a state in 1921. Although the newly formed region of the UK contained within its borders a substantial number of Catholics who were unhappy with their status within Northern Ireland, few efforts were made by the newly elected unionist government to sufficiently address their responsibilities involved in governing a divided society. Such a failure with its concomitant patterns of inequity, biased voting systems, unrepresentative policing, a maintenance of ghettoisation in education, housing, and workplaces, and a significantly alienated minority created the context for the eventual development of a civil war.

In 1972 the Unionist Northern Ireland government was dismissed by the British government, and direct political and security control for the region from London began, Such belated interest from London-which had previously shown little care for on-going inequities in the region-eventually helped to ensure the development of a more equitable and culturally representative society in Northern Ireland.

A LOOK AT THE WORLD OF THE 21ST CENTURY

Multi-track diplomacy, then, enters the 21st century as an established presence; a systems approach to peace-building that embraces a large network of organizations, disciplines, methodologies and venues for working toward the prevention and resolution of violent conflict around the world. It has its success stories, told elsewhere in this book, and its best practices; its challenges and edges for growth.

To understand how multi-track diplomacy might play a role in the world of the 21st century, it is necessary to examine some of the trends in world affairs that are looming on humanity's horizon as potential threats to global security in the coming era. Let us examine eight of these trends in some detail:

The Globalization of Violence

The benefits of globalization that have so affected our communications and economic systems have also been available to those forces in the world bent on destruction, greed and violence. With increased access to world-wide markets, the internet, cellular communication, international banking facilities and other tools for moving information and resources across great distances at high speed, those involved in such nefarious pursuits as drugs, the illegal arms trade, the sex trade, terrorism, gambling, money laundering, the black market, racketeering and other such nasty past times have been able to be more effective in their own endeavours, and to take advantage of the increase in power and reach that comes with working together. The illegitimate industries, like their legitimate counterparts, are cooperating, consolidating and diversifying their interests, forming a shadowy infrastructure that covers the globe, destabilizes vulnerable systems, and thrives on chaos.

Many of these actors are involved behind the scenes in conflict situations, benefitting from the continuation of the violence while having no direct interest in the particulars of that conflict. Though they will never come to the table as part of any formal peace talks, their power is great, especially in certain high political circles without whose connivance they could not operate.

The Breakdown of Systemic Integrity

All kinds of systems are losing the strength and certainty of their boundaries at the end of the 20th century. Cells cannot hold their integrity, as new viruses and diseases pose epidemic threats to large populations. Environmental systems cannot maintain their ability to function properly, as species necessary to the balance of nature die out and the natural world becomes polluted beyond its ability to either sustain or purify itself. Families fall apart; moral systems degenerate; educational systems in some places lose their capacity for operating as learning centres and become, instead, warehouses for the social control of desperate children. Economic systems that have sustained great prosperity over time dissolve in an instant, erasing the possibility of a decent standard of living for millions of people anytime in the near future. Political systems disintegrate, leaving thugs, ad hoc militias and greedy despots in charge of whatever patches of land they can hold by force and threat. Whole nations disappear into the chasm of chaos, or seem poised to do so momentarily.

The Rise of Rogues

Partly as a result of this disintegration of integrity, rogue individuals and nations are emerging in record numbers. People and institutions that function outside any traditional boundaries of law, persuasion or sense of the common good are establishing their capacity to operate across established boundaries at will. Narco-terrorism, nuclear terrorism, the threats of germ and biological terrorism, private armies under the control of warlords and profiteers, maverick states that respond not at all to international pressures or sanctions-these manifestations of uncontrollable, dangerous rogue forces pose untested threats to the world and its institutions of civilization.

The Depletion of Natural Resources

Both a cause and an effect of some of the phenomenon already described, the degradation and depletion of earth's natural resources are posing a major threat to the sustenance and stability of life on the planet. Water, oil, land, forests and breathable air are in increasingly short supply, and reserves of precious minerals necessary for the continuation of modern technology are dwindling. The imbalance of overpopulation with the means to sustain life has already contributed to some of the past decade's worst conflicts, such as in Rwanda. The hole in the ozone layer, global warming and the poisoning of the oceans, direct results of our industrial and economic systems, are, in turn, contributing to the very breakdown of systemic integrity we discussed earlier.

The Institutionalization of Polarization

While there have always been factions and differences in human society, the deepening of polarization as a norm of social, political and economic interaction has become apparent in the last decade. In the U.S., the two main political parties have descended into an entrenched adversarial relationship in which bipartisanship and cooperation are increasingly rare. The North and the South, the developed and the developing worlds, are still deeply divided over power and resources, and the distance between the economic 'haves' and 'have nots' in many countries is growing, and dangerously so. With intensified polarization comes extremism. Throughout the latter part of the 20th century, we have witnessed the threat to regional and global security posed by the rise of nationalistic and religious extremism. As these movements attain power, stature, and resources-such as in the case of the Taliban in Afghanistan, the far-right wing in Israeli politics or, the BJP/Hindu nationalist party in India-they become woven more thoroughly into the fabric of modern life. Less on the fringes, where they can be ignored, they have migrated to the centre of our world screen, where the threats they pose are highly visible-and highly volatile.

Challenges to the Nation State

As empires fall, political boundaries change, and ethnic groups gain access to arms and world attention for their causes, the familiar system of nation states which has ordered the global political and economic systems for so long is being tested from all sides. With between 5,000 and 10,000 different ethnic groups in the world, and only 185 member nations of a UN which affirms in its Charter the right of self-determination, the stage is set for potential conflicts. At both ends of the spectrum, from consolidation to disintegration, the nation state system is facing challenges. As Europe seeks its union, Quebec seeks dis-union. As the Czech Republic and the Republic of Slovakia find a relatively easy way to separate, the Kurds, the Chechens, and the East Timorese have not been so fortunate. The new millennium will require humanity to be creative in designing ways that peoples and national groups can experience the dignity and integrity of their identity while simultaneously maintaining the unity and viability of a world order based on law and mutual respect.

Changing Power Blocs

The fall of the Soviet Union and the rise of the United States as the single superpower in the world is not the end of the story. Far from it. Much is in play in Europe, with the evolution of the European Union and NATO, and in Asia, with the awakening of China to its potential for power in the world. Turkey, poised between East and West, could shift its sizable weight in one of several directions, not all of which bode well for security in Southeastern Europe. The disintegration of Russia could lead to any number of scenarios in which powerful entities might rise from the ashes of that state so recently a major player in world affairs. These are but a few examples of the shifts that are taking place-seismic shifts-in relative strength, alliances and relationships as old and new nations flex their muscles and take or lose advantage on the world stage due to some of the other phenomenon previously mentioned.

The Traumatization of the Human Family

Millions of people around the planet are suffering massive trauma from recent wars and associated famine, displacement and destruction. As civil wars increasingly target women and children, and group massacres, large scale atrocities and rape become common weapons of war, large populations are profoundly wounded, in body, mind and spirit. In some countries, whole generations are debilitated, especially in those places where child soldiers have formed the backbone of the fighting forces. In others, the psychological debilitation is already moving into the second, third and even fourth generations. Post Traumatic Stress Disease (PTSD) is probably the most widespread disease on the planet. This means that many places in conflict remain vulnerable to political manipulation and ongoing cycles of violence, as the people are lacking the personal strength and inner resources to resist the forces that call for retribution and revenge.

8

Domestic Implications of Military Modernization

Military modernization will likely produce two distinct consequences. Politically and socially, the role and influence of the military in Turkey is bound to change once the effects of the modernization program begin to be felt. Economically, the design of Turkey's modernization will have a profound impact on Turkey's industrial development, because it will propel the country's defence industry into a whole new league.

Regarding the military, the modernization program was started to counter specific military challenges that Turkey faces in the post-Cold War era. These include primarily the changing geopolitical role of Turkey as an emerging regional power, the need for greater Turkish military compatibility with the United States and the rest of NATO, and the increasing reliance on the military to provide for internal security as well (the military's objectives in the context of foreign policy will be discussed later). Regardless of the legitimate motivations on the part of the Turkish military, the modernization program also has the potential to partially restore the military's stature in Turkish society and perhaps in politics as well.

The Turkish military views itself as the guardian of Kemalism, the state-based ideology of secularism, Westernization and modernization. In this context, the program will reinforce Turks' historical image of the military as leading the country's overall modernization.

Already considered a source of national pride and ranked as the most prestigious and respectable institution in Turkey today, military modernization will further enhance the army's prestige. Also, the military's perceived success in country's Southeast against Kurdish rebels both strengthened the military's respect within Turkish society, and may have also increased the country's ability to deter future insurgents. Military modernization is certain to further augment this deterrence. Moreover, training with the most up-to-date equipment and earning international respect from other NATO countries will ensure strengthen the military's domestic image of professionalism, which had been declining in recent years following the soft coup of February 28, 1997. This image will once again guarantee large numbers of quality applicants for the officer corps and may re-establish the military as a powerful social and political force.

Furthermore, as Dietrich Jung has pointed out in his examination of Turkish society, the original elite officer class has frequently found itself at odds with the emerging new elite of businessmen. Yet, these two groups' interests may increasingly converge due to military modernization, because the Turkish military will also be an important industrial actor as the military-industrial complex grows.

Domestic military industries typically draw their contracts from the national armed forces and their staff are primarily former military servicemen. Consequently, a network of formal and informal contacts evolves linking the defence industry closely to the military. Through this osmotic process, there is greater awareness among the military class of political-economic considerations that arise from industry ownership.

A major goal of military modernization is precisely to build a substantial Turkish military industry. Currently, Turkey's military industry averages about one billion dollars in sales annually, of which exports made up only $70 million in 1999—equivalent to 0.3 percent of all Turkish exports. Moreover, the lack of a domestic military industry is evident in the fact that only 21 percent of Turkish military needs are met domestically, hence the large procurement of foreign-made equipment. Therefore, "virtually all purchase plans require corresponding offsets by foreign investment in Turkey or a co-production arrangement with local arms manufacturers."

Also, most purchases cover high-technology equipment that could hypothetically be reproduced in Turkey. Initially, these high-technology products will be co-produced with one of the traditional suppliers, leading to a transfer in technology that is hoped will lay the groundwork for future independent Turkish production. The goal is to modernize the military while simultaneously boosting Turkey's fledgling defence industry, allowing it to eventually become independent of increasingly less reliable foreign suppliers.

In fact, when analyzing Turkey's capabilities, it is evident that Turkey fundamentally has the potential to develop a major defence industry. According to Luis Bitencourt, in order to succeed in defence industrialization, a developing country needs to have a perception of threat, access to financial resources, a diversified industrial base, a domestic procurement budget, sufficient domestic education, and superpower support.

Indeed, even if the country's recent economic crisis casts doubt on Turkey's financial and industrial development, Turkey does fulfil all of Bitencourt's prerequisites. If Turkey succeeds, the relationship between the military and private business may improve, contributing to further democratization and economic liberalization.

Ironically, military modernization—i.e., strengthening the military institutions—may produce a more democratic society because it links the military with business interests, which are mainly concerned with creating stable macroeconomic conditions through liberalization and good governance.

TURKISH POLITICAL INFLUENCE FROM MILITARY MODERNIZATION

Turkey will have increasingly less difficulty acquiring military equipment if it embarks on long-term procurement, because the defence industry has the necessary political leverage to ensure deals are not blocked and can even minimize the complications that might arise with additional requirements that countries sometimes include in arms sales. Also as suggested, Turkey may increasingly utilize the defence industry's interests in order to achieve other political goals.

In a sense, Turkey's military modernization project has become the carrot and stick of Turkish foreign policy. Turkey offers or threatens to retract arms supply contracts in persuading Western governments or parliaments. France experienced Turkey's penal retraction of defence contracts after the Assemblée Nationale passed a bill recognizing the Armenian genocide. On October 19, 2000, the U.S. House of Representatives was about to pass a similar bill. This resolution angered Turkish officials who threatened the administration both to review the strategic relationship with the United States as well as cancel all defence contracts and bar U.S. firms from bidding for future tenders. On Capitol Hill, the main argument for withdrawing the bill in the last minute was the threat of canceled military purchases by a strategic ally. Coincidentally, Turkey had just closed a $4.5 billion helicopter deal with Bell Textron. Nevertheless, it is questionable whether "Turkey would have made good on its threat to cancel arms deals with U.S. companies."

THE ELEMENTS OF MODERNIZATION

Despite a decade of extensive reform during the 1980s, the Gulf War graphically demonstrated just how far behind modern militaries the PLA had fallen and how much still needed to be done to close the gap. There is little doubt that the Chinese military leadership has now grasped the totality of the problems and challenges it confronts and has begun to implement sweeping reforms across the spectrum of all services and functional areas. Most services and units are experiencing several transformations simultaneously. In fact, a major challenge is that too much is being thrust on the PLA too quickly. Large, complex organizations, especially militaries, are instinctively resistant to change. Many of these reforms are profound and fundamental in their nature, inasmuch as they are intended to change long-standing practices, regimens, and norms. Naturally, many are being resisted. As is the case with reform in other sectors of Chinese society, there is also a tendency to feign compliance with directives while persisting in entrenched practices. Difficulties of assimilation and adjustment are profound in many areas. Yet the PLA needed reform from top to bottom. The incremental reforms of the late 1980s had proven insufficient, and bolder steps were warranted. Now such reform has truly begun. Just as the rest of China is making the transition to modernity, so too now is the military.

Trends in Military Leadership

"The sense of grievance among armed forces that the civilian bureaucracy has short-changed it and this is reflected in the hierarchy laid down in the pay commission is both sad and dangerous. If allowed to fester it will undermine not just the self-system of the armed forces, but it will engender a sense of rivalry and bitterness between the civil and military wings of the government." Daily News and Analysis (DNA), Pune 13 October, 08.

The editorial goes on "The argument of the top brass in uniform that it is more a matter of honour rather than that of money underscores their sense of being discriminated against." In elaboration it suggests that while as the norm in our country is for the armed forces to report to civil authority, a norm meticulously followed by the services all these years, civil authority cannot be substituted by civil service authority, which the armed forces see as humiliating. It is this confrontationist situation that needs the intervention of the political leadership.

Political leadership in our country is vote-bank-oriented and civil-service-dependent. It has had little awareness of space for the armed forces views and feeling, a cultural baggage to a fault. Armed forces are no vote bank. A large number of them in any case do note vote, they are busy getting on with their job wherever they are, disposed all over the country for from their constituencies, with little time and patience for postal ballot and electoral issues. And what help and service the servicemen can provide to nurture the kinds of politicians and policies our diversity and governance have spawned? The present confrontationist situation has come about because the intake in leadership echelon has gone into an alarming decline, premature retirements on an alarming ascent, and the top brass repeatedly showing hours from the south block in the ears of the government.

The government offered a few sops through the deafeningly silent civil services-sixth pay commission, committee of secretaries and now group of ministers. What the GOM does is yet to be seen, as at the time writing. If increase in pay was one sop (it cannot be called an incentive yet), increase in the number of ranks (colonel to general officers) was another. These were lopped off by devaluing and reducing rank status vis-à-vis civil services personal, that touched the raw serve of the serviceman's sense of honor and recognition as well. It also carried the certain conflict in role-play.

One needs to quote Samuel Huntington (The Soldier And The State) if only because no Indian intellectual or researcher has thought it fit to dwell on soldier-state-society relationship in our country with its own peculiar politico-socio-economic milieu. He writes "The motivations of the officer are a technical love for his skill and the sense of social obligation to utilize this skill for the benefit of society. Society on the other hand, can only assure this motivation if it offers its officers continuing and sufficient pay while on active duty and when retired." In this situation if the society-the government - does not ensure this pay aspect then who is to do it? And if nobody is doing it in a sufficient manner why blame the services leadership for projecting and insisting on it? Our Constitution denies the services the right to form or join unions, indulge in dharna, strikes, public demonstrations, communicate to the press, write books or articles without services clearance etc. In the present instance it is the armed forces top leadership which has (projected the demand directly to the government it is serving and has access to - the one legitimate quarter and the only access-.) Its fault seen in many eyes is its determined insistence on converting sops into equitable incentives with rightful status, honour and recognition the servicemen deserve, the types of responsibilities they carry and effectively operate in the command and control structure the government puts in the sphere of national security, both external and internal.

The whole gamut of pay, status and honour have come to the fore for attracting intake in the armed forces (leave aside high class intake) and retain it for the maximum period of usefulness. Traditional attitude towards the soldier is that he is a second-rate, mentally and intellectually inferior. Physical strength has always counted for more than intelligence and intellectual strength, despite the iconic example of David against Goliath.) In Morris Janowitze's words: "A liberal ideology –holds that since war is essentially destructive, the best minds are attracted to more positive endeavors. The impression exists among educators that the intellectual level of those entering the military profession via the service academies reflected the adequate effective and adequate minimum standards rather than any extensive concentration of students at the upper end of the intelligence continuum." ("The professional Soldier"), further in the same book he refers to a study of US Army lieutenants "which suggests that the brighter ones resign as soon as they complete their obligatory service, while those less well equipped remain,thus military against finding the brighter people in the upper echelons of the military hierarchy."

In this eminent psychological study of military leader ("Psychology of Military Incompetence") Norman Dixon says that intellectual ability has not always counted for very much in training for generalship; that academic requirements of the (military academics) are not wholly relevant to those actually required for competent generalship; and that denigration of progressive thinkers and powering score on men who challenged existing practices must surely have tended to stiffle any exercise of the intellect who wanted to get on, and deterred the gifted from ever seeking a military career. He goes on to add "Of the psychological problems which beset military officers few exceed in severity those associated with leadership. In this respect they are required to fulfil incompatible roles. They are expected to show initiative, yet remain hemmed in by regulation. They must be aggressive, yet never insubordinate. They must be assiduous in cating for their men, yet maintain on enormous social distance. They must know everything about everything yet never appear intellectual. The fact remains that a deliberate cult of anti-intellectualism has characterized the armed services."

This and others like increasing consumerist attitude, big and quick money, and the huge pay packets and perks offered by the corporate, MNCs etc. are some of the main reasons for the declining intake, no doubt. McNamara rightly says; "Brains are like hearts, they go where they are appropriated." In such a situation how are the services and the society going to change the thinking? What should they be doing towards: -

- Identifying intellectual and intelligence contents required in military leadership?
- Fostering, nurturing, encouraging and improving them in the military leadership?
- Retaining and optimally utilizing talent, intellect and expertise obtaining in military leaders?

Basically, it adds up to intelligence (ability to gain and apply knowledge and skills), intellect (power of using mind to reason and understand) and practice of putting both to optimal use that brings a level of satisfaction to the leadership.

That leads to the need of reviewing selection content and methods. The present selection system has been clinically analyzed by Maj Gen Suman in an earlier IDR issue. Such a review is also necessary for the content and methods of training officers progressively all through their service. Intelligence has to be fertile and sharp, while it is intellect, which puts it to good use, necessitating the presence of one and potential and scope for the other. Candidates from varying backgrounds and thinking, ideas and motives appear for selection and initial training. Employment considerations, family traditions, starry ideas of patriotism, serving the nation and suchlike, financial inducements, glamour and many others play their part in attracting or forcing candidates, who do not always have a clear enough understanding of what exactly in retail is required in their persona in order to get selected. Many low and slow starters turn into high fliers later, and vice-versa. Selection content and methods need to reduce the hit-and-miss chances in selection, by fine-tuning it through well thought out identification of requirements, attitudes, psychological make-up and mental horizon. Today's combat scenario needs not only fighters but also administrators, managers, teachers, thinkers and technical experts, all conversant with combat demands and dangers, uncertainties and fatigue, and all having their mixes of intelligence and intellect, brain and brown, aggression and self-control.

Soon after entry the first agenda would be naturally to bring the background influences, attitudes, motives, thinking etc. on to the common denominator, namely, the aspect of soldiering, its content, nature, ethos, demands and characteristics, so as to subordinate individual predilections to the main theme. Excessive emphasis on drill, bull, obsessive orderliness, blind obedience and confirmity beyond rationality destroy individuality.

Pontification on tradition, discipline, immunization to fear by group and mechanical, automatic actions, though necessary to an extent, drive towards attempt to homogenize individuality and destroy the thinking faculty, so essential in developing courage and innovativeness. In our training repertoire there is little emphasis on instruction regarding what professionalism is, what characterizes military profession, what it entails, what parts drill and tradition, discipline and obedience physical toughness and intellectual strength aggressiveness and self-control play and to what extent. Penchant for drill, strict obedience, unthinking conformity and strangle hold of tradition are all authoritarian ingredients that tie down leaders and help perhaps survival. But survival is not the goal of soldierly action; it is to win- a positive, active, aggressive action, and therefore needing sufficient room for ideas, innovative approach, out-of-box thinking and individuality. Our present system, an authoritarian, rigid, conventional, stifling one needs to create scope for individuality thinking, initiative, ideas and intellectual content, difficult though it is to loosen its authoritarian grip (of minimum basic survival demand and survival instinct). It is this authoritarianism-high on drill-bull and low on intellectual and initiative-that deters and put off those who have and want to use their brain.

The army itself also is a culprit. It seems to be deeply and senselessly embedded in routine, drill, waiting inordinately for something to happen or attending to small thing with fastidious meticulousness, wasting enormous energy and time, obsessed with no-mistake syndrome and keeping everybody on the hook all the time, be it in peace or wartime. No-mistake syndrome spawns over supervision, which, in turn, starts the disease of the senior doing his juniors job. The syndrome itself is fecundated by the desire to please his superior and create good impression.

Armed Forces are identified with dealing with violence, killing, destroying etc., for which they have to be ready to sacrifice, imbibe strict discipline, develop unquestioning loyalty and obedience and so on with less than necessary analysis of why these traits are required. Nevertheless these become the bottom line, with stress on the "minimum" and the "hazardous". One wonders at this exclusive emphasis on the minimalist approach. Aren't there other larger, maximal, aspirational lines above it? if so why don't they find urention and emphasis? They don't because they do not seem have been identified, developed and practiced as military service ethos, management imperative and military culture in the rush of meeting the bottom line. Military recruitment advertisements flaunt "can you do it" placards. Do what? Join and stick on to military service? In what expectation? To achieve what, satisfy what? With what avenues available? The above challenge is titilltive of human manliness, a matter becoming less relevant as women too have been entering the profession. Even "challenge" needs replacement by promises of "opportunity, awareness and scope" for the candidate to inspire, motivate and attract him to the profession to realize and enjoy his potential and pursuit. It needs necessary scope for intelligence, excellence and intellectual content, apart from financial recompense for attracting entry into the profession and falling in love with the conditions and restriction imposed by it.

Now what about motivation to continue in service? Financial incentives serve the purpose up to an extent and no further. Thereafter it is job satisfaction, sense of honour, status and pursuit of personal excellence. That is what the service chiefs have highlighted too. Job satisfaction is possible only if ideas, innovative sprit, constructive criticism, frank opinion and exercise of expertise and chosen skills are allowed necessary space, tolerance and understanding; if these are encouraged and sustained and permitted to develop and be practised. More than a thousand officers are wanting to leave the army, nearly ten thousand officer vacancies exist, with hundreds of entry vacancies in the academy going undersubscribed. The existing environment, works ethics and restriction under the garirs of discipline, obedience, tradition and so on deny job satisfaction because of senseless waste of time in adhering to form rather than substance; because of depriving officers of private time and scope for personal pursuits; because of organizational and its higher leadership failure to help subordinates widen their mental, intellectual horizons and pursue their personal inclinations in these spheres. In its holy mantra of "career profile" the system appears to prepare pegs to fit into all kind of geometrical holes. For example engineer officers gathering MES expertise are transferred in their contributive years into general staff. So is it for Border Roads. Those attuned to long years of command experience are thrust into senior staff appointments and vise-versa, an invitation to disaster. Preparing officers at their contributive stage in career as jacks of all trades generates a lot of job disillusionment.

Job satisfaction entails providing opportunity and scope to the officer to develop skill and expertise, and then to put them to practice in his service, particularly when he reaches professional adulthood and contributive period of his career. It has a close relationship with intellectual bent as well as desire for pursuit of personal excellence. Intellectual pursuit does not mean gathering doctorates in science, arts and literature, (though they help to an extent). It means providing berth for a vision, a look- beyond and relating his professional undertaking with other human activities-scientific, social, economic, administrative and many others.

It is in this development that throws up a vision that the armed forces are pretty thin. There is no "vision paper" for officers career, contribution and conduct. Large number of officers want private time, personal study, break from long periods of office routine and escape from over supervision. They want to pursue their interest, hobbies, inclinations, and also contribute to the profession. They listen to what Bertrand Russel says "The performance of public duty is not the whole of what makes a good life, there is also the pursuit of private excellence." It will be of interest to study the part played by vision (more an exception in the leadership than professionally fostered) in The crossing of the Meghna, and lack of it (a general condition of leadership) in the 1962 NEFA debade. Srilanka episode of 1987-90 was probably an example of intellectual weakness and misplaced vision, which resulted in that "march of folly" (Barbara tuchman's monumental work).

For the first time in sixty years the matter of serviceman's view has come to a head. The government and the society have to tackle the financial aspect of soldiers incentive, as is rather firmly being insisted upon by the service chiefs. How far the government and the society tolerate the service chief's pressure in accommodating their demands, and how for the service chiefs stretch their persistence need to be watched. That is likely to lay the first foundation stone of a healthy convention between civil-military relations, if only the politician throws out his apprehension of a military coup. This foundation will also have to include the unique content of the serviceman's demand for due status, honour and recognition. Secondly, both the government and the services, the latter in particular, need to make room for the serviceman's job satisfaction and intellectual development. There is a need to review the identification of requirements in the entry candidates, method of breaking him in for professional imperatives, followed by educating him on intellectual plane, and employing him in an optimal manner that gives him job satisfaction and a sense of contribution, in order to retain him in service and add qualitatively to the military leadership content.

By and large the soldier and the ex-soldier have been progressively devalued and given low priority in the public eye, the government and, much more regrettably, the civil administrative machinery at the state and district levels. In some northen states the soldier continues to remain in their eye, but in the rest of the country he is neglected. Particularly so in matters of revenue, litigation, property and legal cases, where he has to remain away for long periods. Soldier Boards in most states are helpless, powerless, inadequately staffed. Civil officials-DCs, secretaries and ministers have little interest in their functioning, with little or no communication between them for years together, leave aside interaction. This state of affairs has to change. Soldier needs to be at par with other concerns of civil administration, with a couple of concessions, namely those of being heard quickly and disposed off quickly and reducing the legal wrangles he has to go through while he is immersed in the exigencies of service, while paying a heavy price on his return to the ex-serviceman's status.

THE IMPORTANCE OF NEW LEADERSHIP DOCTRINE

At present, our leadership concepts are a constantly changing hodge-podge of old manuals, readings, and faddish briefings from consultants. We mix management, command and leadership concepts from business, from other military forces, or from the public service. Little of this is truly analyzed to see what it adds and none of it is consolidated to cut away the doublespeak and give clarity to how we plan to employ it. We now write business plans for operational units, pay consultants to teach us thirty year old lateral thinking processes or explain

Standards for Harassment and Racism Prevention, and employ civilian experts to teach military officers ethics. We now have principles of leadership (which almost everyone has forgotten), principles of command, principles of management, ethical values and standards for harassment and racism prevention. We seem to have forgotten that this is all leadership, yet we have fragmented it into small packages. It is time we stopped and reviewed all of these concepts and consolidated them into a clear and coherent doctrine that is accessible. Generals, senior executives and Master Corporals need to study different aspects of leadership, but it must all be based on the same vision and philosophy.

The only solution is a clear statement of our leadership vision. The CF must put first things first and state explicitly the leadership concepts that we, as an organization believe in, will teach, promote and most importantly practice. We must promote a new philosophy of leadership that places operational requirements at the forefront, but applies equally well at static headquarters and on bases. It must promote trust and create the conditions for delegation and the development of initiative. This philosophy must be one based upon basic values and ideals and this is where our leadership doctrine must begin.

The Base

The basis of our leadership doctrine must be the core values of our organization. It should be quite simple to define the core values of the CF, but ours are fragmented. There exist lists of ethical principles, a military ethos, the Army's Professional Ethos and certainly others. This basic list must encompass organizational values such as truth, dignity, justice, service, and perhaps accountability. The CF must put its best minds and experience to the task and define such a list as the basis for our leadership philosophy. This list will also become our ethical and moral checklist or compass to be referred to when required. It is only on this base of values that we must build the walls of personal characteristics, leadership concepts, leadership techniques and leader development which will result in the building of strong and effective leadership.

The Four Walls

Personal Characteristics. Canada's military leadership doctrine, to be most effective, must explain the personal characteristics desired of all members of the forces (perhaps loyalty, discipline, honesty, courage, competence and fitness) and then describe the further requirements of all leaders (perhaps intellect, self-discipline, diligence, responsibility, initiative, commitment, compassion, determination, and self-confidence). It must, however also provide a personal guide for mid-career leaders to recalibrate and refocus their personal character towards the daunting tasks of higher command and indirect leadership. Each of the above characteristics must be reinterpreted in the light of the higher level of task and the increased complexity of leadership in large organizations.

Leadership Concepts. While the leadership characteristics will not change greatly from past doctrine, the leadership concepts must. Firstly, our leadership philosophy must build on the idea of trust. Present CF leadership doctrine is transactional and is based on a barter system to elicit the support of the follower. The exchange may be a tangible reward, such as time off, or promotion, but it may also be more subtle: perform well and be accepted as a member of the team. Whatever form it takes, there is an aspect of barter to transactional leadership. Values are not critical for its success. The leader and the follower may have very different base values; however, the leader can overcome these differences and influence the follower to assist in mission accomplishment. There are situations when this method works, but it is not adequate for most operational situations, nor is it best suited for maximum organizational effectiveness.

In transactional leadership situations, the follower participates because it is, in some way, in his personal interest to do so. Greater effectiveness is achieved through a transformational leadership approach. Transformational leaders, *get[s] followers to transcend their own self-interest for the sake of the leader, team, unit or organization. The transformational leader obtains more from his or her followers than superficial change in their attitudes or minor increments in their temporary level of motivation.*

This approach to leadership is based on trust as well as on concepts of pride and self-esteem. It focuses on development rather than evaluation of the followers. It does not come into conflict with the military notions of discipline and duty. In fact, it is particularly well suited for a volunteer, professional military in which members accept altruistic notions of mission before self and service for one's society. Soldiers do not risk their lives on operations for personal reward; they do it for abstract concepts such as honour, duty and integrity. Likewise, staff officers and civilian executives do not work long hours at NDHQ for extra pay or for medals; they do it for the same basic concepts as the soldier in the field. This would suggest that in the vast majority of situations in the Department transactional notions are not required. At times, appeal to higher values may be less successful than an offer of a day off in motivating the duty driver, but as Stephen Covey quite rightly notes:

Obviously both kinds of leadership are necessary. But transformational leadership must be the parent, as it provides the frame of reference, the strategic boundaries within which transactions take place. The goal of transformational leadership is to "transform" people in a literal sense...and bring about changes that are permanent, self-perpetuating, and momentum building.

The transformational approach relies on articulation of the leader's vision and is based on appeal to common values and ideals. At higher levels this approach is most effective, for as the leader rises in rank, or position, so too are the key subordinates increasingly self-motivated and share a common interest in mission accomplishment. The concept of transformational leadership is also however, directly applicable to operations and command at all levels. The acceptance of transformational leadership in our doctrine will place a greater emphasis on the responsibility of our leaders to develop their subordinates and it will correct some of the deficiencies in our present doctrine about the way we understand motivation.

Transformational leadership will aid in the motivation of subordinates and it will create a climate of trust and initiative which will allow our command philosophy of directive control and our decentralized management philosophy to flourish. To fully change the way we lead, however; we must also rewrite our definition of leadership. Since the leader must do more than simply get followers to complete a task, perhaps an initial draft definition might read like this:

Leadership is the art of analyzing issues and tasks; of visualizing missions; of communicating intent; and of directing and guiding the actions of individuals and organizations to complete identified missions. The leader creates a climate that develops the individuals and organizations to prepare effectively for future unidentified missions.

This definition, though long, captures the breadth and complexity of leadership better than did our old definition. It also emphasizes the importance of the follower in the completion of the mission, while emphasizing the responsibility of the leader for both identifying the immediate mission, supervising the accomplishment of that mission, while maintaining a long-term perspective.

A final concept which must be corrected is that of leadership styles. The US Army has long relegated leadership styles to an appendix in their doctrine, and the time has come for us to do so as well. The leader can change his approach to a new situation, or with new followers, but he or she cannot actually change leadership styles. To suggest that it is possible is to promote acting and therefore compromise trust. No leader can shift completely from one style to another, and no situation clearly requires just one style. The leadership styles are only useful as idealized models and are of no pragmatic value. The new CF leadership philosophy must use transformational leadership to create the conditions where a delegating style can be employed, while accepting that not all subordinates are ready for the responsibilities which that entails. It is the leader who must decide the level of delegation and the supervision required. The styles, if they are to be kept at all for pedagogical purposes, must be reviewed and rewritten to conform to our new philosophy of leadership.

Leadership Techniques. Our new doctrine must include up to date instruction of the techniques required by leaders. An emphasis in all areas must be given to operational issues to ensure that while acknowledging the unique leadership situations created on operations, we do not allow ourselves to create a military leadership style for operations and a public service mentality in garrison. The CF has one core competency and that is, when necessary, to fight. If our leadership doctrine does not emphasize the requirements of military operations in all environments, then we should consider contracting our services out. The techniques for planning, for decision making and for command and control must be addressed at appropriate levels and if necessary, with environmentally specific annexes to deal with the specifics of air, land or sea leadership. Techniques to motivate and maintain unit cohesion should be discussed with historical examples. A separate, but related manual might be developed specifically with higher command on operations in mind.

There will also be a requirement to address the more mundane, but no less important techniques of leadership. These will include chapters on communications skills, counseling, supervision, performance review, team development, as well as on specialty areas such as harassment and racism policies, law of armed conflict, ethics and stress. By centralizing all aspects of leadership in one set of manuals, we will correct the fragmentation and redundancy of effort that exists today. In addition, we will become more cohesive as an organization.

Leader Development. The final wall required to build our effective leadership structure is that of leader development. Most of the groundwork for this has been completed and exisits in the Officers' Professional Development Handbook, but that should be expanded to include all leaders. Every leader in the CF must pass through at least one posting where he or she is faced with the responsibility and demands of direct leadership. We have too many officer classifications where senior leaders are developed through a series of follower or staff positions. We send officers to CFC Toronto who have never commanded a ship's division, a flight or an army sub-unit. Those officers, upon graduation are quite likely to command a unit without any previous leadership experience.

Our system must be tightened to ensure that leader development is common throughout the CF. Obviously land, sea and air officers will have different specific experiences, but each must be comfortable in direct leader roles, indirect leadership roles, and in staff roles.

Only then can we be sure of developing senior officers with the breadth of experience to set policy, provide direction, and most importantly, command CF elements on joint operations. Our leader development model must be included with our doctrinal manuals to ensure that both the doctrine and the handbook match and that both are amended together when necessary. Responsibility for leader development throughout the CF must be placed directly on the shoulders of all leaders.

THE POLITICAL CONTEXT OF MODERNISATION

With a backdrop of economic crises and political instability, many Latin American countries which had implemented a package of State reforms in the 1990s were forced to rethink the idea of a minimal State and fiscal discipline as pillars of modernisation, to start rebuilding democratic institutions and meet the increasing demands of their citizens. Accordingly, a 'second generation of reforms' was devised, based on introducing management techniques from the private sector in order to boost efficacy and efficiency in the public sector. This second wave was an improvement on the previous set of reforms, among other reasons because it recognised that the market could not play the political role which legitimately corresponds to the State, and it understood that efficacy and efficiency are not achieved only through the macroeconomic sphere but also with public policies aimed at enhancing human development.

In this regional context, Chile began implementing a set of management measures in 2000, via the State Reform and

Modernisation Project *(PRYME)*, which became a permanent body within the General Secretariat of the Presidency, in order to modernise and incorporate information technology to improve public management. This process also impacted favourably on citizens, and helped enhance standards of administrative management; but success was not a matter of chance: buoyant economic growth and institutional stability constituted the ideal framework in which to implement long-term administrative management.

Furthermore, continuity in the government's line of policy enabled it to maintain the programmes and further pursue reforms, which normally require years of effort to see the first stable results, and a budget worthy of a developed country to achieve them. Both conditions were met in Chile, firstly because public policies established in previous administrations were upheld, and secondly because successive budgets were provisioned for the administrative management projects and policies, and because the Inter-American Development Bank (IDB) lent its financial support to specific programmes.

This approach has been pursued even further recently: President Bachelet reasserted her commitment to modernising the State structure by announcing in November 2006 an 'agenda of probity, transparency and modernisation' in the management of the State. The agenda sets forth specific measures to ensure the constitutional principle of transparency, the imposition of a new system to select senior public management in order to professionalise the civil service, the introduction of supervisory measures such as internal auditing of the government, and regulation and absolute transparency in financial management. The Head of State thereby ensures the permanence of the reforms as part of State policy, but can also optimise any favourable results of management and transparency indices as an achievement of the governing coalition. Until 2005, modernisation was implemented in many State bodies via specific programmes for key administrative areas, mainly pertaining to customer care and results-based management. However, the 'managerial style' did not prosper in the area of

Defence. There were two main difficulties in implementing new management methodologies: first, unlike other State bodies, Defence in Chile is still burdened by the collective image it conjures up of the repression of the years of dictatorship. As a result, despite its democratic institutions, it is clear that the slate is not yet clean; this was made evident, for example, by the division in society during the funeral of General Pinochet.

At another level, the very structure of the Ministry itself hampers implementation of some techniques, such as outsourcing specific services, since National Defence cannot be channelled like a service industry towards a civilian body or private company. This means that some of the measures regularly implemented under administrative reform cannot be transferred automatically into the Defence area. In Health or Education, privatisation of the provision of certain goods or services under State supervision is a solution to the difficult issue of meeting citizens' demands, because of the possibility of finding better management solutions at private corporations. In the case of Defence, not only in Chile but also in the rest of the world's democratic countries, outsourcing is linked only to the procurement of military supplies, the military industry or consultancy; if it were assigned to a private company, this would mean relegating the political role of the State and aligning the administration of the sector with what would be a private military company. Consequently, given the area's complexity, it deserves a special mention, considering its specific properties and the political context of each country. Some initiatives, such as results-based management, the digitalisation of administrative processes and procedures or management supervision may be feasible, while privatisation or viewing the citizen as a client, are infinitely more controversial.

The Reform of National Defence: Consolidating Civilian Command, Transforming the Ministerial Structure

Without neglecting these contextual factors when considering the Defence area's reform, the country is showing political coherence in its approach to modernisation. Within this framework, Bachelet's commitment is to direct the sector's modernisation based on strengthening political leadership in the definition and management of Defence. 'Consolidating political command' means, in specific terms, managing Defence from the executive power, with the Minister's cooperation, while affording the armed forces with a more or less technical and consultancy-related role.

At a seminar on the modernisation of the State and the Defence sector, held in 2003 at the University of Chile, Bachelet announced that her main objectives would be to recover the value of the armed forces and the Ministry as a joint entity, revise the mechanisms for assigning resources set forth in the Copper Law, achieve effective modernisation of the pensions system for the armed forces and national police (*carabineros*) and make headway in enforcing the equality of opportunities for women in Defence, among other significant points. Despite the variety of measures announced by the then Defence Minister, public opinion in Chile insists mainly on the issue of procurements as being at the heart of this debate. Consequently, so far the longest delays have been in formulating an exhaustive procurements policy, defined by the ministerial authority and not as an independent requirement for each of the services. The heated public debate on procurements falls within the framework of the need to democratise and, therefore, to 'politicise' the Defence agenda, sidelining the idea that it is a matter solely for the military and at the same time trying to overcome the distrust which sometimes emerges between political and military circles during decision-making and management processes. One of the thorniest issues for public debate is the destination of the funds from the Reserved Copper Law. This Law, enacted in 1958, distributes 10% of copper revenues among the three armed services with the purpose of maintaining and boosting military supplies. Evidently, it was created in quite another political era at the both domestic and international levels, but it has not yet been adapted to the current context. Consequently, the first bone of contention is that procurements are not guided by Defence policy. Although the 2002 Defence Book still conveys a classic vision of National Defence, which might justify the need to modernise and promote the procurement of military supplies permanently, Chile's good relations with neighbouring countries, plus greater world-wide attention to the emergence of asymmetrical conflicts in the light of the lower proportion of 'traditional' wars, creates an obvious contradiction.

Furthermore, this Law could counterbalance the efforts to consolidate political leadership in the Defence area, since it envisages that the military should define its needs in terms of procurement and maintenance without joint planning within the armed forces, and without a policy defined by the Executive with the advice of the Minister and Chile's Joint Chiefs of Staff. On the first point, under the previous Minister, Jaime Ravinet, work commenced to assess the procurements made under the Copper Law, by implementing a System for the Evaluation of Defence Investment Projects, which began in 2005 with the joint planning of armed forces development. This system employs the managerial methodology of project management, by inviting the armed forces to present their requirements in the form of projects which justify their procurement and the procedures involved, as well as a proposal to meet capacity requirements. Approval of the use of resources depends ultimately on the President, but prior evaluation stages are carried out by a specialist team from the Ministry.

The reform is a significant step in that it enhances the transparency of the internal processes of procurement and maintenance of material, empowering the Ministry's technical experts to evaluate projects; however, long-term joint planning is still pending. It is clear that if Defence policy is defined as a public policy, the percentage and proposed use of the revenues from the Copper Law must be the result of negotiations and the prioritisation of needs, as with any other policy within the framework of a democratic State. A last important point is that the modernisation of military supplies is looked upon with distrust by other international players and this can generate a negative image of Chile abroad, especially within the region. The idea of a country committed to peace missions and international cooperation, which does not, at least in the short term, face any real threats to its security but nevertheless has state-of-the-art weapons and technology, at first glance looks like something of a contradiction. One's first instinct might be to fear a steady militarisation in a regional context which seems to be moving precisely in that direction, as made evident by Venezuela, among others. However, over time the coherence of its procurements policy could offset this image, since despite the still pending public debate, Chile has shown no hostility to other nations and neither has it begun an arms race overnight. Nevertheless, as Bachelet said at the seminar in 2003, the matter of procurements is not the only urgent item on the agenda; there are other questions in terms of modernisation, which are necessary to integrate a wide-reaching reform to optimise management, take into account the sector's specific characteristics, work on the political context and generate a democratic and effective response to the challenges posed on the international stage. In this regard, there is a second debate in Chile, in regard to the transformation of the sector via an integrated plan, involving administrative restructuring, removing the overlapping of public departments and also boosting the decision-making capacity of ministerial authorities.

The result of this debate was a draft bill signed by former President Lagos in 2005 which proposed the Ministry's structural modernisation, with the main aim of strengthening presidential and ministerial authority in managing government processes. Among the most significant changes, the bill proposes to create an Office of the Joint Chiefs of Staff to replace the Defence Chiefs of Staff as the Minister's working and advisory body in matters relating to the preparation and joint use of the armed forces. Furthermore, the aim is to redesign the organisational structure of the Undersecretariats, so as to avoid overlapping tasks, make progress in joint planning and speed up management processes. Accordingly, the Undersecretariats of War, the Navy and the Air Force and the Ministry's Administrative Directorate would be removed and replaced by two new departments: the Undersecretariat of Defence and the Undersecretariat for the Armed Forces. The former would prepare policies and plans for the sector and the latter would perform the tasks of the three old Undersecretariats in managing all questions and processes which the armed forces require to fulfil their tasks. Although the draft bill presented to Parliament is still being processed, it manages to crystallise some of the government's aspirations in respect of administrative modernisation and the need to foster the greater accountability of the armed forces to the political authorities and to society. A significant portion of public opinion is critical of the independence of the military in terms of defining the objectives, plans and requirements for Defence and, at the same time, civil servants at the Ministry are meeting with certain managerial obstacles, due precisely to the armed forces' relative independence of the central administration. If the law were to be enacted, both these conflictive issues would be resolved, since all the reforms are aimed at transferring political responsibility and strategic planning to the Minister, who will act with the cooperation of the armed forces. This would certainly imply reducing the power of the military, which in all instances will have to submit to the Minister for planning sector policies and carry out only secondary planning in relation to the procurement of military supplies and the administration of matters falling within their responsibility.

Finally, a third matter for public debate is the modernisation of compulsory military service. The definition of new objectives, equal access to military service and an effective incentives formula are as yet unresolved issues. Most people think that this system has become an obstacle in terms of the employment and educational outlook for the middle and upper classes and, at the same time, the need for employment or qualifications are the main motivation for completing military service for the young from low income sectors and rural areas. As a result, conscription could start to lose its patriotic sense and gradually become a basic training system for the most marginalised sectors of society.

The maintenance of compulsory military service as a recruitment system was justified by the vulnerability of the country's geographical layout and its strategic defence options, with most conflict hypotheses requiring a significant territorial deployment. This is why most youngsters performing their military service are sent to remote areas and involved in army service, and many of the yearly contingents are trained as infantry. However, the new challenges in international security, the inequality of access to military service among young people and the high costs of its maintenance are specific reasons for a reform.

In 2000, public debate led to the holding of a national forum involving civilian organisations as well as State institutions and the armed forces. The exchange of opinions was resumed one year later for the purposes of the draft bill for modernisation of compulsory military service, whose aim is to promote voluntary recruitment. Without modifying the compulsory nature of military service as set forth in Article 22 of Chile's Constitution, the aim is to foster voluntary recruitment by attempting to make the draft a subsidiary channel. The project seeks to improve ways to encourage people to present themselves as volunteers, and to establish the universal draft merely as a means of making up the necessary numbers.

Despite the planned achievements in terms of volunteer recruitment, they do not resolve the problem posed by public opinion. The poorest young people are still the first to enter the armed forces, in search of better prospects, and this, among other things, might make conscription a social service which is a far cry from the military vocation. Yet so far there are no prospects for a radical transformation of the system, since as the President herself said in regard to the forum's conclusions: 'Neither conditions nor resources are yet sufficient to have a professional army'.

MODERNISING THE INDIAN INFANTRY

Why has it taken the Army so long to conceive an upgrade package for the oldest, most potent and intensely employed fighting arm, the Infantry, even after the so-called revolution in military affairs? The foot soldier, the original and most versatile weapon system that is always taken for granted, has emerged from the dubious shock and awe strategy of recent campaigns as its ultimate arbiter. India has paid dearly for the neglect of its infantry in terms of cost, casualties and over-stretch of battle. But the Infantry has never let us down. Kargil was its finest hour. Gen VP Malik, the Army Chief of the time, wryly noted: "We will fight with what we have."

So when for the first time an international conference of Army and defence industry was launched last week to put the forgotten soldier centre-stage, some misgivings were natural. While Army Chief Gen JJ Singh outlined his vision for the soldier system of the future, the conspicuous and total absence of Government - MoD - robbed the conference of any sanctity. In sharp contrast, for a MoD-sponsored defence finance seminar earlier in the month, Government officials and ministers were stepping over each other at Vigyan Bhavan.

Free India's Army came into being in 1947 and within weeks, the Infantry soldiers landed in Srinagar to save J&K from being gobbled up by Pakistani tribal raiders. Since then, the Infantry has not ceased fighting proxy wars there and later, elsewhere too. A former Army Chief, Gen SR Choudhury, who was not from the Infantry, described the Infantry as the Army and vice versa. Field Marshal Montgomery said: An army is considered only as good as its Infantry.

The experience of four wars, several border skirmishes, two out-of-area missions, the ceaseless campaign to counter cross-border terrorism in Kashmir, numerous other insurgencies in the North-East, internal stability operations elsewhere in the country and UN peace keeping operations make the Indian Infantry the most battle-hardened and combat rich force in the world. The simple and uncomplaining infantryman has given so much to so many for so little. The modernisation of the infantry was first attempted - halfheartedly - in the mid-1980s by the Perspective Planning branch of the Army Headquarters. The bias for mechanised warfare, zealously pursued by Gen Sundarji, was so pronounced that the Infantry modernisation plan was skipped altogether. Guns, tanks, APCs were the weapons in demand. The Infantry was ignored. Had a modest upgrade package been undertaken at that time, infantry would have been more combat contemporary and effective.

Instead, till recently, some soldiers were still using World War II equipment and clothing. Shameful as it was, soldiers had to buy rucksacks and other accoutrements from the market. DRDO is still to come out with a light bulletproof vest. The Army failed to accurately visualize the nature of combat it would fight in the future. Pakistan-sponsored insurgency in Punjab did not alert the nation and the Army to the proxy war brewing in J&K. We defaulted on both counts - anticipating low intensity conflict and cross border terrorism and preparing the Infantry for it.

Despite the sustained counter-insurgency and counter-terrorism campaign in J&K and the North-East since the 1990s, the Army was sluggish in investing in the infantry. The first Gulf War reintroduced the fiction that wars could be won from the air. The air campaigns in Bosnia and Kosovo temporarily turned fiction into reality. But 9/11 broke the myth of supremacy of air power. Operation Enduring Freedom in Afghanistan lasted 76 days; 65 of these were air operations.

The 11-day land offensive secured a temporary and incomplete victory against the Taliban. Operation Iraqi Freedom on the other hand, fought for 20 days was bereft of any preparatory air campaign though a secret air war preceded it. Unhappily for the US/NATO-led coalition forces, despite their pyrrhic military victories, low intensity wars in Afghanistan and Iraq are continuing in full blaze.

The recent 34-day war in Lebanon and the ongoing campaign in Gaza demonstrate the limits of Israel's military power. Used to decisive victories in less than 10 days, Israeli Defence Forces (IDF) were badgered by Hassan Nasrallah's jihadi militia. Reliance on air power, tanks and guns in Lebanon as substitute for ground troops - infantry - was motivated by casualty aversion. We too have to be sensitive to casualties.

The wars in Lebanon, Iraq and Afghanistan spurred by the growing cult of Osama bin Laden and Hassan Nasrallah require a redefinition of the concept of power and military success.

Success would necessarily be an inclusive military victory encompassing post-conflict stability and reconstruction. For this we need Infantry.

The Indian Army should not get overly seduced by high-sounding warfare like 'netcentric' that the West is being diverted into. This is not to suggest we ignore the strides in high-tech warfare. But as a former US NATO Commander noted recently: "This netcentric stuff is great but our men in Baghdad are being blown up with their Humvees by IEDs." He suggested that we address the battle we are fighting before switching to the one we will fight in the future.

India's supreme operational challenge is and will be the maintenance of internal security. Just last month, Prime Minister Manmohan Singh stated this ground reality. The Infantry is at the heart of counterinsurgency and counter-terrorism operations and may well get sucked into anti-Naxal operations as well. Keeping the Army operationally ready for both conventional and unconventional missions is imperative but the emphasis has to be on the business of the day: CI and CT.

The Indian Infantry is belatedly embarking on a modernisation programme to enhance its combat skills through increased lethality, communications, surveillance, mobility and suvivability. These force multipliers will enable the soldier to fight all-weather, 24x7 and on any terrain in the right battle-configuration albeit with the accent on LIC.

The GSQR for the Future-Infantry-Soldier-As a System (F-INSAS) must empower not encumber the soldier. DRDO must compete with domestic and international industry. DRDO has one more chance to make amends for its omissions and commissions. F-INSAS must strike the right balance between the surge of technology and sensibility of the soldier keeping the battle of the future in mind. Defence Minister AK Antony should accord F-INSAS the highest strategic priority.

9

Japanese Military Strategy

The magnitude of Japan's advance into Southeast Asia convinced the British to adopt a more vigilant outlook. Prior to the outbreak of war, the accepted assumption was that, although Japan possessed the strength to conquer Malaya and the Dutch East Indies, its fear of provoking Allied retaliation would compel the IJN and IJA to conduct a piecemeal conquest of Southeast Asia in an effort to sound out British and US reactions. Thus, the Allies could take advantage of a breathing spell that would allow them to bolster their defences. Following Japan's lightning conquests, the British based their forecasts on the expectation that the loss of Britain's territories in Southeast Asia was a foregone conclusion.

By March 1942, the Japanese had established bases within striking range of the Indian Ocean, thereby raising the possibility of operations against areas hitherto considered beyond their reach. In early April, the IJN launched a carrier-based sortie against the Royal Navy's base at Ceylon, highlighting the vulnerability of Britain's position.

The situation was desperate because commitments in Europe and North Africa continued to limit the forces available for operations against Japan. Consequently, for the first half of 1942, the British resigned to the probability that any large-scale Japanese expedition would deal a devastating blow. Nevertheless, while Japan's forces reigned supreme, as early as February, they began to face overstretch, and by June, the consequences became clear. The IJN stumbled from one unsuccessful operation to the next, first at Coral Sea and then at Midway, where the IJN lost its predominance over the US Navy.

Yet, the Japanese continued to possess ample strengths to forestall Allied counteroffensives, and the situation warned against any underestimation of the strength that had to be built up before the Allies could liberate their lost territories. At the same time, inaction entailed the risk of enabling the Japanese to consolidate and render Allied operations more difficult. The cumulative result was the development of a strategy aimed to inflict attrition against weak spots on Japan's outer perimeter. The strategy of limited offensives manifested itself in the decision to launch the disastrous Arakan campaign of winter 1942–1943.

The speed of Japan's advance convinced the defence establishment that Britain's position in Southeast Asia was untenable. By mid January, Japanese troops completed their advance through the Malay peninsula and conquered the southernmost province of Johore, thereby gaining an opportune position for besieging Singapore. The COS discarded their notion that Britain's bastion in the Far East could hold out against the Japanese. In response to Churchill's question about the wisdom of sending reinforcements, Alanbrooke, the CIGS, replied, 'the defence of Singapore is part of a delaying action'. The plan was to play for time while withdrawing to rear positions in the East Indies.

The Allies faced equally poor chances of retaining their positions in other parts of Southeast Asia. Given the weak state of Allied defences, Japan was most likely to secure its conquests by establishing a defensive barrier stretching from the eastern frontier of India to the southwest Pacific, destroying all remnants of resistance. In January 1942, the JIC concluded that the conquest of the Malay barrier not only provided vital supplies of raw materials. From a strategic viewpoint, it also served to push the Allies to their rear bases in India and Australia, securing the outer perimeter of Japan's empire.

Any hopes of holding the Malay barrier were contingent upon last-ditch forestalling actions. In mid February, during the battle of the Java Sea, the British and Dutch fleets failed to intercept the Japanese convoy headed for the East Indies. Pownall, along with and Wavell, who had been appointed the C-in-C Southwest Pacific, concluded that the Allies simply did not have enough strengths to forestall a landing. While British intelligence deduced the scope of Japan's ambitions in Southeast Asia, the possibility of operations beyond the Malay barrier remained open to conjecture. The available evidence was replete of information on Japan's long-term strategy. The structure of intelligence collection and analysis did not undergo major changes at the start of the conflict. The GCCS continued to intercept diplomatic signals intelligence, which simply pointed to strategies that were under consideration.

To illustrate a few examples, as late as the end of 1942, information on the possibility of Soviet–Japanese hostilities was contradictory and did not firmly indicate whether Japan intended to invade Siberia. Neither the JIC nor COS were able to produce conclusions. Signals intelligence also revealed that Japan was seeking ways to secure the Congress Party's cooperation in establishing a pro-Axis government in India. The information came at a time when the political situation in the Indian subcontinent was precarious. The colonial government faced increasing difficulties in stemming the nationalists' demands for full independence, and the circumstances seemed ideal for an Axis campaign of subversion. Nevertheless, information on Japanese intentions did not indicate whether a concrete strategy was likely to materialize, and the material simply exacerbated British fears of impending operations against India. Naval signals intelligence proved equally unreliable. When the fall of Singapore became imminent, FECB headquarters was relocated to Colombo in Ceylon. After March 1942, with the cooperation of the US Navy's sigint unit, OP-20-G, British cryptanalysts deciphered the IJN's JN-25 code. However, naval intercepts provided little apart from warnings of impending attacks. Prior to the Japanese attacks on Ceylon in early April, naval sigint alerted Admiral Sir James Somerville, C-in-C Eastern Fleet, who was able to evacuate his ships. The Japanese were prevented from launching another Pearl Harbour style air raid. Yet, long-term forecasts remained impossible, and defence plans had to be formulated on the understanding that enemy attacks could take place at short notice.

The truth of the matter is that until April 1942, Allied efforts to predict Japanese strategy were complicated by the fact that the IJN and IJA had not decided what they were to do after their operations in Southeast Asia were completed. Japan's leaders did not face an entirely favourable situation. The navy and army were stretched to their limit, and the China venture remained unresolved. The high command needed to make difficult decisions whether to consolidate or pursue further conquests. To complicate matters, no course of action held high promises of a decisive victory. An invasion of the Hawaiian islands was out of the question, given the state of alert the Americans were on after Pearl Harbour. An invasion of Australia was also difficult, because the IJA did not possess the strength to overcome the islands' defences, nor the logistics to support such a complex operation. An occupation of Ceylon and outlying British bases in the Indian Ocean would have provided a springboard for invading the Middle East, and in turn enabled the IJA to link up with Rommel's *Afrika Korps*. This move could have dealt a serious blow to the British Empire. Even then, Japan's eastern flank would have remained open to US incursions.

At the same time, consolidation was an equally questionable strategy, for Japan had yet to fulfil one of its main objectives, namely to neutralize US naval power in the Pacific. The failure to sink the carrier fleet at Pearl Harbour confronted Japan's leaders with a situation they had not anticipated.

To complicate matters, disagreements between the IJN and IJA commands hindered a decision. The navy wished to secure Japan's conquests by occupying Hawaii or Australia and preventing their use as bases for an Allied counteroffensive. The IJA, on the other hand, maintained that Japan's ultimate objective remained to conclude the war in China and prepare for action in Siberia. The army thus argued that its resources were insufficient strengths for large-scale offensives in the Pacific, and proposed to consolidate its southern conquests at the earliest opportunity. The IJA general staff premised its policies on the assumption that the Americans would be incapable of striking back for at least the first two years of the conflict, and hence a pre-emptive attack was unnecessary. The question of how to secure Japan's empire in Southeast Asia had not been seriously considered. Within Yamamoto's naval staff, there were disagreements as to whether Japan's key to victory lay in a main fleet action against the United States or the elimination of British positions in the Indian Ocean. Finally, while the possibility of bringing India into Japan's orbit was discussed at the high command level, the plan never transpired beyond a distant pipedream. At an imperial liaison conference held in January 1942, Japan's leaders issued a document stating, 'the Imperial Government has no hesitation in making wholehearted efforts to help the independence movement irrespective of whether inside or outside India'. Yet, the Japanese government did not have any direct contacts with Indian political parties, and was reluctant to support anti-British movements unless the Axis powers were willing to simultaneously send forces to the Indian subcontinent. Because neither Germany or Italy were ready to undertake operations east of Suez, a concrete strategy was unlikely to materialize.

The difficulties Japan faced in making a decision meant that war plans were formulated *ad hoc*. The Combined Fleet did not order the expedition against Ceylon until the third week of March, when the buildup of the Eastern Fleet at Trincomalee convinced Yamamoto's staff that British naval power in the Indian Ocean had to be neutralized. Only in late April did naval leaders decide to direct the IJN's main thrust against the US Fleet in the Central Pacific, after the Doolittle air raids on the home islands had revealed how the Americans could bring carriers within proximity of Japan. The IJA's plan to occupy Port Moresby was not drawn until mid spring, when mopping-up operations in Southeast Asia were approaching completion.

Under the circumstances, no matter how thoroughly British intelligence tracked Japanese strategy, the evidence was bound to remain contradictory. The absence of conclusive intelligence required British forces to guard against attacks at all possible points. In assessing Japanese strategy, the British looked at the overall situation in the Asia–Pacific theatres, but tended to focus the larger part of their attention on the Indian Ocean areas. This was because the Pacific theatre, including Australia, was a US sphere of responsibility. The loss of Singapore severed Britain's links with the Dominions, and the latter requested US military support in forestalling a Japanese invasion. Roosevelt accepted the request, and on 9 March 1942, Churchill agreed to the US proposal that the Dominions be placed under General MacArthur's Southwest Pacific Command. Thereafter, the British entrusted the defence of Australia to the Americans, and were more concerned about the possibility of Japanese incursions against their imperial possessions in the Indian Ocean.

British appreciations of Japan's strategy reflected a growing realization that efforts to predict enemy strategy were futile. The most important factor to be considered was the enemy's capabilities rather than intentions. The lack of indications of plans for an invasion was not taken to mean that such scenarios would not materialize. While an expedition against areas to the west of the Malay barrier entailed exposing Japan's eastern flank, its forces still possessed ample strengths for operations against British positions in the Indian Ocean, and stood to reap tangible benefits through such actions. In February, the JIC warned that Japan could muster the necessary troops for an invasion of Ceylon at any time, and its naval power and shipping resources were more than adequate. On the question over the probability of such operations, the committee admitted that no data was available for making a definite forecast. However, the Japanese were likely to realize that the loss of Ceylon would deprive Britain of its main base in the Indian Ocean. The uncertainty which plagued efforts to predict Japan's war plans, along with evidence of sufficient forces for further offensives, meant that the only way to ensure security was vigilance.

The increasing likelihood of Japanese expeditions against the Indian Ocean necessitated a closer examination of the strategic balance, and the upshot was that the British were not in a favourable situation. The *R* Class battleships used to reinforce Somerville's Eastern Fleet were relics of the Great War, and did little to help. The carriers *Indomitable* and *Formidable* were equipped with limited complements of aircraft whose performance did not match their Japanese counterparts. Nor was the garrison at Ceylon able to forestall a landing.

To complicate matters, the war against Germany remained Britain's top priority. Shortly after the United States entered the war in December 1941, the British and Americans held their first summit meeting (*Arcadia*) at Washington. Churchill insisted that the Allies needed to concentrate on Germany. The US representatives, in particular Admiral Harold Stark, the chief of the naval operations, argued that offensive operations against Japan should commence immediately. However, Roosevelt accepted Churchill's view that Germany posed a greater threat.

Nevertheless, the 'Germany First' strategy meant that Britain could not substantially strengthen its position against Japan until operations in Europe and North Africa had progressed sufficiently. Under the circumstances, no amount of intelligence could remedy the fact that British defences in the Indian Ocean were precarious, and the prospect of improvement in the near future were minimal. By March, the British conceded that few alternatives existed apart from accepting the consequences which could arise from a Japanese invasion, namely the loss of control over the territories adjacent to the Indian Ocean, and severance of the sea communications to the Middle East. Within India Command and the Eastern Fleet, the prevailing view was that Ceylon could not be defended without adequate air and naval reinforcements. In February, shortly after his appointment as C-in-C India, Wavell warned, 'to attempt to provide against a large scale invasion [by strengthening Ceylon's ground defences] would involve locking up troops which could be better used in offensive operations elsewhere'. The garrison in Ceylon was of little use if the

Japanese gained control of the surrounding ocean and airspace, and the Eastern Fleet could not repel a Japanese foray until sufficient numbers of carriers and their accompanying aircraft could be deployed. However, the Joint Planning Section (JPS), COS and Churchill maintained that until Allied forces had neutralized Germany's threat to the Middle East, and U-boat attacks in the Atlantic had ebbed, Britain could not provide the necessary forces for the larger part of 1942. The IJN's sortie into the Bay of Bengal in April highlighted the vulnerability of British territories in the Indian Ocean. The ease with which the Japanese brought a fleet within striking distance of Ceylon reinforced the conclusions reached previously. Sir Richard Peirse, commander of Air Headquarters India, and Wavell repeated their warnings that Ceylon and the east coast of India were defenceless without substantially increased air strengths. The COS concluded that if the Japanese pressed westward, India would be placed in great danger, and the Middle East and essential supply lines via the Indian Ocean placed under threat.

At the same time, the difficulties involved in strengthening Britain's position were acknowledged, and its strategy continued to be influenced by its global commitments. While Wavell insisted the defence of Ceylon be treated as a matter of the utmost urgency, the COS and Churchill replied that operations in the Middle East were more important, and hence the protection of sea communications with that theatre take priority. The Indian Ocean was to be secured by occupying Madagascar. As the official history on the war against Japan has pointed out, 'Wavell's difference of opinion with the COS was natural'. Churchill and his staff had to view the problem from the broader angle. The security of the UK had to take precedence, and the needs of India related to those of the Middle East.

Churchill and the COS realized that Britain's only hope of protecting the Indian Ocean, in the absence of an adequate Eastern Fleet, was to obtain US cooperation. Urgent requests were made for the US Pacific Fleet to either launch naval offensives on Japan's eastern flank, or send warships to join Somerville's fleet. Naturally, the Americans, who were reluctant to commit their limited strengths to defend the British Empire, made it clear that Britain's proposals were out of the question. The visible indications of Ceylon's vulnerability, and the difficulties involved in bolstering its defences, gave rise to a strategy of withdrawing major British units from the enemy's striking range and minimizing potential losses.

The Eastern Fleet was moved to East Africa on the premise that until adequate capital ships and carriers could be deployed in the Indian Ocean, its presence was more likely to lure further attacks. FECB headquarters was relocated to Kilindini on the assumption that the raids may have heralded an invasion. In reality, Japan had no plans for further incursions into the Indian Ocean.

However, only after Japan's defeats at Coral Sea and Midway had depleted the IJN's surplus of naval and air forces, could the British conclude that the enemy was unlikely to muster the strengths needed to support large-scale invasions. The possibility of Japanese offensive operations could be dismissed only by evidence which pointed to a diminution of its capabilities. During May and June 1942, Japanese naval losses provided reasonable grounds to conclude that the peril of a seaborne landing on India and Ceylon had passed.

Churchill minuted to Pound that the loss of four Japanese carriers at Midway had improved Britain's position in the Indian Ocean and Bay of Bengal, and that a 'severe restraint [was] imposed upon the Japanese' by their need to husband their extensive naval requirements. Pound responded that the position had improved 'inasmuch as the Japanese are less likely to stick their head into [the Indian Ocean]'. Assessments of Japan's strategy also emphasized how its forces had lost the initiative.

In September, the JIC suggested that to win the war, the IJN and IJA had to 'resist whatever counteroffensive Allies may put up', and 'build up her military machine' in the hope that 'the exhaustion of [Allied] resources would force the latter to sue for a negotiated peace'. The shifting balance of power in the

Pacific, along with Japan's shortage of surplus forces, meant that its strategy had shifted to one aimed to consolidate its outer perimeter. Nevertheless, Japan's waning capabilities did not obscure the scale of effort required.

The turning tide of the conflict, accompanied by evidence that Japan was turning to the defensive, meant that the Allies could begin contemplating a strategy for liberating the western Pacific and Southeast Asia. The IJN and IJA continued to possess ample forces to defend Japan's conquests. While naval sigint began to provide comprehensive information on the IJN's strengths and dispositions, information on the IJA remained patchy for much of 1942 and the early part of 1943, because the army employed a more complicated code system. This created continued difficulties for Allied cryptographers and intelligence staffs. However, the British could deduce that the Japanese armies which had successfully ejected the Allies from the Malay barrier remained unscathed, while British strengths in the Far East had not undergone any substantial increase. The scenario supported the contention that an attempt to dislodge the enemy from its conquests was premature.

The situation was further complicated by the Allies' adherence to the 'Germany First' strategy, which relegated operations against Japan to secondary importance in terms of resource allocations. The COS maintained that the Allies did not possess sufficient strengths for simultaneous operations against both Germany and Japan. Whereas Germany could become invincible if it was allowed to recuperate, the same did not hold true for Japan. The Allies thus needed to focus their efforts on a decisive German defeat, while diverting only the minimum force necessary to hold Japan. The argument that operations against Germany necessitated a limited commitment in the Far East was employed at the highest levels of Allied planning. At the January 1943 Casablanca Conference (*Symbol*), Admiral King, chief of naval operations, argued that while Germany was the prime enemy, the Allies should be prepared to move against Japan after the European war had been won. King suggested that the Allies double the quota for force allocations in the Asia–Pacific theatres from 15 to 30 per cent. Alanbrooke agreed, strictly on the condition that the effort against Germany would not be prejudiced. The decision to continue allocating priority to the European and North African theatres meant that British forces in the Far East were bound to suffer neglect and correspondingly limited capabilities.

British appreciations concerning the practicability of large-scale counteroffensives warned that until numerically superior forces could be deployed, Japan's defensive position was virtually impregnable. On 11 July 1942, the COS met with General Harold Alexander, the commander of British army on the India–Burma front, to discuss Wavell's plans for recapturing Burma during the winter 1942–1943 campaigning season (*Anakim*). The plan called for an assault across the Assam border, accompanied by landings on the west coast.

Wavell had already expressed concerns over the lack of air power and the shortage of aerodromes and communications. Without a clear British numerical superiority, defence planners tended to focus on the problems created by the substantial forces which the Japanese could put up. Alexander was not confident that a landing on the Burma coast was feasible since the British did not possess the resources for such a laborious process. The COS feared the plan committed British forces to extended operations supported by unreliable communications, while the Japanese could easily bring reinforcements from the southern regions. Although Churchill criticized his advisors for basing their assessments on worst-case scenarios, on 12 July, after extensive debates, he conceded, 'unless the Japanese air forces available' are 'cut down below the present level and their military forces cannot be reinforced, we need not commit ourselves to *Anakim*'. At the same time, inaction could only allow Japanese forces to consolidate.

In June 1942, the JPS warned that the defeat of Japan would become progressively more difficult if left too late. Its armed forces would have the opportunity to strengthen the defences of the conquered territories. The most economical strategy was to 'concentrate sufficient force in one area to threaten Japan's vital interests', and attacks on sea communications were the best means to achieve this objective. The COS warned that it was important to seek measures to maintain pressure and thereby prevent the IJN and IJA from developing threats against Allied forward bases. The Allies also had to deal with the possibility of minor offensives against the Southwest Pacific and Indian Ocean areas, as part of a Japanese attempt to disrupt Allied preparations for counterattacks, even though Japan's offensive capabilities had faded.

In August, the IJN and IJA staged a landing on the South Pacific island of Guadalcanal. The aim was to secure a base for conducting attacks on the lifeline between the US west coast and Australia, thereby hindering the Allies' ability to use Australia as a base. The ensuing contest was not a guaranteed victory for the US Navy, which was unable to put up a numerically superior fleet. The IJN also demonstrated a high level of skill at conducting raids during hours of darkness, while US forces remained inept at conducting night engagements. The deadlock was not broken until mid November. Back in London, the JPS estimated the Americans would not achieve parity with the IJN until 1943. Without carrier support, the US Fleet had to remain on the defensive.

On the India–Burma front, the Congress Party passed the 'Quit India' Resolution in August 1942, sparking civil unrest and threatening Britain's hold on its main base for operations against Japan. The prospect of revolution rekindled concerns over the possibility of an invasion, and while Japan had no clear ideas how to exploit the 'Quit India' movement, the unrest came at a time when Congress leader Bose was in Berlin, courting Axis support. Germany never made a firm commitment to the campaign; however, Bose's efforts created the impression that the European Axis powers were seeking to undermine Britain's hold on India, and wished to see Japan attack in the near future. The JIC and India Command warned that Japan possessed sufficient forces for a landing in the Bengal regions, and the operation was most likely to coincide with local disturbances. Although there were no indications that the Japanese considered the prospects of success to be high, it was important to monitor the situation. Evidence of Japan's capabilities for further offensives thus continued to warn that British forces needed to take the necessary precautions.

The twin dilemmas of the shortage of forces for large-scale offensives, and the inherent dangers of staying on the defensive, led the British to conduct limited advances against Japan's outer perimeter. While the strategy of steady attrition reflected a realization of the need to take all possible measures to gradually weaken Japan's defences, it also signified an overestimation of how limited operations could affect the enemy's war effort. In November, the COS decided to dispatch the carrier HMS *Victorious* to the Southwest Pacific Area (SWPA). The move was based on the grounds that the Eastern Fleet's strengths were insufficient to counter a Japanese incursion into the Bay of Bengal, and the carriers could be put to better use if they joined the US counteroffensive in the Pacific. While the US fleet achieved significant progress in pushing back Japan's forces, by the end of 1942, the IJN's defeats at Guadalcanal resulted in a depletion of its strengths, to the point where the *Victorious*' presence was superfluous. Incidentally, the *Victorious* did not engage the Japanese fleet during its entire tour of duty.

Decisions concerning operations on the Burma front revealed a similar lack of vision. In autumn 1942, Wavell concocted a plan to reconquer Japanese outposts in the Arakan regions. The plan stemmed from an oversight of the fact that Japanese armies in the region were well entrenched, and supported by a line of communication that enabled them to bring reinforcements from rear areas at short notice. Against such opponents, limited offensives were unlikely to yield favourable results.

Operational ineptitude played an equally significant role in laying the grounds for Wavell's decision. Prior to the Pacific War, Britain's military involvement in the Far East was confined to policing actions in its colonies. British forces had not conducted campaigns in Southeast Asia which required the provision of substantial forces and logistics. In the expansive jungles of the region, mobility was restricted due to rugged terrain and poor communications. In close country warfare where movement was slow, attacks needed to be conducted on a wide front and accompanied by diversionary moves. Such measures were necessary to prevent the enemy from consolidating, and also to guard against interference with the attacker's communications. Although Wavell realized the inherent dangers, his plan was based on the hope that a rapid advance could secure his objectives. In late August, he informed the COS that he planned an overland advance against Akyab, aimed to bring the Japanese air services into battle and inflicting losses. In addition to depleting enemy air strengths and thereby helping Allied operations in other theatres, the operation also appeared to hold prospects of preparing the way for further operations into Burma, and lessening the threat to India.

In mid September, Wavell justified the operation on the grounds that Japanese army strengths in the frontier regions of Burma were weak, and the IJA was too tied down in the SWPA and China to provide any reinforcements. Although the COS replied that air requirements could not be met, Wavell maintained that risks had to be accepted. Despite their objections that British positions were likely to be untenable, the COS acquiesced. The operations faced further difficulties when diversionary attacks in the form of amphibious landings and long-range penetration operations behind the enemy's positions were scrapped owing to shortages of landing craft and manpower. Thus, the attack was confined to a narrow axis on which British forces faced the risk of being held up and outflanked. The campaign was nonetheless launched on the belief that the attackers could prevail with their preponderance of strength.

While the first Arakan offensive ranked as one of Britain's greatest blunders during the Far Eastern conflict, the decision has to be viewed in light of the fact that adequate precedents for determining the effort required to deal with Japanese defences were lacking. British planning for counteroffensives during the opening year of the conflict reflected the fundamental dilemma which its military planners faced. In short, estimates of the strategic situation only permitted broad conclusions concerning the challenges faced by the Allies. The most effective methods for overcoming enemy opposition could be determined only with the help of adequate firsthand combat experience.

TACTICAL AND TECHNOLOGICAL CAPABILITIES OF JAPAN'S ARMED FORCES

The efficiency demonstrated by Japan's forces during their invasion of Southeast Asia convinced the British to acknowledge their opponent's tactical skill. The failure to hold out against the IJA, IJN and Japanese air services also highlighted how British forces needed to undergo extensive improvements in order to overcome their opponent. As far as the British army in the Far East was concerned, the prevailing opinion was that its tactical skill and discipline were no match for the IJA. In regard to the Royal Navy and RAF the British realized that they could not fight properly without significant steps towards re-equipment and modernization.

Although Japan's reverses during the latter half of 1942 dispelled the contention that its armed forces were invincible, they continued to demonstrate a high level of proficiency. Assessments on Japanese capabilities urged that a considerable level of caution be exercised when engaging the enemy. Most importantly, Allied successes had been entirely in the form of limited advances by US and Australian forces in the South Pacific. Britain's forces in Southeast Asia, on the other hand, remained idle and lacked firsthand experience defeating their adversary. Consequently, while the opening year of the conflict provided reliable indications of the challenges which the British were likely to face at the battlefield level, even at the start of 1943, there remained a great deal of misunderstanding over the tactics and equipment that were needed to overcome the obstacles.

Bureaucratic obstacles also continued to hinder the intelligence machinery. The FECB was forced to relinquish responsibility for handling material on Japanese tactics and technology as its headquarters at Singapore was forced to relocate in the face of invasion, and its activities fell into disarray. The British navy, air force and army began to set up their own intelligence services in the Far East, but their development was slow. The problem stemmed from the absence of an effective staff which could fully utilize the lessons which the British had learned from their defeats. This was especially true within the army. The intelligence directorate at General Headquarters in India had focused its attention on the possibility of a German invasion via the Middle East, and did not acquire a team of Japanese specialists until autumn 1942. Whitehall carried out the bulk of the analysis and dissemination, and its staffs were removed from the front lines. As a result, Japanese capabilities were often exaggerated and weaknesses not fully appreciated.

At the level of dissemination, the more seasoned British staff officers in the Far East found it difficult to educate their subordinates on the lessons they learned, mainly because the rank and file lacked the experience needed to properly apply the information on the battlefield. True, a large number of British and Commonwealth officers who fought in Malaya and Burma ended up in captivity and were unable to share their stories. At the same time, a number of senior personnel, including Wavell and Pownall, did manage to escape. Drawing upon the information compiled from their field officers, they produced a fair number of critical accounts concerning the lessons to be learned. However, for much of 1942, the middle and lower ranks of Britain's armed forces consisted of raw recruits who had little idea of the threat which the Japanese posed, nor could they fully grasp the proper countermeasures they needed to employ. The lack of battle experience meant that the British needed to climb a difficult learning curve before they could develop the capacity to overcome their opponents.

Despite the difficulties, the aftermath of Singapore and Burma saw intelligence staffs and defence planners adopting a more judicious view of Japanese tactics. Due heed was paid to the fact that the Japanese possessed strengths which the British were yet incapable of coping with. For example, the Allies' failure to halt the Japanese amphibious landings in Southeast Asia convinced the British that their enemy exerted a threat which was not to be ignored. B.H. Ashmore, a senior commander on Percival's staff, noted how the Japanese amphibious forces at Kota Baru conducted their landings with little concern for losses, and commenced their inland advance without awaiting reinforcements. The efficiency demonstrated by Japanese amphibious methods was also acknowledged by intelligence staffs as well as the highest sections of the defence establishment. On one hand, the Japanese continued to carry out their landings against minimal resistance, and enjoyed complete security of sea communications, along with naval and air superiority. Because beach defences in Southeast Asia were often nonexistent, the IJA and IJN did not need to conduct opposed operations.

However, as far as the British were concerned, the most noteworthy fact was that Japanese forces were fully capable of achieving their objectives with remarkable efficiency. In March 1942, the War Office propagated the conclusion, 'the suitability of the Japanese landing equipment and the thoroughness of their preparations... largely account for the rapid attainment of the objective with small loss'. Japanese landing parties were likely to prevail in weakly protected areas, no matter how tenaciously the defenders fought.

A report on the experience of American forces in the Far East in March received an 'A' grading, as it provided an accurate account of how Japanese landing operations were preceded by thorough reconnaissance of the beaches and hinterland, enabling amphibious parties to exploit weak spots while bypassing strong-points. Japanese army tactics on land forced similar reassessments. Although the IJA had not been particularly trained for operations in the jungles of Southeast Asia, its unimpeded advances proved that its infantry troops were capable of achieving a high level of mobility in undeveloped terrain. More importantly, the failure to hold out against the Japanese onslaught spawned a general consensus that British and Commonwealth armies possessed a lamentable standard of efficiency.

Experiences in Malaya and Burma proved beyond doubt the IJA's ability to outmanoeuvre British positions. In December, the War Office warned that enemy troops were capable of overcoming any natural obstacle. Scenarios of this nature quickly broke the myth that the jungle acted as a reliable barrier. The aspect which posed the greatest challenge was the IJA's practice of outflanking Allied forces by circumventing the main roads. Ten days following the Japanese landing, Brooke-Popham conceded that in light of the Japanese army's skilful manoeuvring, British forces had few choices apart from withdrawing and consolidating themselves in more tenable positions in southern Malaya. The IJA's tactical skill entailed equally slim hopes for defending Burma. Poor communications had not deterred the Japanese from launching invasions. Hutton, the GOC, concluded that given the IJA's practice of enveloping its opponents and their ability to live on the country without proper maintenance facilities, it was reasonable to assume that the enemy would 'deploy the greatest possible strength' on 'as many approaches as possible'.

Postmortems on the British defeats in Southeast Asia invariably attributed the IJA's successes to its high level of training, and credited the Japanese army as a top-rate force. Wavell cited the Japanese army's practice of fully utilizing 'the primary infantry virtues of marching and fighting', which placed 'minimum reliance on mechanized transport', as one of its key assets. H.P. Thomas, an OBE (Order of the British Empire) from the Indian Army, acknowledged, 'as an Asiatic power, maintaining European standards of efficiency, and at same time operating on Asiatic soil, the Japanese had a great initial advantage'.

The most important lesson drawn from the defeats in Malaya and Burma, however, was that the combat effectiveness of British armies was substandard. The IJA did suffer a number of weaknesses, including a lack of concern for providing reinforcements, and a tendency to underestimate enemy opposition. However, the experiences of defeat forced the British to admit that their own forces faced problems, and had yet to develop the skills needed to exploit their opponent's disadvantages. In contrast to prewar assessments which suggested that the IJA's weaknesses undermined its ability to engage its Western rivals, appraisals following the setbacks in Southeast Asia signified a realization that poorly trained armies were not a match for the IJA. For instance, the British army's traditional method of employing fixed defences was unlikely to work if the positions could be outflanked and were not held with adequate strength. The Japanese success in carrying out infiltration movements showed how the defenders needed to conduct an aggressive patrol of their surroundings, and in situations where poor communications restricted mobility, the proper use of infantry was vital. Jungle warfare was a 'matter for feet rather than wheels', and Japanese troops clearly demonstrated their skill. They wore rubber belts which could be inflated for use as river transport, and used captured bicycles for transport.

British troops, on the other hand, depended on motor transport, and hesitated to march through the jungle by foot. This characteristic rendered them incapable of countering the IJA's rapid movements. Major-General H.G. Bennett, commander of the Australian forces, alleged that British empire commanders suffered a 'retreat complex'. As a result, the slightest Japanese attack was enough to compel defenders to abandon their positions. The development of adequate countermeasures against the Japanese not only entailed an alteration of methods. Equally important was to reassess the quality of troop training within the British army. Commanders in the Far East conceded that their failures were due to a prevailing lack of discipline. Pownall pondered upon the British soldier's dependence on creature comforts and aversion to strenuous work, both of which gave rise to a situation where training was conducted without preparing troops for battle conditions. Brooke-Popham acknowledged that a key feature which enhanced the IJA's efficiency was the way in which its indoctrination programme aimed to instil sentiments of hatred for the enemy, whereas British troops were not exposed to such types of instruction.

British army commanders made urgent demands for measures to instil a more aggressive attitude among soldiers. Reflecting upon lessons drawn from encounters with the IJA, Wavell warned that British soldiers needed to overcome their fears of long periods of isolation in the jungle and the disorientation caused by the enemy's deception methods. Field commanders in the Far East insisted that troops needed to develop individual initiative. Upon taking command of the 15th Corps in autumn 1942, Slim set up a programme at his headquarters in Ranchi to train infantry units to hold their ground in the face of the enemy's encirclement and surprise tactics. The IJN's establishment of superiority in Southeast Asia and the western Pacific led to reassessments similar to those which took place regarding the IJA. Encounters in Southeast Asia provided visible proof that the technology onboard Japanese capital ships and auxiliary vessels was top quality, while training among naval crews was high.

Japanese capital ships were proficient at delivering fire over extended distances and outranging their Allied opponents. This achievement owed itself largely to the fact that for much of the interwar period, the IJN's doctrine was fixated on securing its decisive victory by fighting a surface action along the lines of Tsushima. The Gunnery and Antiaircraft Warfare Division was aware of the extensive efforts which the IJN had made to equip its fleet with improved guns and stressed that, although there was no information regarding recent progress, there was 'no reason why they [the Japanese] should not be superior' in long-range direct fire and medium-range blind fire. In light of the IJN's effective performance, the Admiralty was compelled to acknowledge the strong possibility that British vessels needed extensive modernization before they could stand up to their opponents. Capital ships had to be refitted with radio direction-finding equipment and longer-range guns if they were to possess adequate firepower and accuracy. Objections against the operation of the battleship *Malaya* with Somerville's main fleet for the defence of waters adjacent to Ceylon were based on the grounds that it possessed low endurance and limited gun range, and only the most modern ships could engage a concentration of Japanese vessels.

Naval operations also had to be undertaken by crews with adequate training. In February 1942, Somerville minuted to Pound that operations in the Far East needed to be commanded by flag officers who were well informed on gunnery matters. Assessments of Japan's air services also revealed how combat experiences provided the British with unquestionable signs that the enemy's performance posed a formidable contest. Japanese fighter aircraft demonstrated a high standard of manoeuvrability and an ability to undertake both coordinated and independent attacks against ground targets. The Air Ministry's praise for enemy fighters was clearly reflected in a report on the Zero, titled 'a formidable fighter'. The comment was based on inspections of downed aircraft, which revealed a high engine output and fuel capacity. Findings of this nature quickly dispelled the notion that the Japanese were unable to produce aircraft that could match their Western rivals.

The failure to provide adequate defences against the JAF led both intelligence staffs and air commanders to reconsider whether their opponent's weaknesses justified complacency. The Air Ministry continued to emphasize shortcomings by noting how the Japanese used a number of obsolete aircraft in Malaya. British commanders in the Far East took a less condescending view, and realized that and Allies were defenceless unless they remedied their own weaknesses, namely numerical inferiority and poor efficiency in the air. Wavell concluded that the JAF's successes in Southeast Asia were largely due to its establishment of local air superiority. While Japanese fighter aircraft raised concern, British reactions to the IJN's air arm was one of alarm. The sinking of the *Repulse* and *Prince of Wales* demonstrated the exceptional skill of Japanese torpedo bombers. Within a week after the capital ships were lost, the Air Ministry observed, 'recent spectacular results... indicate that intensive training and practice have been carried out'. The aircraft involved was the Mitsubishi T-96, whose aiming was described as 'very accurate'. The accuracy of Japanese attacks against naval targets also highlighted the necessity of bolstering the antiaircraft (AA) defences onboard British vessels. During the interwar period, the Admiralty did not fully grasp the extent to which aircraft could develop the range and striking power to attack capital ships in the high seas. The result was a misperception regarding the types of vessels the Royal Navy would have to operate when confronting the Japanese. Because Britain's war plans in the Far East before December 1941 had been based on the assumption that the main fleet would operate under the cover of aircraft based in the Malay peninsula, the Admiralty adhered to its belief that the battleship was the centrepiece of its strategy. As a result, little attention was paid to the need to develop carrier tactics. Experiments during the interwar period also revealed that fighters were incapable of providing full protection. Naval officers concluded that AA cover provided the most reliable defence, with supporting aircraft filling the gaps. When adequate fighter cover was unavailable, ships were vulnerable against determined attacks.

The Royal Navy's AA capabilities were further handicapped by its lack of the resources and technology needed to develop accurate fire control systems. The devastation inflicted on Force Z gave rise to a dramatic rethinking about the threat which air attacks could pose. The incident demonstrated not only that aircraft had become a highly effective naval weapon, but that the Japanese had developed it beyond all expectations. The terms of reference for the enquiry into the sinking of the *Repulse* and *Prince of Wales* explicitly stated that the main objective was to review the circumstances attending the loss of capital ships since the beginning of the war. In order to do so, it was of the utmost importance to consider the measures to be investigated or pursued, with 'the intent to improve the defence of British warships against existing or anticipated enemy weapons'. During the IJN's attacks on Ceylon in April 1942, its air arm managed to sink a number of British vessels, including the light carrier HMS *Hermes*, as well as the heavy cruisers *Dorsetshire* and *Cornwall*. The encounter reinforced British views that Japanese pilots and aircraft possessed a high standard of efficiency, while acting as a reminder that British vessels needed to be equipped with the most up-to-date radar and AA guns. Naval commanders in the Eastern Fleet were overawed by the force and precision of Japanese naval aircraft. The captain of the *Dorsetshire* was impressed with the way in which enemy pilots overcame British AA defences by exploiting blind spots. The captain of the *Hermes* commented that the attack on his ship was carried out 'perfectly, relentlessly and quite fearlessly... '. Within the Admiralty, opinions did not show the same level of trepidation; however, the incident reinforced the view that Japanese methods and technology were commendable. The Director of the Naval Air Division (DNAD) commented that the degree of accuracy achieved by the Japanese 'could only be obtained by highly trained personnel'. The Director of Gunnery and AA Fire (DGF) noted how ships possessing inadequate armament and lacking proper radio direction finding and gunnery ranging sets had 'little chance of survival against massed air attack'. All ships destined for the Far East had to be equipped with the most updated material before setting off.

At the same time, efforts to provide adequate protection for seagoing vessels were complicated because British fighters such as the *Seafire* were too heavy for carrier-based operations, while the performance of aircraft with lighter designs such as the *Hurricane* could not compete with the Zero. The production of the *Barracuda* fighter, which had the right combination of speed, manoeuvrability and weight, had faced delays. Upon realizing that the British did not possess adequate fighters, Churchill lodged urgent requests to Roosevelt for the loan of suitable American aircraft. The JAF's demonstration of its capabilities was not only taken as a reason to reassess the enemy. More importantly, the British realized that their forces were in need of extensive improvement.

The turn of the tide against Japan's armed forces during the latter half of 1942 dispelled apprehensions insofar as to prove that the enemy could be defeated at the tactical level. The IJA, IJN and air services continued to demonstrate skills that urged wariness. In addition, because the Allies had yet to acquire sufficient experience, precedents for gauging the effort required for success were patchy. To further complicate matters, British forces in Southeast Asia remained largely inactive for the latter part of 1942. Intelligence was thus mainly derived from reports on US and Australian operations in the Pacific theatres. The information did not permit accurate appraisals as to whether the British had developed the capabilities necessary to confront their opponent. Assessments on the matter revealed continued unease as well as a lack of understanding of the appropriate methods for defeating the Japanese.

On the ground, the Allied successes in New Guinea and the Solomons during autumn 1942 proved that the IJA was not invincible. However, in both offensive and defensive operations, its performance continued to reveal competence. Accounts of US and Australian encounters in the South Pacific urged due caution.

In the South Pacific, the IJA continued to demonstrate their proficiency, while US ground forces were 'poorly prepared for what they had to face'. American soldiers, while high in morale, were not trained to conduct the battles of attrition they faced at Guadalcanal and New Guinea. Although Australian soldiers were trained by officers who had battlefield experience from the 1914–1918 conflict, their performance showed room for improvement.

The Japanese army's offensive operations continued to demonstrate their expertise at surprise moves. Engagements on the Kokoda Trail in New Guinea showed the enemy's adeptness at deploying infiltrators to encircle Allied positions, often using jungle cover to conceal their presence so that the defenders could not notice. At the same time, Allied troops proved highly adaptable, and displayed ingenuity. The Americans and Australians managed to repel their attackers with increased frequency. Intelligence bulletins and field manuals thereafter highlighted a number of Japanese weaknesses that could be exploited. The War Office concluded that although enemy soldiers were skilful at conducting surprise moves, their success depended on catching opponents off guard. A chapter in the

Handbook of the Japanese Army (*HJA*) in December 1942 pointed out that the tenacity with which the Japanese conducted their envelopment tactics frequently gave false impressions of their strength, and enabled the attackers to overcome considerably larger forces than their own. Combat experience also revealed that so long as the defending forces undertook a number of basic countermeasures, Japanese assaults could be repelled.

A meticulous reconnaissance of the environs was important. At Milne Bay, US marines deployed scouts against enemy night attacks. The parties prepared to meet the Japanese onslaught, and the ensuing encounter often threw the enemy off balance. Such developments dispelled the view that Japanese forces were formidable in the attack.

However, British forces had yet to prove their capabilities, and needed to practice due caution against the obstacles likely to be encountered. A chapter in the *HJA*, based on observations in New Guinea and Guadalcanal, summed up the situation: 'Defence against Japanese attacks must be principally against infiltration. It must be organized with strong points properly adapted to terrain features. If possible, they should [provide] all round defence'.

Positions had to be protected with barbed wire and landmines, while intervals were to be covered by strong automatic fire. Most importantly, defending troops needed to fight without becoming panic stricken by enemy attacks. Evidence of the IJA's weaknesses therefore did not obscure the arduous effort required to defeat it.

Intelligence on the IJA's defensive capabilities gave equally few reasons to alleviate images of a resilient opponent. Allied encounters during the Solomons campaign quickly disproved the preconception that the IJA's lack of experience rendered its defensive operations ineffective. Experiences in the SWPA gave rise to the conclusion that the Japanese army was capable of inflicting significant delay and attrition on its attackers. Positions were made to provide all-round fields of fire and maximum protection from bombardment. Defences were laid out so as to create systems of mutually supporting bunkers, using whatever materials were available.

The War Office disseminated an account of enemy fortifications at Buna and Sanananda in New Guinea, describing them as 'simple, but effective'. Significantly enough, without visible indications of deficiencies open to exploitation, assessments focused on the obstacles arising from the IJA's proficiency. For example, JIC appreciations and intelligence bulletins reinforced the contention that the IJA was a difficult adversary, regardless of whether the Allies achieved numerical superiority.

A section in the *Handbook of the Japanese Army* in February 1943 exhaustively described how experiences in the Pacific had highlighted the need for thorough preparations against camouflage, surprise methods, counterattacks and defences prepared in depth.

For British field commanders, the absence of sufficient combat experience tended to result in a misperception of how to surmount the challenges, in spite of their awareness that Japanese defences were difficult to reduce. After the Eastern Army was established in autumn 1942, field officers attempted to learn how to overcome the IJA, but their efforts encountered a number of initial setbacks. The problem stemmed from a habit which prevailed within the British Army, namely an undue dependence upon overwhelming firepower to neutralize enemy forces. The practice was a byproduct of the carnage suffered in the trenches on the Western Front during the Great War, which gave rise to an accepted belief that assaults against prepared positions could only result in mass casualties.

While the doctrine of relying upon heavy weaponry aimed to avoid excessive losses, it had the unfortunate result of rendering British commanders slow to grasp the need to fight a combined arms battle, which was crucial when engaging a well-entrenched opponent. Enemy defences needed to be neutralized through a combination of artillery fire, aerial bombardment and armoured attacks, while ground troops mopped up the remnants of enemy resistance. The Eastern Army was certainly not alone in facing difficulties in scaling the tactical learning curve. Following the defeat at Dunkirk, British field officers in the home army and North Africa upheld the belief that heavy weaponry alone could overcome the Germans, and the misunderstanding resulted in further setbacks during the early phases of the desert campaign.

Indeed, one of the British Army's greatest shortcomings during its campaigns against the *Wehrmacht* was the absence of a uniform doctrine for combined arms tactics. Infantry units suffered excessive casualties because they were not trained to manoeuvre against enemy positions unless the defending forces had been completely neutralized.

Although British forces in the Far East eventually achieved a higher standard of efficiency than their counterparts in Europe and North Africa, the Eastern Army's experience during the opening stages of the Burma campaign reveals parallels. While the defeats in Malaya and Burma exposed the deficiencies British armies had suffered in defensive operations, precedents for planning counteroffensives against the IJA were nonexistent.

The Japanese invasion of Malaya and Burma clearly highlighted how the skilful use of infantry often had a decisive effect on the outcome of battles in jungle conditions, where poor communications and the prevalence of natural obstacles restricted the use of heavy weapons.

However, appreciations on the lessons to be drawn from the Allied setbacks were prepared at a time when Britain's immediate objective was to forestall further Japanese advances. Even in the autumn of 1942, when British forces began to recover from the shock brought about by their defeats, commanders had not had enough time to come to grips with the lessons to be drawn from the IJA's operations.

The situation was further complicated by a lack of experience involving operations in jungle terrain, which in turn created difficulties in grasping the methods which the British needed to employ. Throughout the interwar period, the garrison in India remained committed to its traditional role of acting as a police force against local disturbances in areas such as the Northwest Frontier. Training was focused on mountain warfare against weakly defended guerrilla forces. Insofar as foreign invasions were concerned, the scenarios which raised the most concern were a German or Soviet advance via Afghanistan and Persia. Consequently, minimal efforts were made to prepare troops for operations in the jungles of Burma. British field officers were thus forced to concoct tactics for unfamiliar battlefield conditions. Any lessons which staff officers did learn from the early phases of the war were not enforced upon troops. The Directorate of Military Training did not commence creating a uniform doctrine in its manuals until autumn 1942. The absence of communication between the SWPA and India regarding the lessons that had been obtained during operations in New Guinea and the Solomons also negated the prospects of obtaining the necessary information.

The tactics employed during the first Arakan campaign of winter 1942– 1943 illustrated the dilemmas facing the British. While army commanders were aware of the dangers posed by the IJA's resilience, they did not comprehend the necessary countermeasures. The Eastern Army's decision to advance down the Mayu Peninsula in November 1942 was made on the assumption that the Japanese soldier's tenacity could be overcome by artillery fire and tank support. The stalling of the advance at Donbaik and Rathedaung during early January 1943 revealed how Japanese bunkers were impervious to bombardment. Following this, Wavell ordered Noel Irwin, the GOC of the Eastern Army, to launch a second attack on the peninsula, on the assumption that with a fresh British brigade and improved covering fire, enemy defences could be neutralized. Irwin and Lloyd, the GOC 14th Indian Division, executed the operation on the same conjecture.

That British commanders based their plans on a faulty understanding of the tactics necessary to defeat the IJA, rather than an ignorance of the challenges their troops faced, is also illustrated by documentary evidence. In their correspondence between January and March 1943, Wavell and Irwin clearly stated that one of the main purposes of the operation was to acquire valuable experience of Japanese methods, which could allow for future successes.

Reminiscing upon the first Arakan campaign, Wavell admitted that while the difficulties of launching the operations without properly trained troops had been realized, he miscalculated how numerical superiority and a rapid advance could help his forces attain their objectives. The decisions leading up to the first Arakan offensive therefore illuminate how evidence pointing to the IJA's strengths could rarely provide accurate information on how to defeat the enemy. In the absence of combat experience, the evidence was open to various interpretations. The development of appropriate methods could take place only through experimentation.

In regard to the IJN, the shortage of information, compounded by the Eastern Fleet's lack of engagements, rendered accurate assessments virtually impossible. Naval intelligence continued to be a grey area. As late as December 1942, evidence was obtained primarily from US sources, which provided little beyond rough figures on Japan's naval construction. The shortage of reliable intelligence precluded accurate estimates.

For example, when Churchill ordered an enquiry into the reasons why Japanese carriers were able to hold more aircraft than their British counterparts, Pound was unable to go further than to suggest that the actual tonnage was probably greater than disclosed. The situation was further complicated because of the continued shortage of firsthand encounters between the Royal Navy and the IJN. An example of this dilemma arose in June, when the Admiralty disseminated possible methods of countering enemy submarines. The recommendations were accompanied by what amounted to a disclaimer that the report represented only the opinion of US commanders. In the absence of combat experience, the available intelligence could not provide a clear picture of the IJN's capabilities against its British counterpart. Naval intelligence staffs hesitated to suggest that Japanese vessels possessed shortcomings open to exploitation, and were more likely to highlight evidence of the IJN's proficiency.

In the air, as late as the end of 1942, the available intelligence was thin on signs of weaknesses likely to hamper the JAF's ability to challenge its British counterparts. Owing to the RAF's relative inactivity following the defeats in Southeast Asia, information was primarily derived from accounts of Allied operations in the Pacific. Accurate evaluations continued to be hindered by the lack of data. Information on crucial aspects, such as the production of new prototypes, was scanty. Optimism was further precluded by continued indications that Japanese pilots and aircraft were capable of putting up a serious challenge. Commenting on the Battle of Midway, the DNAD noted how American fighters were particularly vulnerable owing to their practice of conducting individual attacks on enemy bombers. This practice enabled the Zero pilots to take advantage of their aircraft's manoeuvrability, and pursue planes flying out of formation.

When the Allies began to bolster their airpower in the South Pacific during autumn 1942, they did not immediately establish air superiority. According to Eric Bergerud, 'for most of the time between spring 1942 and winter 1943–1944, neither side was completely dominant'.

Because the topof- the-line US fighters were dispatched to Europe and North Africa, Allied air forces in the Pacific consisted mainly of P-39s, whose manoeuvrability, range and speed were inferior to the Zero. Only when the more advanced fighters of the US air fleet, such as the F4F *Wildcat*, P-51 *Mustang*, P-47 *Thunderbolt* and *Corsair*, were dispatched to the South Pacific in large numbers during late 1942, did the balance begin to gradually shift against the Japanese. The situation demanded due caution in assessing enemy capabilities. In December, the Air Ministry propagated an account of US encounters in Guadalcanal. US aircraft 'could not stay with [the Zero] at all and dog fight at any altitude'. Japanese pilots were highly trained, and aircraft output had kept pace with losses. The only source of comfort was that intensified battles were likely to take a heavier toll on the enemy.

The RAF's ability to confront its Japanese counterpart was also questionable. In the absence of significant successes, the most notable feature was likely to be the high level of efficiency the enemy had demonstrated during the onset of the conflict. Pilots arriving in the Far East were inducted with tales by veterans who had confronted the JAF in the skies over Malaya, Burma and Ceylon. They almost invariably emphasized how enemy aircraft were manoeuvrable, and described Japanese tactics as 'excellent'. Any indications of the JAF's weaknesses had to be viewed alongside the fact that British pilots and aircraft in the Far Eastern theatres had yet to equal their opponent.

10

Strategic Planning for Military Technology

The Joint Capabilities Integration and Development System (JCIDS). The JCIDS, required by the Chairman of the Joint Chiefs of Staff Instruction (CJCSI) 3170.01C, provides an integrated, collaborative process for developing new warfighting capabilities through changes to doctrine, organization, training and education, materiel, leadership, personnel, and/or facilities (DOTMLPF). Manpower officials shall help identify DOTMLPF solutions to operational deficiencies. If a materiel solution is required, manpower officials shall work with other Defence officials to identify which concepts and technologies can be developed into affordable Defence acquisition systems. During the JCIDS staffing process, DoD Component manpower officials shall comment on the adequacy of the capabilities documents and Key Performance Parameters (KPPs).

Because of the interrelationship of manpower, personnel and training requirements, manpower officials shall confer with Program Managers (PMs) of Defence acquisition programs and personnel and training officials to ensure that materiel solutions are affordable from a manpower perspective, maximize use of human resources, and help solve or, at a minimum, do not exacerbate systemic manpower, personnel, and training problems.

Threat Changes and Operational Risk. As required by section 153(a)(3)(C) of title 10, U.S.C., the Chairman of the JCS shall advise the Secretary of Defence of critical deficiencies and strengths in force capabilities (to include manpower) identified during the preparation and review of contingency plans (CONPLANS). Combatant Commanders shall assess threat changes and determine whether the manpower policies of the armed forces support changing strategic plans and whether the planned number of non-combatants in theatre during a conflict is appropriate for the threat-level and situation.

As required by DoD Instruction 3020.37, Commanders shall assess the probability that private sector contractors will continue to perform critical support services during a mobilization or war.

If there are concerns about non-performance or inappropriate risks, Commanders shall prepare contingency plans for obtaining the essential services from another source. These determinations shall be made in conjunction with manpower and contract officials, as appropriate, to ensure the work can be converted to another category of manpower or to another private sector contractor.

STRATEGIC PLANNING FOR DEFENCE ACQUISITION PROGRAMS

Consistent with DoD Directive 5000.1, DoD Components shall plan acquisition programs based on realistic projections of the resources (funds and manpower) likely to be available in future years. Manpower officials are responsible for assessing program affordability from a military end strength (ES) and civilian full-time equivalent (FTE) perspective. Preliminary assessments of manpower affordability shall be based on (1) long-range forecasts of the Defence workforce; (2) plans for retirement or transfer of "predecessor" systems; (3) broad estimates of the manpower required for the new capability; (4) Congressional constraints placed on military ES and civilian FTEs; and, (5) restrictions placed on resources for special programs, such as resources "fenced" for the National Foreign Intelligence Program (NFIP). If out-year projections indicate there will be significant shortfalls, manpower officials shall work with other Defence officials to determine what resources the DoD Component will invest to operate, maintain, support, train, and dispose of the system. These determinations shall consider all available information—e.g., priority of the new system, possible trade-offs for manpower in lower priority programs, and program goals set for comparable systems and capabilities.

Manpower Estimates (MEs)

MEs for Defence acquisition programs shall be approved by the DoD Component manpower authority, or designee. Manpower affordability shall build on preliminary judgments of program affordability made during the JCIDS process. However, MEs shall provide more detailed assessments of the manpower required for the new system and for the retired or replaced "predecessor" systems. In all cases, judgments about manpower affordability shall be consistent with information reported in the ME. Also, since manpower costs (both direct and indirect) are often major contributors to total ownership costs, the MEs shall be used to inform the Independent Cost Estimates (ICEs) and other cost estimates required by DoD Instruction 5000.2.

Consistent with DoD Instruction 5000.2, DoD Components shall establish program objectives and thresholds for a minimum number of cost, schedule, and performance parameters for Defence acquisition programs.

As directed in DoD Instruction 5000.2, cost parameters shall be established for system life cycle costs or, if available, total ownership costs. The user representatives shall assess system affordability when establishing these requirements. Because manpower can be a major determinant of program costs and affordability, manpower parameters should be established in the Capability Development Documents (CDDs). When there are critical manpower or skill requirements that warrant a key performance parameter (KPP), the KPP should be established in the CDD and reflected in the Acquisition Program Baseline (APB). Manpower goals and parameters shall be based on manpower analyses and studies and established to ensure that:

(1) design options that reduce workload and are essential for ensuring program affordability are pursued and not passed-over in favour of other lesser priority design features; (2) ownership costs and manpower are kept at desired levels; and, (3) future-year resources designated for other higher priority programs are preserved.

Performance parameters are established to ensure systems are designed and developed to provide an operationally useful capability. Performance parameters in the CDD, such as reliability, availability, and maintainability (RAM) rates and operating tempos, shall be used to establish the manpower requirements and directly link them to operational requirements. This linkage is critical to readiness reporting, mobilization planning, and programming/budgeting.

Human Systems Integration (HSI)

Acquisition policy in DoD Directive 5000.1 stresses the importance of a "total system" approach. HSI focuses on the human component of the total system by addressing and integrating requirements for manpower, personnel, training, human factors, occupational health, safety, habitability, and personnel survivability. Since all aspects of HSI are interdependent, PMs are encouraged to establish HSI Integrated Product Teams (IPTs) to support the Defence acquisition process and ensure that, as trade-offs are made, systems are designed to optimize total system performance, minimize total ownership costs, and accommodate the characteristics of the population that will operate, maintain, and support the system.

Manpower officials shall participate in the Defence acquisition process and work with personnel officials and human factors engineers to ensure that PMs pursue engineering designs that minimize manpower and control increases to skill requirements. Consistent with guidance in DoD Instruction 5000.2, PMs are required to ensure human factors engineering/cognitive engineering is employed during system design to provide for effective human-machine interfaces and assure systems are built to meet the parameters in the capabilities documents and KPPs in the APBs. Manpower and personnel officials shall assist PMs with identifying and eliminating system design characteristics that require excessive cognitive, physical, or sensory skills or workload intensive tasks.

Training and safety and occupational health hazards contribute directly to manpower in the Individuals Account and time away from work. Consistent with guidance in DoD Instruction 5000.2, PMs are required to consult with the training community to develop options for individual, collective, and joint training with special emphasis on alternatives that enhance user capabilities, maintain skill proficiencies, and reduce individual and collective training times. PMs are also required to address habitability issues, prevent environmental, safety, and occupational health (ESOH) hazards, or manage these hazards when they cannot be avoided. Manpower officials shall assist both communities and the PM with identifying design options that minimize training time and ESOH hazards so that manpower and time away from work are kept to a minimum.

Long-Range Forecasts of Defence Manpower

Manpower officials shall develop comprehensive, long-range forecasts of Defence manpower to assist with strategic planning following the procedures at enclosure 2. These forecasts shall project manpower and contract support far enough into the future and provide information in enough detail to assist:

Principal Staff Assistants and other Defence officials with: (1) maintaining oversight of the Defence workforce; (2) developing strategic plans for human resources and Training Transformation Strategic Plans; and, (3) assessing the affordability of alternative concepts and technologies for future joint warfighting capabilities;

The Joint Staff with determining the extent to which the major programs and policies of the armed forces in the area of manpower conform to the strategic plans as required by title 10, U.S.C.;

Manpower mobilization planners with calculating wartime demand and supply to support mobilization planning and programming and estimating potential wartime casualties based on the number of military, civilian, and contract personnel exposed to hostile fire and collateral damage;

Training and personnel officials with maintaining oversight of planned changes to skill requirements so they can revise training and education programs and restructure career fields to accommodate the future needs of the Department; and,

Manpower authorities with: (1) establishing the availability of manpower resources in future years; (2) addressing the affordability of acquisition programs from a military ES and civilian FTE perspective; and (3) identifying, minimizing and, if possible, eliminating critical out-year shortfalls.

RESPONSIBILITIES

The Deputy Under Secretary of Defence (Civilian Personnel Policy) shall provide civilian personnel policies to facilitate detailing, reassignment, or relocation of civilian personnel not needed by one DoD Component to satisfy the critical workload of another DoD Component.

The Assistant Secretary of Defence (Health Affairs) shall, in support of mobilization planning, facilitate reassignment of military medical personnel in excess of the materiel or facility capabilities of one Military Department to the medical facilities of another Military Department, as practical.

STRATEGIC PLANNING FOR RESTRUCTURING THE DEFENCE WORKFORCE

Structuring Career Fields and Developing Critical Expertise. Manpower, personnel, and training officials shall confer to ensure manpower, training programs, and career fields are structured to: (1) support the vesting of title 10, U.S.C., functions, powers, and duties; (2) support the delegation of management responsibilities and approval authorities; (3) provide for career development of both military and civilian personnel; and, (4) keep manpower, personnel, and training requirements at a level to efficiently and effectively accomplish the mission.

Development of Military and Civilian Expertise. Defence manpower, shall be designated, and training and career fields structured, according to the roles and responsibilities assigned to each category of personnel—civilian and military. As a rule, civilian knowledge and facility shall be developed to engender a "profession of governance;" whereas, military knowledge and skills shall be developed to engender a "profession of arms." Manpower shall be designated as civilian to: (1) assist in maintaining civilian authority, direction, and control over the DoD as required by section 401 of title 50, U.S.C.; (2) develop management and leadership skills; (3) provide technical advice and counsel to support civilian governance of the DoD; and, (4) accomplish civilian essential line functions. Manpower shall be designated as military to: (1) maintain military command and control of combat and crisis operations; (2) develop command and leadership skills; (3) provide military advice and counsel to support civilian governance of the DoD; and, (4) accomplish military essential line functions. Career fields for both civilian and military shall: complement but not duplicate or compete with each other; provide for career progression for both categories of personnel; and, avoid over-specialization and excessive training.

Designations for Career Development

It is Department policy to indoctrinate new recruits for military service through initial training and to provide education, training, and developmental assignments for critical technical and leadership skills (military and civilian) that cannot be obtained directly from the private sector. Personnel and training officials shall assess new missions and evolving technologies to determine whether new or additional training, education, or experience will be needed to cultivate the required skills and expertise. Manpower officials must be advised if career development positions are needed to produce an adequate pool of candidates for each ascending level of proficiency or leadership. All such positions shall be part of an approved career development program. However, personnel officials shall ensure manpower requirements for career development positions are held to a minimum by combining occupational specialties and restructuring grade requirements to narrow career ladders whenever possible.

Designations for Rotation Base

It is Department policy to provide for the rotation of civilian career-conditional and career employees assigned outside the United States consistent with section 1586 of title 10, U.S.C., and to maximize stability of military assignments and minimize personnel and unit turbulence caused by excessive permanent change of station (PCS) moves consistent with DoD Directive 1315.7. Accordingly, personnel officials shall review how changes in force structure and unit/ship deployments affect overseas and sea-to-shore assignments.

If there is turbulence detrimental to unit or personnel readiness or service member quality of life, personnel officials shall confer with manpower authorities concerning the size of the rotation base. Manpower necessary for maintaining a rotation base to support an equitable assignment system for overseas and sea-to-shore assignments shall be determined by civilian series and military occupational specialty using a formal process that considers assignment, rotation, and career development policies and military time on station (TOS) goals.

Additional Manpower for Career Progression and Rotation

If there are insufficient positions for military career progression or rotation, manpower authorities shall convert civilian manpower with related skills and grades to military performance except if: (1) civilian incumbency is required by law; (2) the manpower is designated as "key;" or, (3) the manpower is required for civilian career progression or rotation.

If there is insufficient civilian manpower available for conversion to military performance, or if additional civilian positions are needed for rotation or career progression, manpower authorities shall convert contracted services in similar skills and grade-levels to civilian or military performance to meet these requirements. Once converted, this manpower shall be designated for career progression or rotation to ensure it is not inadvertently identified for conversion or elimination.

STRATEGIC PLANNING FOR TRANSFORMATION OF BUSINESS PRACTICES AND ORGANIZATIONS

As missions, priorities, and technologies change and Principal Staff Assistants and functional managers develop plans to transform business practices; restructure organizations; transfer, privatize, or contract activities; or, divest non-core functions; manpower officials shall be consulted concerning manpower adjustments. Manpower officials shall assess how plans for transforming or reengineering roles, missions, and management strategies will affect workloads or alter the lines of authority, span of control, or delegated management responsibilities and require a change to the manpower.

MANPOWER MOBILIZATION AND CRISIS PLANNING

DoD Components shall develop mobilization and crisis planning systems that support the military objectives of the Department. Manpower mobilization planning shall be conducted in consonance with operation planning and shall be flexible, responsive, and adaptive to management changes and emergency situations.

The objective of manpower mobilization and crisis planning shall be to provide reasonable assurance that: (1) manpower in the military forces is programmed at levels necessary to provide needed capabilities in the shortest (most demanding) timeline required by the war plans; and, (2) sufficient military and civilian manpower with the requisite knowledge, skills and abilities (KSAs) are available in the infrastructure, Individuals Account, and Reserve Component, or can be recruited or contracted to meet all mobilization and wartime demands. The manpower mobilization and crisis planning process must provide a range of phased, incremental improvements in force readiness, deployment capability, and sustainability necessary to support JCS approved operation plans (OPLANS), contingency plans (CONPLANS), and CONUS sustaining missions.

The Strategic Planning Guidance, Contingency Planning Guidance, and Unified Command Plan provide strategic guidance, contingency taskings, and force listings for Combatant Commanders. Based on this guidance, Combatant commanders prepare OPLANS and/or CONPLANS, some of which are supported by the time-phased force deployment data (TPFDD) file. Wartime demands—i.e., manpower resources that are needed for a full mobilization and war and to provide filler and replacement personnel for losses sustained over the course of a conflict—shall be determined consistent with the JCS joint operation planning system and the wartime manpower planning systems of the Services.

Planning Process

Manpower authorities shall use a process that has been formally approved by the DoD Component for determining wartime demands consistent with DoD Directive 1100.18 and DoD Instruction 1100.19. Mobilization planners shall: (1) identify wartime demands by quantity, grade, and skill; (2) identify overages and shortages that result when the Department transitions from peacetime to wartime operations; (3) develop plans for realigning available resources to meet the most urgent needs; and, (4) address serious shortfalls during the PPBES process that cannot be offset from other sources. Because a mobilization can expand the military forces beyond the programmed force structure, manpower authorities shall consider the entire wartime demand when making these determinations.

Consistent with DoD Directive 1100.18 and DoD Instruction 1400.32, DoD Components shall ensure that civilian and military personnel inventories are sufficient to meet critical wartime demands. If there are insufficient civilian and military personnel with the requisite knowledge, skills, and grades for critical wartime assignments, manpower authorities shall undertake corrective action.

During peacetime, mobilization planners shall identify and plan to defer or curtail programs and tasks not essential to military contingencies or emergency situations and plan to transfer the associated personnel to higher priority tasks. Manpower officials shall work with personnel and training officials to provide for the efficient and expedient use of these resources by designating the manpower for wartime assignments and, if appropriate, cross-training the personnel for their wartime responsibilities.

Emergency-essential (E-E) manpower for critical support services shall be designated as "key" consistent with the guidance in DoD Directive 1200.7 to ensure the manpower is not identified for conversion or elimination and to ensure the positions are not filled by Ready Reservists that can be called to Active duty.

Civilian manpower in infrastructure activities that provide continuity of operations during a mobilization, contingency, or war shall be designated as "key" consistent with the guidance in DoD Directive 1200.7 to ensure the manpower is not identified for conversion or elimination and to ensure the positions are not filled by Ready Reservists that can be called to Active duty.

If there are Active military personnel that are needed in the operating forces during a mobilization or war that cannot be fully utilized or properly trained in the operating forces during peacetime (such as with medical personnel), DoD Components shall consider cost-effective alternatives. They shall first consider whether members of the Ready Reserve can be used or if conversion to civilian or private sector performance is appropriate. If Active military personnel are required, DoD Components shall assign the military to infrastructure activities during peacetime where they can develop their skills while remaining available in the event of a war or other emergency. If there are insufficient military positions for these assignments, manpower authorities shall convert civilian manpower with related skills and grades to military performance except if: (1) civilian incumbency is required by law; (2) the civilian manpower is designated as "key;" or, (3) the manpower is designated for civilian career progression or rotation. If there is insufficient civilian manpower available for conversion to military performance, manpower authorities shall convert contracted services to military performance to meet these requirements consistent with the DoD Component's manpower policies. In all cases, these conversions must be in activities that enable military personnel to develop or remain proficient in skills required by their wartime assignments. Once converted, this manpower shall be designated for wartime assignments to ensure it is not inadvertently identified for conversion or elimination.

Manpower authorities shall plan to augment infrastructure activities that have critical missions that expand during a mobilization or war with surplus personnel from activities that are deferred or curtailed, non-unit Reservists, recalled retirees, volunteers, or contingency contracts, as appropriate. Manpower authorities shall plan to back-fill positions in the infrastructure that are vacated by E-E civilians and Active military who have wartime assignments in the operating forces with surplus personnel from other areas, non-unit Reservists, recalled retirees, or volunteers provided the positions are critical to a mobilization, military contingency, or war. Contingency contracts may also be used, if appropriate.

PLANNING ASSUMPTIONS AND GUIDANCE FOR FULL AND TOTAL MOBILIZATION

Enactment of emergency legislation empowers the President to limit civilian employment in any industry, occupation, or labor market area or to set employment ceilings in the interest of national defence. The supply of manpower to the military services and Defence contractors will be coordinated to balance requirements for inductees and civilian workers in the industrial base. As the supply of skilled manpower becomes limited, the Defence Resource Board may establish national priorities.

WARMAPS will continue to be updated by the Services (as capability permits) and provided to OSD by HQDA (AHRC-MOC). MACOM military and civilian requirements will be subject to analysis by HQDA (SAMR-MBA). OSD will require the Army to:

(1) Defer manpower growth in functions not critical to the war effort.

(2) Report deferred manpower demands (workyears by Defence Planning and Programming Category).

(3) Report total overages and shortages of civilian manpower by skill.

OSD will direct the Services to reallocate manpower from lower to higher priority functions. Priorities will be defined initially by the Army and will consider —

(1) The DA Master Priority List.

(2) Joint Chiefs of Staff geographic/theatre priorities based upon national or combined strategy.

The OSD will redistribute civilian skills among the military services and Defence agencies. OASA(M&RA) will redistribute Army civilian skills by directing the flow of oversea returnees and tasking CONUS movements.

Programming of manpower in the FYDP will be abbreviated. For operational theaters involved in high intensity conflict, HQDA (SAFM-BU) may suspend publication of the PBG. Programming of manpower will become a component of programming of real assets (equipment and trained personnel) to attain the planned force structure.

End-strength controls on the Army will be suspended. HQDA (SAMR-MBA) will notify each MACOM and agency of the decision of higher authorities to lift such restrictions.

Numerous peacetime programs that require military manpower will be suspended. These include:

(1) CONUS TDA positions maintained in support of the overseas MOS rotation base.

(2) Augmentation requirements.

(3) Career progression and development.

MACOM commanders will —

(1) Allocate a major share of manpower management efforts to workload forecasting. The mobilization requirements

model will be updated by both HQDA and CONUS MACOMs in support of this effort.

(2) Review actual workloads frequently and adjust manpower requirements and authorizations without delay.

(3) Reallocate manpower to higher priority activities. This will require a combined effort with local civilian personnel and public employment offices to obtain critical military and civilian occupational skills.

(4) Restructure jobs to reduce the need for critical skills or skill levels, both military and civilian.

(5) As necessary, change workweek for civilian personnel located at activities not in a hostile fire area to a 60 hour scheduled workweek through M+30 days. Thereafter, the workweek will be 48 hours as necessary.

(6) Delegate appropriate responsibilities to subordinate levels to ensure rapid update of manpower requirements and authorizations.

Commands within the active theatre of operations will assume complete control of indirect hire and foreign national direct hire civilian manpower, since the employment of civilians with these identities is governed by theatre availability, mission priorities, and agreements with host nations. Commands will continue to report to HQDA (SAMR-MBA) the number and types of civilian personnel hired. Manpower managers at MACOM and subordinate levels will assist civilian personnel officers in the allocation of manpower by skill. Manpower managers will:

(1) Provide information extracted from TDAs (as updated) concerning numbers and locations of positions by skills or functions under limitation.

(2) Revalidate requirements for critical skills as requested through survey or workload sampling.

(3) Identify excess positions from reduced or deleted functions.

Defence contractors have the right to seek DOD assistance in defending their work force requirements and priorities during total mobilization. In peacetime, manpower managers should provide contracting officers with the same planning data used for MOBTDA preparation. This will permit inclusion of mobilization expansion requirements in contracts. Manpower managers will continue to provide planning data to contracting officers during full and total mobilization. In addition, they may assist contracting officers in validating the contract work force expansion by projecting the requirements of an in-house work force for the total mobilization workloads using either of the following:

(1) Army manpower staffing standards.

(2) Staffing guides modified to reflect the availability factors.

PREPOSITIONED EMERGENCY AUTHORITIES

The emergency authorities contained in this chapter are arranged into the following three groups:

Group A. These actions and controls are suspended or delegated to MACOMs and separate agencies during a partial mobilization after HQDA transmits instructions to implement "Group A" emergency authorities in this chapter.

Group B. These actions and controls are suspended or delegated to MACOMs and separate agencies only after authority has been given to implement MOBTDA.

Group C. These actions will be taken only under those specific conditions described in parenthesis after each action statement.

Group A

a. Suspend Defence Officer Personnel Management Act controls on officer grades.

b. Suspend manpower survey program and submission of manpower survey schedules and reports by manpower requirements authorities.

c. Delegate authority for blanket approval of workweek or overtime by project without the analysis of alternatives require.

d. Delegate authority to establish or change officer grades 03 and above in TDA.

e. Delegate authority to temporarily detail military to civilian positions.

f. Delegate authority to establish military positions in MWR activities not governed by AR 215-1 of this regulation.

g. Delegate authority to change grade, strength, or abolish Army Medical Department commissioned officer positions with coordination of TSG (DASG-HCM).

h. Delegate authority to transfer manpower allocations with funds between appropriations and major programs.

i. Delegate authority to change strength, grade, or abolish Judge Advocate positions.

Group B

a. Suspend the FYDP and the POM.

b. Suspend end-strength and workyear limitations.

c. Suspend maintenance of CONUS TDA positions in support of SIMOS/rotation base, augmentation requirements, and career progression and development.

d. Delegate authority to change AMHA strength within UIC or AMSCO.

e. Delegate authority to eliminate chaplain positions, with coordination with the Chief of Chaplains (DACH-ZA).

f. Delegate authority to hire to authorized levels (PSRC or partial) of the MOBTDA.

g. Within operational theaters only, delegate authority to the theatre Army command for control of indirect hire and foreign national direct hire employment.

h. Delegate authority to change strength or ASI/specialty skill identifier of commissioned officer operational flying positions.

i. Delegate authority to convert civilian positions to military.

j. Delegate authority to establish SES positions.

Group C

a. Reallocate manpower to higher priority activities. (Army Staff or higher decision to establish priorities or defer manpower by function or location.)

b. Assist base operations contractors in validating their work force expansion requirements (decision to institute civil sector mobilization). Department of Labor and Federal Emergency Management Agency will provide program requirements.

c. Assist local public employment offices in allocation of the civilian work force by skills in order of Army priorities (decision by Department of Labor to allocate civilian labor by skill.)

MILITARY MANPOWER MANAGEMENT

As the Army continues to modernize its forces without increasing active military end-strength, manpower managers must seek every opportunity to manage positions more efficiently and effectively and to eliminate overlapping functions and unnecessary organizational levels in order to achieve greater force readiness.

Special duty

Command and operating agencies are often tasked to perform missions for which no personnel resources have been allocated. When this occurs, they may be forced to borrow Soldiers from one unit to accomplish a higher priority mission in another unit. This borrowing is called special duty. Special duty (SD), and its two subsets, borrowed military manpower (BMM) and troop diversion (TD), are defined in the glossary. BMM is the use of Soldiers borrowed from an MTOE unit to perform duties within a TDA activity for which a MACOM approved manpower requirement exists but for which no manpower space has been authorized; or where the manpower space has been authorized but the position is unfilled. Usually, the absence of Soldiers from an MTOE unit for any reason will have a direct effect on the state of readiness of that organization. Thus, when new missions are identified, commands and operating agencies should first consider temporary hire or other management initiatives before resorting to the use of SD.

An exception to this general rule exists when SD can be beneficial to both the Army and the individual. During peacetime, the most practical means to train some individuals or entire units is through SD; for example, by having MTOE finance units perform installation finance and accounting functions or by having MTOE medical personnel work in the medical department activity. This use of SD may be the most effective means to maintain a Soldier's proficiency. Whenever SD is necessary, it should be made as beneficial as possible to the Soldier by matching the individual's occupational specialty to the needs of the requirement. When commanders determine special duty is required to meet an urgent military need, it will be limited to 90 days, after which the Soldier must be returned to duties in his or her primary military occupational specialty (PMOS) or career progression military occupational specialty (CPMOS). Extensions will not be granted. The following utilization rules apply:

(1) Soldiers who have graduated from the Defence Language Institute will be utilized in positions authorized and requiring foreign language ability.

(2) Non-bonus first-term Soldiers will serve in their PMOS during their first term of service.

(3) Noncommissioned officers should be used only when absolutely necessary.

(4) Mandatory utilization is required of school-trained additional skill identifier (ASI) assets for the minimum service-remaining requirement.

(5) Soldiers who are bonus recipients will be used in their PMOS or a comparable MOS.

(6) Soldiers with Enlistment Bonus or Selective Reenlistment Bonus must serve in the MOS for which the bonus was awarded or in a comparable MOS.

(7) Intelligence career program Soldiers will not be utilized in duties other than their PMOS without a Commanding General (CG), AHRC approved waiver.

(8) Soldiers who have a PMOS in the 02 series (bandpersons) will not be assigned or utilized in an MOS outside that series without prior approval of HQDA (DAPE-EPM-A).

BMM should not be confused with TDs. They are similar in that both BMM and TDs involve performing duty with a unit or organization other than the one to which assigned, while the individual continues to be administered and accounted for by the unit or organization of assignment. Duties given both BMM and TD personnel are required to be performed on a constant or recurring basis throughout the entire year.

(1) The differences between BMM and TDs are as follows:

(a) BMM personnel must be MTOE Soldiers working against vacant, MACOM-approved, TDA requirements.

(b) TD personnel may be either TDA or MTOE Soldiers. It may be a TDA Soldier performing duties in a vacant TDA or MTOE position that either has been approved or could be documented in the requirements base. It may be an MTOE Soldier performing duties in a vacant, approved MTOE requirement or one that could be (but has not been) documented in the requirements base. Or it may be an MTOE Soldier performing duties in a vacant TDA position which could be (but has not been) documented in the requirements base.

(2) The following are examples of TDs:

(a) MTOE to MTOE unit: battalion clerk working at brigade level.

(b) TDA to TDA organization: service school instructor working in combat development.

(*c*) TDA organization to MTOE unit: hospital medics supporting MTOE units during training exercises, running aid stations.

(*d*) MTOE unit to TDA organization: Soldier working as gym attendant in support of extended (24-hour) operations of a gym which was permanently staffed only for 8-hour operations (in other words, beyond that recognized in the requirements column of the TDA).

e. The impact on training caused by the diversion of unit personnel to meet special duty requirements is reported in the Unit Status Report. An effective time management system for training can help to eliminate the adverse effects of special duty when commanders determine that an urgent military requirement exists for special duty. An effective time management system for training (Green-Amber-Red) is discussed in FM 7-0.

Directed military overstrength

Directed military overstrengths (DMOs) are HQDA active component manpower authorizations used for unforeseen, high-priority temporary manpower requirements of 12 months or less not budgeted or documented in TAADS.

DMO positions are designed to support unprogrammed requirements for durations of one year or less until the need can be supported through one of the following:

(1) MACOM reassignment of priorities.

(2) Command Plan/TAA Process.

(3) The requirement terminates.

The process for requesting a DMO involves submitting the following information through command channels to OASA(M&RA), SAMR-MBA:

(1) Mission and function changes necessitating the overstrength.

(2) Organization, duty station, and UIC.

(3) Grade and specialty or MOS.

(4) Inclusive dates (desired start and end date). It generally takes a minimum of 180 days for ODCS, G-1/U.S. Total Army Personnel Command (AHRC) to fill a DMO authorization; therefore, DMO start dates must be requested far enough in the future to allow assignment of personnel so they may complete the full term of the DMO prior to termination. When there is an immediate need for personnel to fill an approved DMO position, ASA(M&RA) and ODCS, G-1/AHRC will attempt to make an appropriate assignment as expeditiously as possible.

(5) A point of contact in the requesting organization.

(6) Special qualifications required and supporting justification.

(7) Detailed supporting justification for the DMO, to include the reason that authorized resources cannot satisfy the requirement and when authorizations will be provided.

(8) Notification to OASA(M&RA), SAMR-MBA, if DMO requirements terminate earlier than scheduled.

(9) Endorsement of DMO requests at the general officer or Senior Executive Service level.

Responsibilities:

(1) The ASA (M&RA) is the DMO manager and approval authority for the entire DMO program (HQDA, staff support agencies (SSAs) and FOAs, MACOMs, and Joint and Defence Activities) and is responsible for the following:

(a) Approving and maintaining the appropriate level of authorizations to support the DMO account.

(b) Maintaining a database to account for all DMO requests.

(c) Staffing all DMO requests with the appropriate HQDA offices.

(*d*) Approving or disapproving all DMO requests.

(*e*) Notifying the ODCS, G-1/AHRC when DMO positions are approved and authorize assignment of personnel.

(2) The ODCS, G-1/AHRC will —

(*a*) Upon notification by ASA(M&RA) process requisitions to include military grade, specialty or MOS requirements, and special qualifications.

(*b*) Assign personnel to approved DMO positions only when notified by OASA(M&RA). If DMO requests are received directly from an agency or major Army command, submit those requests to OASA(M&RA).

(*c*) Monitor personnel assigned to DMO positions to ensure they are properly reassigned upon termination of the DMO authorization according to existing time-on-station and permanent change-of-station requirements.

(*d*) Maintain and update the DMO TAADS document based on guidance from OASA(M&RA).

(3) USAFMSA will maintain and update the SAMAS database for the DMO account based on guidance from OASA(M&RA).

Military police

The primary role of military police is combat support. Military police units established to perform wartime missions will be MTOE units.

Military police units performing garrison law enforcement or secondary missions will be recognized and documented on installation TDAs.

Military police employment priorities are listed below.

(1) Combat support. (This includes battlefield circulation, enemy prisoners of war, and rear area operations against Level I and Level II threats.)

(2) Countering terrorism.

(3) Physical security of nuclear and chemical weapons and nuclear reactors.

(4) Physical security management and evaluation for protection of assets required for Army readiness (that is, physical security inspecting and planning, including the management of contract security guards.)

(5) Drug suppression.

(6) Fraud investigation.

(7) Law enforcement.

(8) Security at critical essential facilities, such as MACOM or unified command HQ residences of designated high risk personnel and facilities that require restricted access to accomplish their mission.

(9) Confinement and correctional treatment of military prisoners.

Military manpower borrowed from military police MTOE units for garrison law enforcement activities will be kept to a minimum.

Military police units may be used as honor guards, provided:

(1) They are not established or maintained for this purpose.

(2) They are not used exclusively when other types of units are available.

In the development of TDAs, care will be taken to organize guard and law enforcement functions in distinct position and work centers. Guard functions within CONUS are subject to CA review. Law enforcement functions are governmental and not subject to review. Military police positions will not be established for the garrison support functions listed below.

(1) Interior guards for nonsensitive installations or activities, such as unit facilities, airfields, conventional ammunition storage areas, communication facilities, and installation medical activities.

(2) Gate guards. One exception is where gate guards are approved on the basis of national defence exemption, for

sensitivity of the activity, from cost study. A second exception is overseas areas where there is a high criminal threat or the sensitivity of activities on an installation requires that military police control access.

(3) Military escorts on school buses, except to combat terrorism.

(4) Vehicle and weapons registration, except overseas where required by international agreements. (Subject to CA review.)

(5) Animal control. (Subject to CA review.)

(6) Information services. (Subject to CA review.) (Privacy Act and Freedom of Information Act requests are excepted.)

(7) Vehicle impoundment operations. (Subject to CA review.)

(8) Intrusion detection system monitoring. (Subject to CA review.)

(9) Money escort for routine bank deposits. (Subject to CA review.)

(10) Other non-law enforcement functions.

Requirements for military police may be recognized, and only military personnel will be used for the governmental functions and positions listed below.

(1) Provost marshal and military police company/ detachment (executive officer, first sergeant, platoon leader, platoon sergeant).

(2) Confinement and corrections involving direct handling of prisoners (that is, incarceration/guard functions).

(3) Security of nuclear weapons and nuclear reactors.

Requirements for military police may be recognized and military personnel may be used for the governmental functions listed below.

(1) Chief of security.

(2) Provost marshal staff or chief of security staff.

(3) Law enforcement patrols.

(4) Military police desk operations.

(5) Absentee and deserter apprehension in selected cases.

(6) Liaison with civilian police and court officials.

(7) Physical security management and evaluation.

(8) Enforcement of wildlife and game laws.

(9) Security of chemical agents.

(10) Military working dog patrols.

(11) Security of critical-essential facilities, to include MACOM or unified command HQ and medical centers.

(12) Investigations.

Military staffing should be given priority over civilian staffing where the governmental functions involve military police/security support to populations with large troop concentrations. Commanders must be aware of the need to maintain developmental opportunities for junior military police officers and enlisted Soldiers that will prepare them to perform at supervisory levels later in their careers.

MANPOWER AND PERSONNEL ANALYSIS OF MILITARY

The analytic process begins with the front end (more art than science), in which the problem is identified and structured. The problem first has to be stated appropriately and clearly, at which point it becomes critical that the objectives be articulated so as to spawn more-precise criteria. What is the desired outcome? Almost all objectives deal with some variant of effectiveness or cost. One part of the front end entails devising a broad, creative range of alternative policies that can be evaluated. A large part deals with sorting out ends from means from alternatives from constraints. Constantly asking "why" helps to construct a hierarchy that allows for analysis to enter a structured picture.

In the second part of the process, the analytic middle (muddle?), science replaces the art of the front end. The science does not have to be complex; logic is often sufficient and may be adequately done on the back of an envelope. This analytic middle sorts through consequences: How well do alternatives meet criteria? Models, methods, data, and qualitative assessments are brought to bear. Once the consequences of alternatives are known, tradeoffs can be made. Rarely are all objectives satisfied by one dominant alternative, so tough choices and compromises must be made when all objectives cannot be met at once.

Which objectives are more important than others? An alternative that provides more effectiveness at a lower cost is a no-brainer, but such an alternative is seldom found in the real world; and the reverse, less effectiveness at a higher cost, is seldom chosen. Alternatives that offer more effectiveness at a higher cost or a lower cost for less effectiveness or other possible combinations require hard thinking aimed at determining which alternative appears to best meet the ultimate objectives. Then, one must deal with uncertainties. What could change the assessed consequences? Specific cases can be examined or certain parameters can be judgmentally varied to see how the consequences and thus the conclusion might change. Last, what is the appetite for risk? Is it better to do nothing if there is no stomach to see the consequences through?

At this point, the back end of the analytic process is reached. Analyzing stops, and decisions or recommendations are made—which includes linking them to other problems and solutions in useful ways. Art and science give way to decision and judgment, a process that in the public sector, is not simply about selecting the "best" alternative for maximizing or minimizing criteria related to objectives, but involves consensus. What can the disparate stakeholders within DoD or across the executive and legislative branches agree to? What can be implemented?

The various parts of the manpower community go about their work differently. The personnel community, which seeks the best answer for the long term, studies the long-range, ideal effects of policy or changed parameters. This steady-state analysis applies constant rates and planning factors to see what happens in the steady state when all the transitional effects are settled out. Of course, no state is steady; transitional effects form a constant stream. But steady-state thinking is the best analytic tool for policy optimization. The program and budget community, however, is more interested in the dynamic effects of a changed policy. What happens over a par174 ticular time horizon as rates and factors change successively? Not surprisingly, the five-to seven-year horizon of the program objectives memorandum (POM) process is frequently used. Models show the effects of policy choice projected out for about five years, but not beyond (the famous "straight-lined" from the fifth year).

Program and budget analysts are more concerned with the immediate resource consequences than with long-term effectiveness issues. And as for the managerial community, it is more interested in execution: How do we get to a chosen new policy over a period of time? What decisions have to be implemented and when if we are to gain the benefits and avoid the costs? Unfortunately, deciding on a course and implementing it are not one and the same, so tough choices often are not followed through on. The reality is a bewildering agglomeration of half-completed past policy implementations that confound not only the managerial community, but the personnel and program and budget communities as well. Personnel policy tends to accrete over time in marginal ways.

Once the front end portion of the process is finished, the middle portion begins, the purpose being to determine the consequences associated with the different alternatives. In what ways do the measures or criteria change as choices are made? Here, more formal techniques are introduced. Each analysis leads to its own methods for determining the consequences of the alternatives vis-à-vis the objective criteria. Because this sample analysis was complex, a formal simulation model was built to capture all of the complicated relationships among the objectives, alternatives, measures, and policies. Any given model will only capture a subset of all the possible relationships; doing more would take more time and effort.

Like all good models, this one permits sensitivity analysis—i.e., it explicitly shows how the objectives would be affected if different alternatives were chosen. In this sample case, analysis ceased at this point, and a good decision dealing with uncertainties, risks, and implementation issues followed. This case dealt with broad objectives and large-scale alternatives; much of manpower and personnel analysis is narrower and more precise. While trends and broad forces do not change quickly, there is much to be learned by analyzing their impacts when seeking improvements to manpower, personnel, and training policies and processes that will increase military effectiveness and reduce costs.

PLANNING THE FUTURE MILITARY TECHNOLOGICAL WORKFORCE

Planning the workforce is about ensuring that manpower needs are met with trained people at reasonable costs. In past years—as a result of practices from World War II through conscription and the draft-induced volunteerism that ended with Vietnam—planning the workforce was largely about determining its size: forecasting who would stay if they were currently part of it, and calculating how many new entrants would be needed each year. "Manning" the force was the mantra; "aligning" the force by numbers and grades was the goal. Planning the future force is currently shifting away from recruiting and toward overcoming the retention shortfall. Today, workers are scarce throughout the economy—not overall, but among those who are skilled and committed. Emphasis is shifting away from pure recruiting and retention strategies to strategies aimed at developing existing workforces to carry out emerging work. The goal is to develop a cadre of personnel who have the skills needed to meet the requirements of the national military strategy. Human capital accretes; it is smarter to build on what exists than to start anew.

This chapter focuses on manpower, personnel, and training. Manpower deals with the numbers and types of people needed to accomplish missions, personnel involves managing people either directly (e.g., via assignments) or through incentives (e.g., via compensation), and training and development affects knowledge, skills, and behaviors. The chapter also addresses questions about the size of the force; its grade, skill, and experience composition; and the cost and optimal methods to procure, enter, train, develop, assign, advance, compensate, and remove personnel.

To illustrate these issues, an example of how to analyse manpower and personnel policies is worked through. The specific example explores manpower, personnel, and training policy alternatives for achieving an available, qualified, stable, experienced, and motivated future force. Some policy choices can be applied servicewide; others can be applied to military units or to individual soldiers, sailors, airmen, or marines. The example illustrates controllable and uncontrollable variables involved in policy alternatives, relationships among policy choices and desired outcomes, complexity and conflicts among competing objectives, and how undesired outcomes can emerge. Frequently, the complex relationships among variables are not sufficiently considered in the process of choosing policies. As a result, what appears to be a reasonable decision to save budget dollars can have unforeseen future personnel and training consequences.

HUMAN CAPITAL OF MILITARY

Human capital comprises the skills, knowledge, and abilities of individuals and groups and has value inside an organization and to an organization's customers. The United States has always gained a military advantage by being able to draw on large pools of human capital.

Inside an organization, the correct skills, knowledge, and abilities lead to greater efficiency; outside an organization, they lead to greater effectiveness with customers. In the U.S. military, the combatant commanders take skills, knowledge, and abilities developed by the services and apply them to seek military effectiveness around the globe for diverse missions. The military needs a proper mix of skills and knowledge to gain internal operating efficiencies and to be effective on battlefields, however defined.

Human capital can be thought of as a "stock," much as we think of a stock of materiel. It must be built, maintained, and upgraded; left alone, it deteriorates and becomes obsolete. The next few sections review what the stock of military human capital is now, how it got that way, and what it is likely to undergo in the future, specifically:

- The historical size, source, and composition of the active military
- The present composition, characteristics, and attributes of the active military
- The future effect of the present under likely conditions.

Historical Size, Source, and Composition of the Active Force

Consider, one at a time, various characteristics of the active force: size, enlisted/officer mix, skill mix, and source of manpower. Size largely depends on external events; type of manpower and mix of occupations depend on mission, organization, and technology; and source of manpower—conscription or volunteer—depends on the size of the military relative to the size of the population.

For most of U.S. military history, the number of soldiers, sailors, airmen (after the 1920s), and marines largely depended on external events, with "bumps" in the size of the active-duty force associated with the nation's earliest wars. When the nation needed to increase the size of the military, it enlisted or conscripted recruits from the general population; when the need abated, these recruits were equally quickly separated. For example, the military increased from 28,000 in 1860 to nearly 2,000,000 by 1864; by 1866, the force had decreased to 77,000. The more recent surges in manpower appear as spikes in the data. Notice the sharp spike by 1945, as the nation mobilized for World War II and the military grew to over 12,000,000. Three years later, however, the force had shrunk to about 1,400,000, a level close to today's.

Since World War II, external events have continued to shape the size of the force—the post–World War II drawdown in the late 1940s; the Korean War in the early 1950s, with its own subsequent drawdown; the Berlin crisis, which added manpower in the early 1960s; the Vietnam conflict, with its own era of growth and drawdown. The debacle at Desert One was followed in the 1980s by the Reagan buildup, the fall of the Berlin Wall, Grenada, and Panama. In the 1990s, the breakup of the former Soviet Union, the Persian Gulf conflict, and participation in humanitarian and other nonwar operations were significant. The 1990s witnessed a sharp reduction in the size of the active military.

The number of enlisted personnel increased by a factor of almost six, to about 225,000, for the Spanish American War. After that war, the level fell by one-half, to about 115,000, which was a consistent level up until World War I. The "standing" active military began in this era. However, officer strength did not increase as much during this period, which accounts for the high enlisted-to-officer ratio for the first 20 years of the century. Before World War I, brawn still mattered most on the battlefield; coal-fired ships, dismounted infantry, and horse-drawn artillery required proportionally more enlisted personnel. An air force did not exist.

Since World War I, there has been a significant shift from enlisted to officer manpower. The introduction of the airplane, tank, modern steam ship, and radio shifted work toward more use of brain than brawn. New technologies tend to be "officer heavy" when first introduced, because initially they are complex and require doctrinal and organizational change. Technological innovations also initially require a larger, officer-rich support tail to provide service and supply. Since World War II, the ratio's trend has been downward, with less frequent spikes, as officers have come to represent a larger proportion of a large active military. Moreover, beginning in World War II, the need to coordinate, integrate, and sustain military forces numbering in the millions, rather than tens of thousands, has led to officers being substituted for enlisted personnel, in part to staff increasingly larger and more hierarchical organizations. These broad trends continue to the present. The organization of work and the composition of the military force are never static; they change with mission, organization, and technology. The precipitous decline in jobs classified as general military is as striking as the increase in technical occupations and craftsmen. During the early years of the military, the demand for occupational specialization was small. Almost all soldiers were infantry riflemen, with a few serving in support activities. The Navy was the first to experience the effect of the Industrial Revolution, and the shift from sails to steam was a far-reaching technological change. The Army lagged for several decades, until the World War I mobilization, but its subsequent transformation was dramatic. By 1918, the combat soldier was for the first time in a numerical minority.

Following World War II, several factors dramatically changed the occupational requirements of the services—e.g., the acceleration of weapons and military technology to include the nuclear military, the application of electronics to communications and logistics, and the emergence of missiles and air defence. Organizational structures changed to take advantage of the new armaments and processes, and there was a noticeable occupational shift from infantry, artillery, and seamanship to technicians. By the early 1980s, technical workers constituted the largest of the five separate groupings, as they do today. As of 2000, 18 percent of enlisted personnel were in a general military specialty, 35 percent were blue collar workers (service and supply workers and craftsmen), and 47 percent were white collar workers (clerical and technical workers).

The United States has used conscription and voluntary enlistment to raise manpower but has never used universal service (although that concept was hotly debated between World War II and Korea). The active military as a percentage of the population from 1800 to 2000. The horizontal bar running across the lower part of the figure has four lightly shaded segments showing the four times (which together total only 30 out of 210 years of federal history) conscription was used. The Civil War and World War I were both periods of wartime conscription; the first use of peacetime conscription was in 1940, shortly before World War II. The nation had a volunteer force from 1946 to

1950, but Korea saw a return to conscription. Vietnam manpower policy was dominated by conscription to meet the needs of the Army; the needs of the other services and the reserve component were met largely with volunteers (though many of these were draft induced).

The size of both the active enlisted force and the population related to the use of conscription (shown in lightly shaded part of bar) over time. The nation has always used conscription when it required an active enlisted force larger than about 1.4 percent of the population, something that has occurred only during the four periods described above. Since 1973, when the last period of conscription ended, the population has grown and the active military has shrunk. Currently, the active force represents about 0.5 percent of the population. Using the 1.4 percent as a rule of thumb means that the need for an active force of above 3.7 million would lead to conscription—a highly unlikely event in the foreseeable future. Also, conditions outlined below will most likely make the rule of thumb obsolete.

The lessons from this history are central to assessments about the future. However, the durability of these lessons cannot help but be affected by more-recent fundamental changes that must be incorporated into any synthesis of the future: the greater use of civilians and reserves, and the greater education and higher aptitude of the enlisted force.

NUCLEAR STRATEGY

Nuclear warfare strategy is a set of policies that deal with preventing or fighting a nuclear war. The policy of trying to prevent an attack by a nuclear weapon from another country by threatening nuclear retaliation is known as the strategy of nuclear deterrence. The goal in deterrence is to always maintain a second strike capability (the ability of a country to respond to a nuclear attack with one of its own) and potentially to strive for first strike status (the ability to completely destroy an enemy's nuclear forces before they could retaliate). During the Cold War, policy and military theorists in nuclear-enabled countries worked out models of what sorts of policies could prevent one from ever being attacked by a nuclear weapon. Different forms of nuclear weapons delivery allow for different types of nuclear strategies. The goals of any strategy are generally to make it difficult for an enemy to launch a pre-emptive strike against the weapon system and difficult to defend against the delivery of the weapon during a potential conflict. Sometimes this has meant keeping the weapon locations hidden, such as deploying them on submarines or rail cars whose locations are very hard for an enemy to track and other times this means protecting them by burying them in hardened bunkers.

Other components of nuclear strategies have included using missile defence (to destroy the missiles before they land) or implementation of civil defence measures (using early-warning systems to evacuate citizens to safe areas before an attack).

Note that weapons which are designed to threaten large populations or to generally deter attacks are known as strategic weapons. Weapons which are designed to actually be used on a battlefield in military situations are known as tactical weapons.

There are critics of the very idea of nuclear strategy for waging nuclear war who have suggested that a nuclear war between two nuclear powers would result in mutual annihilation. From this point of view, the significance of nuclear weapons is purely to deter war because any nuclear war would immediately escalate out of mutual distrust and fear, resulting in mutually assured destruction. This threat of national, if not global, destruction has been a strong motivation for anti-nuclear weapons activism.

Critics from the peace movement and within the military establishment have questioned the usefulness of such weapons in the current military climate. The use of (or threat of use of) such weapons would generally be contrary to the rules of international law applicable in armed conflict, according to an advisory opinion issued by the International Court of Justice in 1996. Perhaps the most controversial idea in nuclear strategy is that nuclear proliferation would be desirable. This view argues that, unlike conventional weapons, nuclear weapons successfully deter all-out war between states, and they are said to have done this during the Cold War between the U.S. and the Soviet Union. Political scientist Kenneth Waltz is the most prominent advocate of this argument.

The threat of potentially suicidal terrorists possessing nuclear weapons (a form of nuclear terrorism) complicates the decision process. The prospect of mutually assured destruction may not deter an enemy who expects to die in the confrontation. Further, if the initial act is from a rogue group instead of a sovereign nation, there is no fixed nation or fixed military targets to retaliate against. It has been argued, especially after the September 11, 2001 attacks, that this complication is the sign of the next age of nuclear strategy, distinct from the relative stability of the Cold War. In 1996, the United States adopted a policy of allowing the targeting of its nuclear weapons at terrorists armed with weapons of mass destruction.

Governance, control, and law

Because of the immense military power they can confer, the political control of nuclear weapons has been a key issue for as long as they have existed; in most countries the use of nuclear force can only be authorized by the head of government or head of state.

In the late 1940s, lack of mutual trust was preventing the United States and the Soviet Union from making ground towards international arms control agreements, but by the 1960s steps were being taken to limit both the proliferation of nuclear weapons to other countries and the environmental effects of nuclear testing. The Partial Test Ban Treaty (1963) restricted all nuclear testing to underground nuclear testing, to prevent contamination from nuclear fallout, while the Nuclear Non-Proliferation Treaty (1968) attempted to place restrictions on the types of activities which signatories could participate in, with the goal of allowing the transference of non-military nuclear technology to member countries without fear of proliferation. In 1957, the International Atomic Energy Agency (IAEA) was established under the mandate of the United Nations in order to encourage the development of the peaceful applications of nuclear technology, provide international safeguards against its misuse, and facilitate the application of safety measures in its use. In 1996, many nations signed the Comprehensive Test Ban Treaty which prohibits all testing of nuclear weapons, which would impose a significant hindrance to their development by any complying country. Due to the strict entry into force criterion of the convention however, it had as of 2011 not entered into force.

Additional treaties and agreements have governed nuclear weapons stockpiles between the countries with the two largest stockpiles, the United States and the Soviet Union, and later between the United States and Russia. These include treaties such as SALT II (never ratified), START I (expired), INF, START II (never ratified), SORT, and New START, as well as non-binding agreements such as SALT I and the Presidential Nuclear Initiatives of 1991. Even when they did not enter into force, these agreements helped limit and later reduce the numbers and types of nuclear weapons between the United States and the Soviet Union/Russia.

Nuclear weapons have also been opposed by agreements between countries. Many nations have been declared Nuclear-Weapon-Free Zones, areas where nuclear weapons production and deployment are prohibited, through the use of treaties. The Treaty of Tlatelolco (1967) prohibited any production or deployment of nuclear weapons in Latin America and the Caribbean, and the Treaty of Pelindaba (1964) prohibits nuclear weapons in many African countries. As recently as 2006 a Central Asian Nuclear Weapon Free Zone was established amongst the former Soviet republics of Central Asia prohibiting nuclear weapons.

In the middle of 1996, the International Court of Justice, the highest court of the United Nations, issued an Advisory Opinion concerned with the "Legality of the Threat or Use of Nuclear Weapons". The court ruled that the use or threat of use of nuclear weapons would violate various articles of international law, including the Geneva Conventions, the Hague Conventions, the UN Charter, and the Universal Declaration of Human Rights. In view of the unique, destructive characteristics of nuclear weapons, the International Committee of the Red Cross calls on States to ensure that these weapons are never used, irrespective of whether they consider them to be lawful or not.

Additionally, there have been other, specific actions meant to discourage countries from developing nuclear arms. In the wake of the tests by India and Pakistan in 1998, economic sanctions were (temporarily) levied against both countries, though neither were signatories with the Nuclear Non-Proliferation Treaty. One of the stated *casus belli* for the initiation of the 2003 Iraq War was an accusation by the United States that Iraq was actively pursuing nuclear arms (though this was soon discovered not to be the case as the program had been discontinued). In 1981, Israel had bombed a nuclear reactor being constructed in Osirak, Iraq, in what it called an attempt to halt Iraq's previous nuclear arms ambitions.

Disarmament

Nuclear disarmament refers to both the act of reducing or eliminating nuclear weapons and to the end state of a nuclear-free world, in which nuclear weapons are completely eliminated.

Beginning with the 1963 Partial Test Ban Treaty and continuing through the 1996 Comprehensive Test Ban Treaty, there have been many treaties to limit or reduce nuclear weapons testing and stockpiles. The 1968 Nuclear Non-Proliferation Treaty has as one of its explicit conditions that all signatories must "pursue negotiations in good faith" towards the long-term goal of "complete disarmament". However, no nuclear state has treated that aspect of the agreement as having binding force.

Only one country—South Africa—has ever fully renounced nuclear weapons they had independently developed. A number of former Soviet republics—Belarus, Kazakhstan, and Ukraine—returned Soviet nuclear arms stationed in their countries to Russia after the collapse of the USSR. Proponents of nuclear disarmament say that it would lessen the probability of nuclear war occurring, especially accidentally. Critics of nuclear disarmament say that it would undermine deterrence and could lead to increased global instability. Various American government officials, who were in office during the Cold War period, have recently been advocating the elimination of nuclear weapons. These officials include Henry Kissinger, George Shultz, Sam Nunn, and William Perry. In January 2010, Lawrence M. Krauss stated that "no issue carries more importance to the long-term health and security of humanity than the effort to reduce, and perhaps one day, rid the world of nuclear weapons".

In the years after the end of the Cold War, there have been numerous campaigns to urge the abolition of nuclear weapons, such as that organized by the Global Zero movement, and the goal of a "world without nuclear weapons" was advocated by United States President Barack Obama in an April 2009 speech in Prague. A CNN poll from April 2010 indicated that the American public was nearly evenly split on the issue.

Controversy

Even before the first nuclear weapons had been developed, scientists involved with the Manhattan Project were divided over the use of the weapon. The role of the two atomic bombings of the country in Japan's surrender and the U.S.'s ethical justification for them has been the subject of scholarly and popular debate for decades. The question of whether nations should have nuclear weapons, or test them, has been continually and nearly universally controversial.

Radioactive fallout from nuclear weapons testing was first drawn to public attention in 1954 when the Castle Bravo hydrogen bomb test at the Pacific Proving Grounds contaminated the crew and catch of the Japanese fishing boat *Lucky Dragon*. One of the fishermen died in Japan seven months later, and the fear of contaminated tuna led to a temporary boycotting of the popular staple in Japan. The incident caused widespread concern around the world, especially regarding the effects of nuclear fallout and atmospheric nuclear testing, and "provided a decisive impetus for the emergence of the anti-nuclear weapons movement in many countries". Peace movements emerged in Japan and in 1954 they converged to form a unified "Japanese Council Against Atomic and Hydrogen Bombs". Japanese opposition to nuclear weapons tests in the Pacific Ocean was widespread, and "an estimated 35 million signatures were collected on petitions calling for bans on nuclear weapons".

In the United Kingdom, the first Aldermaston March organised by the Campaign for Nuclear Disarmament took place at Easter 1958, when several thousand people marched for four days from Trafalgar Square, London, to the Atomic Weapons Research Establishment close to Aldermaston in Berkshire, England, to demonstrate their opposition to nuclear weapons. The Aldermaston marches continued into the late 1960s when tens of thousands of people took part in the four-day marches.

In 1959, a letter in the *Bulletin of Atomic Scientists* was the start of a successful campaign to stop the Atomic Energy Commission dumping radioactive waste in the sea 19 kilometres from Boston. In 1962, Linus Pauling won the Nobel Peace Prize for his work to stop the atmospheric testing of nuclear weapons, and the "Ban the Bomb" movement spread.

In 1963, many countries ratified the Partial Test Ban Treaty prohibiting atmospheric nuclear testing. Radioactive fallout became less of an issue and the anti-nuclear weapons movement went into decline for some years. A resurgence of interest occurred amid European and American fears of nuclear war in the 1980s.

Non-weapons uses

Apart from their use as weapons, nuclear explosives have been tested and used for various non-military uses, and proposed, but not used for large-scale earth moving. When long term health and clean-up costs were included, there was no economic advantage over conventional explosives.

Synthetic elements, such as einsteinium and fermium, created by neutron bombardment of uranium and plutonium during thermonuclear explosions, were discovered in the aftermath of the first thermonuclear bomb test. In 2008 the worldwide presence of new isotopes from atmospheric testing beginning in the 1950s was developed into a reliable way of detecting art forgeries, as all paintings created after that period may contain traces of cesium-137 and strontium-90, isotopes that did not exist in nature before 1945.

Nuclear explosives have also been seriously studied as potential propulsion mechanisms for space travel.

EMERGING TRENDS IN INTERNATIONAL FORCE LEVELS

With economic power gradually edging out military power as the key determinant of national strength and geo-political status, international force levels have witnessed a downturn since the end of the Cold War. In planning future force levels and equipping these forces, most modern armed forces have taken their bearings from the transformation process that is underway in the United States (US) as well as the lessons of the 1991 and 2003 Gulf Wars and the intervening campaigns like the ones in Kosovo in 1999 and Afghanistan in 2001. A number of emerging trends, some clear and certain, other nascent or incipient and some others that are still hazy are discernible in international force levels.

But there is one trend that is clearly discernible in the re-structuring efforts that are currently underway in most modern armed forces, It is that of qualitative upgradation of forces to Revolution in Military Affairs (RMA) technologies, doctrine and organisations and their quantitative downsizing. As military manpower becomes more and more expensive to recruit, train and retain, planners are increasingly opting for technological solutions at least in low risk areas and relying more on 'mean and lean' conventional forces for deterrence. However, at the same time, conventional forces are increasingly proving to be inadequate for facing up to the challenges of sub-conventional conflict.

"In particular, Iraq, Afghanistan and Chechnya demonstrate the limitations of modern conventional forces in complex environments that depend more of them than traditional warfighting." Due to the decreasing emphasis on gaining and holding territory, capability-based re-structuring of conventional forces, as opposed to the old threatbased organisations, is leading to downsizing, particularly of army fighting formations and units. Emerging threats like international fundamentalist terrorism, especially from non-state actors, are also guiding this trend. Simultaneously, the strength of reserve troops has gone up almost across the board.

The transformation of conventional forces is in progress to bring them in conformity with RMA concepts and technologies. Special efforts are being made to upgrade ISR capabilities, particularly those of space-based platforms, and to attain the ability to wage network centric warfare (NCW). At the higher end of the technology trajectory the trend is towards introducing weapons platforms and ISR systems that are either completely unmanned or require minimum manpower for prolonged employment and usage.

Modern armed forces are carefully integrating individual Services to prepare them for joint warfare for greater synergy in orchestrating operations. This is invariably undertaken in the face of heavy opposition as individual Services resent and stubbornly resist change.

The reduction in conventional force levels is leading to greater reliance on coalition warfare as nations pool in their capabilities to make for deficiencies and shortfalls and to gain diplomatic strength. However, this is not always the best solution, as coalitions tend to have disparate objectives and often lack cohesiveness. The increasing proclivity to seek to achieve military aims and objectives by domination from the air through FGA (fighter-ground attack) aircraft and missiles is leading to enhancement of these capabilities. For example, the US and Coalition forces enforced an exclusion zone over Iraq for over a decade exclusively from the air.

Rapid deployment and rapid reaction forces are being added to the inventories of almost all the modern armies. China, for example, is in the process of upgrading one division each to the status of a rapid deployment division in all military districts. Similarly, the European Union has constituted a rapid deployment force. There is noticeable accretion in the force levels of Special Forces the world over as greater reliance is being placed on the low-visibility employment of military force, especially against terrorist cells and fundamentalist insurgents. Some of the armed forces are gravitating towards raising specialised internal security and counter-insurgency forces as a new branch that is being added on to the existing armed forces in the country. This is being seen as a means to separate a 'lean and mean' conventional force for deterrence from fluctuating force levels for subconventional conflict. However, this is not yet widespread.

In some countries, in real democracies as well as those that hold sham elections or have never held an election, the trend is towards a huge expansion of paramilitary forces for internal security duties. In Asia, India leads in this reliance on second tier forces. Almost all the central police and paramilitary forces (CPMFs) like BSF, CRPF, ITBP, CISF and SSB, have added a large number of battalions to augment their fighting strength since the mid-1990s when realisation had first dawned on the military and civilian bureaucracy that insurgency and terrorism are here to stay.

The US, Japan, France, the UK and India have formulated plans to enhance strategic sealift and airlift capabilities for power projection as well as for disaster relief. Additional capabilities are being gradually created for littoral warfare and assault from the sea as the seas and oceans become more important for trade and commerce.

Special efforts are being made to reduce the logistics footprint of armed forces by outsourcing the supply and maintenance chain to civilian trade wherever it can be done without compromising operational readiness. After the American experiment in Iraq, armed forces the world over are considering outsourcing the perimeter security of airfields, logistics bases and other similar nodes and convoy protection duties, when deployed out-of-area for peacekeeping, peace-support and stabilisation operations, to private companies so as to reduce the need for the large-scale employment of regular troops on rear area security duties that are not optimally suited to their skills and training.

In view of the sophisticated hi-tech weapons systems that are now in service with almost all modern armed forces, the technological threshold of the men and women in uniform needs to be much higher than was the case even a decade ago. Hence, it is becoming increasingly more important to recruit and train well-educated youth to serve in the armed forces. Among the Services, the Navy and the Air Force need more educated personnel than the Army because of the greater complexity of their weapons systems.

In fact, these Services are looking to raise entry level educational qualifications to graduation (B.A./B.Sc.) in most trades while the Army could perhaps manage with XIIth standard pass soldiers in arms like the infantry till about 2015 or so with better training. As such personnel are likely to be found predominantly in urban areas, the recruitment base is likely to shift to such areas for Army personnel as well. In case some of the central police and para-military forces (CPMFs) also seek to upgrade their entry-level manpower, this will lead to a new set of socio-economic problems as the armed forces and the CPMFs provide fairly extensive employment opportunities to rural youth at present.

Addressing Shortage of Officers

As India's economy is booming and lucrative career options are available to the youth in the private sector, the Indian armed forces are being increasingly faced by an acute shortage of officers. The worst affected is the Indian army that has a staggering shortage of approximately 13,000 officers out of an authorised cadre strength of about 40,000 officers. In August 2004, the Central Government had announced a proposal to select aspiring IAS and allied services candidates after the 12th standard with a view to catching them young for a career in the bureaucracy.5 Presumably, a new academy is proposed to be established for this purpose because the Mussoorrie academy has a different charter.

The best option and one that is readily available is to train the young recruits at the National Defence Academy (NDA), Khadakvasla, Pune, which provides the finest all round education at the under-graduate level in India. In fact, it would do the budding central services officers a world of good to do some national service in the armed forces for about five years during which they would be exposed to a disciplined way of life, gain hands-on experience of man-management and good leadership, imbibe values and ethics and learn to be officers and gentlemen. They would also contribute handsomely to national security and help to reduce the officers' shortage in the armed forces. The endemic shortage of officers in the armed forces continues to have a deleterious effect on their warfighting capability, particularly on the army's performance in counter-insurgency operations in Jammu and Kashmir and the north-eastern States.

As the shortage of officers is primarily in the ranks of Captain and Major, the solution apparently lies in a re-vamped short-service entry scheme which offers lateral induction into civilian jobs after five to eight years of service in the army. Such a scheme would confer the twin benefits of filling all the vacant positions and reducing the pension bill.

The most pragmatic option is for the central government to absorb all the officers scheduled for early release from the three services. The best method with multifarious benefits to the nation would be to make "military service" compulsory for all aspirants for the Central Services, including the Indian Foreign Service (IFS), the Indian Administrative Service (IAS), the Indian Police Service (IPS), other Allied Services, the Central Police and Para-military Forces (CPMFs) and other similar organisations.

Recruitment to the IAS, IFS and the Allied Services should be channelled only through the armed forces, for men as well as women. Entry into the army, the navy and the air force should be through the Combined Defence Services examination for the NDA conducted by the Union Public Service Commission (UPSC). On graduating from the NDA, the cadets should receive further training at the respective academies of the three services and then join these as commissioned officers. After five years of service, all volunteer officers should be given three chances each to appear for the UPSC examinations and interviews for lateral transfer into the IAS, IFS and the Allied Services. Those who do not wish to leave or do not qualify would continue to soldier on in their respective service.

Assuming that the bait of eventual transfer to the central services would be a lucrative enough inducement for talented young men and women to join the armed forces, such a step would not only completely eliminate the shortage of officers over a few years, but also considerably enhance the quality of the junior leadership of the three services and, later, of the central services.

However, such a move is bound to meet stiff resistance and would require supreme political will to implement. Since the Prime Minister is himself eager to improve the quality of intake and the training standards of the central services, he must provide the leadership to ensure that this pragmatic measure can be pushed through politically.

Graduates of the NDA receive B. Sc. degrees, as the armed forces require a fairly high threshold of the knowledge of science. The NDA syllabus can be suitably modified to accommodate the special managerial requirements of the central services. Particularly at the Indian Military Academy (IMA), Dehradun, and the corresponding academies of the navy and the air force, a recognised management diploma can be included in the syllabus and, if considered necessary, the duration of training can be increased to two years to enable the Gentlemen Cadets to acquire an MBA degree.

At present, officers from the NDA get commissioned at 21 to 22 years of age. Those selected for the central services after five to seven years of active service in the armed forces would be absorbed into the IAS at about 27 to 29 years of age. This would be only marginally higher than the present average age of IAS officers on joining. Services officers joining the central services will be trained leaders of men, some of them baptised under fire, and would have had the unique privilege of commanding men – perhaps the greatest honour that any man can strive for. Above all, they will have the opportunity to serve the national cause in many strife-torn corners of the country and will gain first hand experience of the problems of the local people. Their acquaintance with and insights into the unique diversity of India's culture and traditions, reflected in the armed forces, would surely stand them in good stead in the remaining 30 to 32 years of their service.

It has been accepted by all perceptive observers of the national scene that in these times of a failing national character, with rampant corruption, political expediency and widespread nepotism ruling the roost, the three services have played a stellar role in holding the nation together as a viable political entity.

A disciplined way of life, highly advanced and pragmatic man-management techniques, a no-nonsense approach to problem solving and active secularism, have helped the services to avoid falling prey to the maladies afflicting the other organs of the state. The officers transferring to the central services from the armed forces will carry with them these impeccable attributes and will undoubtedly succeed in transforming the manner in which the bureaucracy conducts the business of administration. Compulsory military service for entry into the central services will also give civilian bureaucrats a better understanding of India's defence and security interests and will create a permanent bond of camaraderie between the civilians and the servicemen. It is a win-win situation and an idea whose time has come.

11

The Challenge of Future War

Given the proliferation of military theory and uncertain political conditions, what then are the possible contours of future warfare over the next decade? While accurate prediction of events is impossible, it is possible to speculate cautiously about emerging trends. In September 1999, the bipartisan US (Hart–Rudman) Commission on National Security/ 21st Century stated: The future strategic environment will... be one of considerable turbulence... The international system will be so fluid and complex that to think intelligently about military issues will mean taking an integrated view of political, social, technological, and economic developments. Only a broad definition of national security is appropriate to such a circumstance. In short we have entered an age in which many of the fundamental assumptions that steered us through the chilly waters of the Cold War require rethinking... *The very facts of military reality are changing, and that bears serious and concentrated reflection.*

If the Hart–Rudman Commission's judgment about the a change in the facts of military reality is correct—and many, including the author of this chapter, believe that it is—then those concerned with preparing for armed conflict in the early 21st century must expect to confront a range of old, new and hybrid forms of armed conflict. During the Cold War, the West confronted a uni-dimensional threat from Soviet Marxism–Leninism—an adversary whose motives were certain and whose moves were expected. In the new century, such predictable conditions no longer apply. In the words of the present US Secretary for Defence, Donald H. Rumsfeld, new military thinking is now required to arm Western societies 'against the unknown, the uncertain, the unseen, and the unexpected'.

It has become imperative for all concerned with security issues to pay greater attention to the merging of previously discrete forms of war across a spectrum of conflict. The conceptual basis for the study of warfare in the West must now be broadened to include a rigorous study of the interaction between interstate, sub-state and trans-state conflict, and the diffusion of contemporary military capabilities. We have to recognise that, in an age of interconnectedness, linkage and interdependence seem to pervade all aspects of armed conflict. Military analysts and force structure specialists have to concentrate on the multifunctional use of force in highly complex operations. In addition, military professionals must learn to embrace the challenges of proportion, coercion and dissuasion as well as the older traditions of battlefield destruction. In particular, what the US Hart–Rudman Commission has described as 'the spectrum of symmetrical and asymmetrical threats we anticipate over the next quarter century' must receive increased attention from both military theorists and policy makers. In short, the challenge is to prepare for full-spectrum conflict.

Such a preparation is more difficult to undertake than many defence analysts realise. It is true that the notion of a spectrum of conflict is not a new idea, but for most of the Cold War, an understanding of war in the West was based on generic intellectual categories of conventional (highintensity) and unconventional (low-intensity) conflict. Most of us engaged in the field of strategic studies thought in terms of separate worlds of conventional inter-state (or high-intensity) and unconventional intra-state (or low-intensity) military activity. Unfortunately, the spectrum of conflict that is emerging in the early 21st century is distinguished by its merging categories, by its multidimensionality and by its unprecedented interaction.

In an era when all security issues are interconnected and when the national security of Western states has become critically dependent on the health of international security, single-scenario strategies and rigid military force structures have become anachronistic. Traditional concepts of deterrence and defence need to be supplemented by new doctrines of security pre-emption, security prevention and expeditionary warfare. Moreover, the clear separation of peace and war needs to be supplemented by an acknowledgment that modes of war have merged. In a new age marked by networks and instant communications, the need is for advanced military forces with a broad range of skills across a spectrum of conflict. These skills may involve preventive deployment, pre-emptive strike, war fighting, peace enforcement, traditional peacekeeping and peace building, and counter-terrorism.

The intellectual challenge facing military professionals is not as Martin van Creveld would have us believe, to consign Carl von Clausewitz and 2000 years of Western military knowledge into the dustbin of history. Rather, the task is to learn how to fight efficiently across the spectrum of conflict. No responsible Western military theorist can accept at face value the thesis of the 'obsolescence of conventional war' or the paradigm of asymmetric warfare as main force-planning or doctrinal determinants. In a dangerous and unpredictable world, military professionals and their political masters must prepare to fight in conditions of a 'high–low mix'. This preparation is still best accomplished by always being ready in the alleyways of war to tame the big wild cats and not simply the vicious little kittens. Advanced militaries must be able to fight Iraq's Republican Guard as well as Taliban and al-Qa'ida militia and terrorists. As every good operational commander knows, in the military art, one can 'trade down' but one can never 'trade up'. Moreover, all the evidence that we have indicates that success in peace support operations requires the kinds of conventional firepower, mobility and force protection that can only be drawn from military establishments that are optimised for conventional warfighting.

Readying ourselves for conventional war does not, however, absolve us from undertaking a major transformation in the way we think about, and conceive of, the use of military force. The most pressing intellectual task facing all of us at the crossroads of the old and new centuries is one of rapid adaptation to new and merging forms of conflict. In the West we have to reconcile how we would *like* to fight with how we might *have* to fight. We have to try to synthesise relevant features from the massive literature on the Gulf War—RMA high-technology classical model of warfare with the changing reality of conflict—both conventional and unconventional—as it presents itself at the beginning of the 21st century. We have to undertake an intellectual exploration of the growing interaction between interstate, sub-state and trans-state conflict, and conduct a rigorous investigation of the phenomenon of merging war forms: internal, international, postmodern, modern and pre-modern.

The merging of modes of armed conflict suggests an era of warfare quite different from that of the recent past. Fighting in the future may involve conventional armies, guerrilla bands, independent and statedirected terrorist groups, specialised anti-terrorist units and private militias. Terrorist attacks might evolve into classic guerrilla warfare and then escalate to conventional conflict. Alternatively, fighting could be conducted on several levels at once. The possibility of continuous, sporadic armed conflict—blurred in time and space, waged on several levels by a large array of national and sub-national forces—means that the reality of war in the first decade of the 21st century transcends a neat division into distinct areas of symmetry and asymmetry.

Indeed, it is arguable that the main reason for much of the intellectual confusion surrounding war at the turn of the century stems from the lack of a conceptual synthesis between the requirements of traditional conventional war and the emerging blend of interstate, trans-state and non-state modes of conflict in the 21st century. It is no accident that the most productive areas of military theory have been those that have attempted to concentrate on the expanding phenomenon of war. The most interesting new approaches have come from those who have endeavoured to examine the growing complexity of conflict, its holistic yet multidimensional character and its sociological, as well as technological dynamics. Conceptual progress has come from analytical work into war's connection to society and the state; from assessing the convergence of modes of conflict and the growing requirements to control armed violence in an age of instantaneous media imagery; and in the area of developing multipurpose forces that can wage warfare across a spectrum of conflict.

In short, it is the interactive character of war—Clausewitz's famous chameleon 'that adapts its characteristics to the given case'—that has proven to be the most original avenue for analysis. The immediate future of war lies perhaps in two key areas. The first area lies in the realm of multidimensional theories of war and conflict, which call for multifunctional forces for intervention missions. Second, the evolving theory of counter-war or 'mastery of violence' demonstrates a potential to assist military practitioners and policy-makers to understand and deal with armed conflict as a multifaceted phenomenon.

A MULTIDIMENSIONAL APPROACH TO WAR AND CONFLICT

According to the leading Russian theorist, Makhmut Gareev, 21st century war is becoming 'multi-variant'. Under these circumstances, advanced armed forces need to develop a multidimensional approach to conflict. The most interesting American and British military theory reflects a growing recognition that, in a new age of multiple threats, the discrete categories of conventional and unconventional conflict are becoming blurred, along with corresponding legal and moral restraints. Much of the West's present drive towards preparing to meet an accelerating convergence of military challenges is shaped by three ideas. First, armed forces must become multifunctional in order to possess the ability to adapt to differing modes of war right along the conflict spectrum. Second, as questions of both national and societal security merge and interpenetrate, it is clear that possessing a reactive operational strategy alone is inadequate as a means of deterrence. Security in the new era of liberal globalism also requires a willingness to undertake intervention and a corresponding need for proactive military forces. Third, if political and technological conditions now permit radical groups and rogue states to use ballistic or biological weapons to inflict mass casualties on democratic societies, then this new challenge must be met by military preemption in ways that have not been seen since the late 19th century.

In other words, those that espouse a doctrine of asymmetric or unconventional warfare aimed at the mass murder of innocent civilians in cities and suburbs must be destroyed wherever and whenever pre-emption is possible. As President George W. Bush stated recently, it is necessary for the West and its allies to act decisively against the new threat emanating from 'the perilous crossroads of radicalism and technology'. In short, a real threat has arisen from the diffusion and proliferation of advanced technology—from standoff missiles to commercial space systems to possible weapons of mass destruction. Preventing such weapons systems from falling into the hands of smaller armies, paramilitaries, militias and other armed groups puts a premium on Western expeditionary warfare. Two leading American military theorists, Huba Wass de Czege and Richard Hart Sinnreich, have recently given an unequivocal view of the merging of conventional–unconventional conflict:

Clear distinctions between conventional and unconventional conflicts are fading, and any future major conflict is almost certain to see a routine commingling of such operations. Similarly, once useful demarcations between front and rear or between theatre and strategic operations will continue to evaporate as the instrumentalities of war become more interdependent and, as is increasingly true of communications and space systems, less easily separable from their civilian and commercial counterparts.

As a result, the future requirement will be for joint-forces designed for multidimensional expeditionary-style operations—

what the US Army now refers to as 'operational manoeuvre from strategic distance'. Such operations are vital to control theatres where forces might expect to encounter a range of 'high–low' threats and varied forms of conflict. Consequently, the main trends in contemporary Western military theory are towards operations with multinational joint taskforces with a reduced level of headquarters—from corps, division and brigade to force and formation. Future force structure will become more modular and capable of rapid taskforce organisation in order to provide a 'golf bag', or variety, of military capabilities.

In expeditionary warfare, the main need is to reconcile operational versatility with organisational stability. Western forces must be capable of undertaking joint multi-dimensional missions ranging from shaping the environment to air–ground operational manoeuvre through to all-out conventional warfighting. The demands of operational versatility are likely to place a premium on the need for organisational change. The need is for smaller combat formations, such as the combined-arms brigades, to be formed to serve as modular building blocks for forces in the field.

WINNING THE BATTLE OF IDEAS

Like Rome after the fall of Carthage, America wields supreme power in the world. But like the victorious Romans, Americans confront new threats and challenges to prosperity and security. America does not hold the patent on innovative ideas or a monopoly on new technology. History demonstrates that an early lead in any one area of military affairs does not convey permanent advantage; Britain introduced the tank in 1916, but Germany exploited it fully.

It is one thing to experiment with a technology or a concept, however, and quite another to displace existing assets or doctrine to make way for the new. Efforts at far-reaching change produce powerful resistance. As Niccolo Machiavelli observed, There is nothing more difficult to take in hand, more perilous to conduct, or more uncertain in its success, than to take the lead in the introduction of a new order of things. Because the innovator has for enemies all those who have done well under the old conditions, and lukewarm defenders in those who may do well under the new.

Difficulty is no excuse for inaction, however. Transformation is not an option; it is an imperative. The difficulty of change on the strategic level is what makes the President's commitment to transformation so important and difficult. Clearly, the Executive Branch cannot make this strategic change alone. Congress must also understand the need and sign on to the policy and plan. The nation's elected representatives are obliged for domestic political reasons to think about people, bases and the defence industry. Many in Congress would, however, welcome the Administration's lead if they believed that true and comprehensive transformation were a top priority and were made participants in the process. Since the early 1990s, Congress has sounded a constant theme urging real change inside the Armed Forces (the Army in particular) during hearings and private sessions with the nation's military leaders because Members of Congress do not view a smaller Cold War force as either prudent or affordable for the times.

Members would support Administration efforts if they saw evidence that they were dealing with true and comprehensive transformation and were not being asked to support piecemeal reductions in selected defence programs or preserve today's forces in an obsolete Cold War configuration.

HISTORIC OPPORTUNITY

America's victory over Spain in 1898 marked the beginning of a new era in world affairs. Overnight, America became a world power. Realising that American national-security institutions had reached block obsolescence, President Theodore Roosevelt instructed Secretary of War Elihu Root to devise a new strategy and structure that would position the United States to play its role in the world as a great power. Then, as now, American military thinking lagged behind the technology of war. Then, as now, new thinking and new organisations were required to propel the nation into the new century.

When the Roosevelt Administration Bill for Army reform and reorganisation came before Congress, many senior officers opposed Root's plan to create an Army General Staff, to convert the 25 000-man Army of cavalry, infantry and artillery regiments to a force of 100 000 troops and six divisions. They asked, 'Why change; after all, we won the Spanish–American War, didn't we?' Despite the opposition to change, Roosevelt skilfully manoeuvred his Bill through Congress, and within two years, Root's successor, Howard Taft, quietly retired the opponents of the Bill. America's military leaders know in principle that obsolete paradigms lead to military disaster. They can cite historical examples of governments and armies that brought catastrophe on their nations by basing their forces and policies on imperfect or delusional models of the world. Now they have the opportunity to demonstrate that they are not prisoners of the past and that they will not repeat those mistakes.

Few historical figures have had Theodore Roosevelt's ability to recognise changes in the strategic landscape, to conceive the measures necessary for military forces to fight and win in the new environment, and to summon the resolve in himself and others to overcome the inevitable resistance to fundamental change. As America's first President of the 20th century, Roosevelt transformed the Army and Navy when there was no immediate threat to American survival. The result was imperfect, but it provided the foundation for American victory in two world wars. The question is: Will the first American President of the 21st century, under similar circumstances, break the deadlock in defence, resurrect transformation and convert today's disjointed armed services into a truly joint force that can guarantee American security and influence for the remainder of this century?

FUTURE CHALLENGES

In February 1921, the Journal of the Royal United Service Institution published a lecture by Captain B. H. Liddell Hart, titled 'The Man-in-the-Dark Theory of Infantry Tactics and the Expanding Torrent System of Attack'. Since that time, the man-in-the-dark analogy has been a vivid and useful way of thinking about battlefield tactics. With the US Army's recent advances in developing and acquiring information technologies, however, perhaps the time has come to shed some light on the man-in-the-dark. In his lecture, Liddell Hart began by offering a simple analogy with which to examine modern tactics. Due to his experience as an infantry platoon leader and company commander in World War I, Liddell Hart had a solid foundation for both understanding and teaching small-unit infantry tactics. He likened battle between two opposing units to hand-to-hand fighting between two men in a dark room. Since neither opponent could see the other in this fictional contest, each had to adapt his stance and fighting techniques to the fundamental uncertainty of darkness. Liddell Hart showed that the problems faced by the men in the dark were conceptually the same as those faced by military units on the battlefield.

Imagine standing in a pitch-dark room, and all you know is that your opponent is somewhere in the room with you. Instinctively, you crouch. Why? Because you want to lower your centre of gravity and assume a defensive posture in the event that the enemy surprises you. Liddell Hart noted that, just as the man-in-the-dark would crouch, so also armies on the battlefield assume a constantly defensive stance—even when they are moving or attacking. Good armies are constantly thinking about the possibility of ambush.

The man-in-the-dark will tend to move slowly—much more slowly than he is actually able to move. He does this because he cannot see the floor or the opponent, and he does not want to stumble or wander into the enemy unprepared. Likewise, on the battlefield, armies move much more slowly than their components could move. An M1 tank can reach speeds of 50 miles per hour. In battle, however, a tank battalion will move at perhaps a tenth of that velocity. The unit moves slowly and cautiously, taking time to use overwatch tactics and to post air guards and flank guards, and so forth.

Among the techniques used in the blind fight is the outstretched arm. We can easily visualise ourselves standing in the dark, knowing that our opponent is nearby but being unable to see him. Instinctively, we raise the arm and extend the hand. In essence, the hand must assume the duties of the eyes. The first purpose of the extended hand is to find the enemy. In military parlance, this function is called 'reconnaissance'. Reconnaissance is an enemy-oriented function because, in order to perform it, the unit must go where the enemy is and collect detailed, precise information on enemy dispositions and capabilities.

The second purpose of the extended hand is to avoid a surprise attack. Again, this concept has a military term that defines it: 'security'. Security is oriented on the friendly force and seeks to prevent observation by the enemy and attack on friendly formations. There is a third purpose for the extended hand: grasping the enemy. In military terminology, this is called 'fixing' the enemy. Just as a man in the dark would grasp the throat of his foe to immobilise him and set him up for the decisive punch, so military units on the battlefield must immobilise enemy units. The fixing function serves to hold an enemy in place and divert his attention so that another attack—such as a decisive envelopment—can be more effective.

With this germane comparison, Liddell Hart went on to explain the principles of infantry tactics in detail and provided a useful perspective for thinking about war. Yet recent developments in information technologies and related advances in weaponry suggest that a new analogy may be appropriate. It is time to consider the 'man-in-the-light'. As the US Army continues experimentation with digitisation and related information technologies, it will probably face a spectrum of threats in the future. Future adversaries may employ information technologies equal to, or perhaps better than, those of the US Army, while others will have advanced little in this regard. It is instructive, then, to think first about what might happen to tactics when facing the latter. What would occur if US forces were enhanced with information technologies, while those of the opponent were not? With apologies to Liddell Hart, we must begin by modifying his analogy. In this case, one of the contestants can see, and the other cannot. Again, we must admit that the situation on a real battlefield will rarely be so clear-cut. Advantages in perceiving the battlespace would be relative, not absolute. For the sake of our exploration, however, let us proceed at first with the absolute: we can see, and the enemy is blind. It is obvious from the start that such a fight is asymmetrical in the extreme. This is a key point, and one that has its good and bad sides. It is almost inconceivable that the friendly force would not prevail in such an encounter. The blind opponent is at an overwhelming disadvantage. If, however, future US military units obtain a clear edge in information operations, what would be the effect on battlefield tactics?

To begin with, the stance of the man-in-the-light would change. If we were to picture ourselves in a well-lit room in which we could clearly see our blind opponent, it is unlikely that we would crouch, tense and extend the arm as we did in the dark. With our eyes functioning properly now, we would not use our hand for reconnaissance. Although reconnaissance would still be a critically important function in the fight, we would use our eyes rather than our hands to do the work. On the battlefield, then, we should expect that a clear-cut advantage in information dominance would lead to less reliance on manoeuvre forces for reconnaissance in favour of other battlefield sensors. The information dominance resources of future commanders may include 'eyes' processing data fused together from an array of sources: optics, radar, imagery, electronic intelligence, local populace, and so on. If realised, this notion would offer welcome respite since reconnaissance by ground forces can cost time and lives.

Anyone with experience in combat or at a combat training centre understands the arguments against a reduced emphasis on ground reconnaissance. In the past, there was no viable substitute for having stealthy groups of soldiers or combat vehicle patrols probing enemy positions. In the past, existing technology was neither responsive nor precise enough to supplant ground reconnaissance. Hence, while commanders would exploit whatever intelligence they could garner from other assets, they would rely on their own soldiers to gather the detailed intelligence necessary to prevail in combat. We simply do not yet know whether emerging technology will overcome this challenge; if it does, then the reconnaissance function must move from the hand to the eye. A clear example of this dynamic can be drawn from the Battle of Britain in 1940. One of the problems the Royal Air Force (RAF) faced was how to detect incoming German aircraft. Although Ultra and ground observation teams helped considerably, the RAF would have had to rely on fighter pilots conducting surveillance from the air. The pilots and the aircraft would have quickly been worn out using this method. Fortunately, the British had developed radar. The Chain Home radar system allowed the RAF to keep pilots on the ground until they were needed for the interception. Hence, by using information technology, they were able to reserve pilots and aircraft for the decisive fight.

The outstretched hand would remain an effective security measure even in the now well-lit room, but again, the eyes would take over some of the security function. The man-in-the-light who can observe his blind opponent will not feel compelled to raise the hand for security until he has closed the distance to striking range. Hence, by using his eyes, the man-in-the-light employs the hand more precisely to protect himself. This analogy, if sustained in experimentation, may have a fundamental effect on tactics. In short, by employing the eyes to detect a threat, the man-in-the-light does not need to remain in a crouching, battle-ready stance continuously. Instead he can relax (thus using less energy), plan and stalk his blind opponent—tensing himself only moments before he strikes.

In battlefield terms, this phenomenon may mean that units can avoid the inefficiencies that attend current security measures and instead move, strike, protect and refit more economically. For example, let us consider a mechanised infantry brigade combat team operating in a theatre of war. In the context of current technology, the brigade is in a similar position to the man-in-the-dark and it must compensate for the uncertainty of the situation with active security measures. Units must patrol aggressively; establish manned observation posts; and develop, supervise and execute sentry procedures. All these activities take time, consume resources, tire soldiers, and sometimes result in death or injury. If future technology can instead provide the brigade with battlefield visualisation that is good enough to detect threats reliably in a timely manner, we could perhaps dispense with many such security measures, thereby saving time, supplies and lives. Security is an economy-of-force activity, and the principle of economy of force directs that we garner our energies, time and resources for the decisive action. Future technology may move us closer to the goal.

Again, we must be circumspect. The unit that relies solely on technology for security, allowing the organisation to ignore other measures, will be annihilated by an attacker that defeats or avoids the technological defences.

Therefore, as we move from theoretical extreme to practical reality, we must recognise that information technologies may lead to a relative reduction of security measures. Even so, relative changes will result in tangible economies. In the asymmetrical fight of the man-in-the-light against the blind man, the concept of fixing must also change. Because enemies in war will always have their own intentions, capabilities and strengths, US Army doctrine calls for tactics in which the army 'fixes' enemies as it seeks to defeat them. The fixing function accounts for enemy strength and attempts to immobilise or divert it, so that it cannot be brought to bear against the friendly plan.

With its recent emphasis on information operations, the US Army must now consider whether it is feasible to fix the enemy in a way that is different from before. Whereas the US Army used to have to fix the enemy with ground forces, it may now be possible to fix the enemy with his own ignorance. Consider our analogy. The man-in-the-light looks across the room and sees his blind opponent groping about, trying to sense and understand the battlespace while avoiding destruction. Armed with his perfect intelligence, the man-in-the-light stalks his opponent, perhaps sneaking behind him, while the blind man is completely unaware.

When it comes time for the decisive blow, the man-in-the-light does not need to spend the energy to fix his opponent, because the blind man is fixed by his own ignorance of the situation. The attempt to grasp the blind man would more likely serve only to alert him of the danger. In a similar manner, it may be possible for the US Army to employ information operations on the future battlefield to fix the enemy with less reliance on ground combat for this critical function. In the asymmetric fight, the friendly force is planning, mounting and executing operations more quickly than the blind force. Through active and passive command-and-control warfare, the friendly force could conceivably manoeuvre and shape the battlespace to the point at which a decisive operation could be launched without first having to engage enemy forces to fix them. Instead, for example, the commander launches a high-tempo enveloping attack, exploiting the enemy's lack of awareness. The enemy is fixed by his own ignorance. Once again, we must consider the counter arguments. In real warfare, the enemy is rarely fixed in the absolute sense even when engaged in ground combat. Fixing in practice is relative and produces relative advantages. The same would be true with information operations.

The enemy will not cooperate and is likely to be not totally ignorant of the battlespace, but merely partially so. If we employ this concept, what we must avoid is using the 'fixing by ignorance' idea simply to wish the problem away. Fixing by ignorance will not work unless we combine aggressive information operations with high-tempo manoeuvre and fires. In common practice, it is likely that future fixing operations in an asymmetric scenario will combine information operations and ground operations to achieve the desired outcome.

The asymmetry of the 'one man-in-the-light' scenario should result in an unprecedented display of the principle of economy of force. The friendly force in such a contest should adapt itself to exploit the advantages that it has, resulting in real savings in time, logistics and lives. Precision warfare—particularly when pitted against its converse, mass warfare—should lead to economies in every dimension. It should also lead to overwhelming victory. Therein lies the danger of the asymmetric scenario. It is human nature to adapt when confronted with a challenge. The enemy will do the same. As we investigate future warfighting concepts, we must put ourselves in the enemy's shoes and ask the question: If we were faced with an enemy who had overwhelming advantages in battle, would we simply give up? Usually, the answer is a resounding 'no'. Instead, humans figure out a way to adapt themselves to the new situation.

It is this innate capacity to adapt that underlies the theory of combined arms and, incidentally, confounds theorists who envision a future battlefield dominated by a single arm or weapon system. No single system will ever prevail in real war because, no matter how effective it is, the enemy will eventually adapt to it. It is also true that the greater the effectiveness of the friendly force, the more quickly and urgently the enemy will react to diminish the advantage. Since the asymmetric fight we envisioned here confers such an overwhelming advantage to the friendly force, we can anticipate that future adversaries will race to defeat or avoid that scenario.

How would an enemy react to the asymmetry of the one man-in-the light scenario? Obviously, the US Army can count on opposing nations and groups to continue their own technological innovation programs. When we demonstrate a technological advance in battle, we can be certain that future adversaries will attempt to develop their own technologies in order to defeat that capability, or at least to imitate it.

Technological adaptation takes time and money, however. The enemy will also adapt itself through battlefield tactics. If the fight is too asymmetrical, the enemy will urgently avoid battle altogether and prosecute unconventional warfare instead. In extreme cases, the US Army will see its battlefield advantages become nullified through political realignments or even cultural revolution. By various means, potential enemies will adapt themselves to the US Army's successes, with the result that the asymmetric scenario will be short-lived.

Bibliography

Ahmad, Imtiaz: *State and Foreign Policy: India's Role in South Asia*, New Delhi, Vikas, 1993.

Appleby, Paul H.: *Policy and Administration*, Birmingham, AL: University of Alabama Press, 1949.

Arend, A.: *International Law and the Use of Force*, London, Routledge, 1993.

Basu, Prahlad K.: *Governance and Public Administration for Poverty Reduction*, Salvador, Brazil, 1997.

Burnes, Alexander: *Cabool: a Personal Narrative*, London, J. Murray, 1842.

Chandra, R.: *Judicial System in Mechanical Warfare*, Lucknow, Print House (India), 1992.

Dixit, Prabla: *Communalism: A Struggle for Power*, New Delhi, Orient Longman, 1981.

English, Barbara: *The War for a Persian Lady*, Boston, Houghton Mifflin, 1971.

Entner, Marvin L.: *Russo-Persian Commercial Relations 1828-1914*, Gainesville, University of Florida, 1965.

Fraser, James B.: *Narrative of a Journey into Khorasan in the Years 1821 and 1822*, London, Longman, 1825.

Friedman, G.: *The Future of War: Power, Technology and Western Military*, N.Y., Random House, 1996.

Habberton, William: *Anglo-Russian Relations Concerning Afghanistan 1837-1907*, Urbana, University of Illinois, 1937.

Hans J. Morgenthau: *Politics Among Nations: The Struggle for Power and Peace*, New York, Knopf, 1960.

Huntington, S.P.: *The China Modernisation Military and the State*, N.Y., Vintage Books, 1964.

Huntington, S.P.: *The Military and the State*, N.Y., Vintage Books, 1964.

Hurewitz, Jacob C.: *Diplomacy in the Near and Middle East: A Documentary Record 1535-1914*, Princeton, New Jersey, 1956.

Imlah, A. H.: *Economic Elements of the Pax Brittanica*, Cambridge, Harvard University Press, 1958.

Jones, W.H.: *The Government and Politics of Indian Military*, London, Hutchinson, 1971.

Keane J.: *Democracy and Civil Liberty*, London, Verso, 1988.

Kelly, John B.: *Britain and the Persian Gulf 1795-1880*, Oxford, Clarendon Press, 1968.

Moseley, Philip E.: *Russian Diplomacy and the Opening of the Eastern Question*, Cambridge, Harvard University Press, 1934.

Norris, James A.: *The First Afghan War 1838-1842*, Cambridge, University Press, 1967.

Peterson, B.R.: *The Sources of Military Space Force*, Cornell Univ. Press.

Posen, B.R.: *The Sources of Military Doctrine*, Ithaca, 1984, Cornell Univ. Press.

Puryear, V. J.: *International Economics and Diplomacy in the Near East*, London, Oxford University, 1935.

Rosen, P.: *Societies and Military Power: India and its Armies*, Ithaca, Cornell University Press, 1996.

Selden, S.: *The Promise of Representative Bureaucracy: Diversity and Responsiveness in a Government Agency*, New York, M. E. Sharpe, 1997.

Simon, D. : *Societies and Military Power*, Ithaca, Cornell University Press, 1996.

Singh, Kushwant: *A History of the Sikhs*, New Jersey, Princeton University Press, 1966.

Singhal, D. P.: *India and Afghanistan: 1876-1907. A Study in Diplomatic Relations*, St. Lucia, University of Queensland, 1963.

Stoker G.: *The Politicals of Local Government*, Basingstoke, MacMillan Educational, 1988.

Index

N

O

P

S

T

□□□